REPRINTS OF ECONOMIC CLASSICS

A TREATISE CONCERNING
CIVIL GOVERNMENT

A
TREATISE

CONCERNING

CIVIL GOVERNMENT

BY

JOSIAH TUCKER

$$[1781]$$

REPRINTS OF ECONOMIC CLASSICS

AUGUSTUS M. KELLEY · PUBLISHERS
NEW YORK · 1967

First Edition 1781
(London: T. Cadell, *in the Strand*, 1781)

Reprinted 1967 by

Augustus M. Kelley · Publishers

354.42
TH997

Library of Congress Catalogue Card Number
65 - 26384

Printed in the United States of America
by Sentry Press, New York, N. Y. 10019

A

TREATISE

CONCERNING

CIVIL GOVERNMENT,

IN

THREE PARTS.

PART I.

THE NOTIONS OF MR. LOCKE AND HIS FOLLOWERS, CONCERNING THE ORIGIN, EXTENT, AND END OF CIVIL GOVERNMENT, EXAMINED AND CONFUTED.

PART II.

THE TRUE BASIS OF CIVIL GOVERNMENT SET FORTH AND ASCERTAINED; ALSO OBJECTIONS ANSWERED; DIFFERENT FORMS COMPARED; AND IMPROVEMENTS SUGGESTED,

PART III.

ENGLAND'S FORMER GOTHIC CONSTITUTION CENSURED AND EXPOSED; CAVILS REFUTED; AND AUTHORITIES PRODUCED: ALSO THE SCRIPTURE DOCTRINE CONCERNING THE OBEDIENCE DUE TO GOVERNORS VINDICATED AND ILLUSTRATED.

BY JOSIAH TUCKER, D. D.

DEAN OF GLOCESTER.

LONDON:

PRINTED FOR T. CADELL, IN THE STRAND.

M.DCC.LXXXI.

THE
PREFACE.

THE long preliminary Difcourfe, which I had printed in the Specimen difperfed among my Friends, is now totally fuppreffed. It was their Opinion, that fuch an Enumeration of Errors, as were there collected together out of Mr. LOCKE's Writings, was needlefs at prefent; becaufe the Degree of Infallibility, which had been afcribed to his Name and Works, is now greatly leffened. They likewife thought, that fuch a Catalogue of Miftakes might be made Ufe of by a fubtle Adverfary, as an Handle to divert the Attention of the Reader from the main Point, to that which was foreign to the principal Defign. I am perfuaded of the Juftice of thefe Remarks; and I do hereby requeft my worthy Friends to accept of my grateful Acknowledgments.

My prefent Defign is to fpeak to another Subject. Some there are, who think it impoffible, that fuch a Man as Mr. LOCKE, ever meant to patronize thofe dangerous Confequences, which his Followers, and particularly Mr. Molineux, and Dr. Price, have deduced from his Principles. They wifh, therefore, that all the Cenfure might fall on the Difciples, and not on the Mafter. In Reply to this, I fubmit to them and the Public the following Confiderations.

1ft.

1*ft.* -- That Mr. Molineux was Mr. Locke's Acquaintance, Correfpondent, and bofom Friend; that he fent him his famous Book, the *Cafe of Ireland*, as a Prefent ;—that he defired his Opinion thereon; which though Mr. Locke declined or rather *deferred* to give ;—yet he never once hinted, that Mr. Molineux had miftaken his Principles, and had afcribed Confequences to him, which he muft difavow. [See the whole Correfpondence carried on between them in Mr. Locke's Works.] Moreover, I defire it may be taken Notice, that Mr. Locke furvived Mr. Molineux feveral Years ;—during which Time the Proteftants of *Ireland* were worked up into intemperate Heats by thofe very Notions of unalienable Rights and Independence, which Mr. Locke's and Mr. Molineux's Writings had infufed into them, and which they have fince adopted in fo decifive a Manner ; yet during all this Time Mr. Locke was filent. and made no Remonftrance againft fuch Proceedings. He never intimated to any one, as far as I can learn, that they were miftaken in their Inferences ; nor did he retort upon them, by faying, that if they thought they had a Right to deduce fuch Confequences from his Principles.—the Papifts of *Ireland* [the original Natives of the Country and the vaftly greater Majority of the People] had a much ftronger and clearer Right to fhake off the Proteftant Yoke, and to affert their native Independence, and unalienable Birth-right.

This

This he probably would, or at leaft this he *ought* to have done, had he really thought, that Mr. MOLINEUX and the *Irifh* deduced fuch Conclufions from his Premifes, as it was incumbent on him to difavow.

2*dly*. GRANTING for Argument's Sake, that the DEAN of *Glocefter* is either fo illiterate, or fo blinded with Prejudice, that he cannot fee the obvious Meaning of the plaineft Propofitions in Mr. LOCKE's Work,—yet what fhall we fay of Dr. PRICE, his warmeft Advocate, and profeffed Admirer? Is he too in the fame Situation with the DEAN of *Glocefter*? All the World muft allow, that Dr. PRICE is a very learned Man, and a clear Writer: And if his Prejudices *for* Mr. LOCKE, and the DEAN of *Glocefter's* Prejudices *againft* him, fhould make them agree in the fame Opinions; it muft at leaft be allowed, that fuch a Clafhing of oppofite Prejudices hath produced that marvellous Effect, which oppofite Prejudices never produced before. The Doctor and I fee Mr. LOCKE's Principles with the fame Eyes; we underftand them in the fame Senfe; and all the Difference between us, is, That he admires them, and *glories* in the Confequences of them, which I do not, and think them to be extremely dangerous to the Peace and Happinefs of all Societies.

BUT 3*dly*, And to end this Controverfy at once: Let fome Friend to Truth, bleffed with

greater

greater Difcernment than the DEAN of *Glocefter*, or even than Dr. PRICE, take Mr. LOCKE's Book in hand, and fhew from the natural Con-ftruction of the Words, and the Scope and Tenor of the Context, that both of us [and in-deed, that all in general, Admirers, and Non-Admirers] have hitherto miftaken Mr. LOCKE's true Senfe and Meaning: And in the next Place, let this happy Interpreter or clear-fighted Com-mentator point out, how fuch and fuch Paffages ought to have been underftood; and what Con-fequences ought to have been deduced from his Writings, different from all thefe, which have been deduced before.

THIS would be coming to the Point; and when *fatisfactorily* performed, a moft ufeful Work it will be.—I, for my Part, fhall be exceed-ing glad to have it proved, that I was miftaken. [For I never wifh to find Fault without great and urgent Caufe] Therefore if this Point can be fatisfactorily proved, I do hereby pledge myfelf to make a public Recantation. This I promife to do, becaufe I think it to be no Manner of Dif-grace to the Character of an honeft, fallible, well-meaning Man to fay, I am now convinced that *I was in an Error; and I afk Pardon.*

Two Things more I fhall beg Leave to add and thefe I borrow from Mr. LOCKE's own Pre-face to this very Book on Government.

" FIRST,

" First, that cavilling here and there, at
" fome Expreffion, or little Incident of my Dif-
" courfe, is not an Anfwer to my Book.

" Secondly, That I fhall not take Railing
" for Argúments ; nor think either of thefe worth
" my Notice :—Though I fhall always look on
" myfelf as bound to give Satisfaɛion to any one,
" who fhall appear to be confcientioufly fcrupu-
" lous in the Point, and fhall fhew any juft
" Grounds for his Scruples."

The PRINCIPAL ERRATA.

Page 224.---Line 20, for *Armenian*, read American.
287.---Line 23, for 5*thly*, read 6thly.
288.---Line 3, for *Innations*, read Innovations.
293.---Line 6, for *the*, read that.
Ditto, in the Note for *Monterate*, read Montacute.
295.---Line 7, for *are*, read were.
301.---Line penult. after *Disingenuity*, place a Full-point, and begin the next Word with a capital Letter.
305.---Line penult. for *and*, read in fact.
306.---Line penult. for *Elector*, read Electors.
309.---Line 10, for *Discord*, read discordant.
312.---Last Line, after *Hands*, read and whilst.
318.---Line 6, of the Note, for *more*, read meer.

THE
NOTIONS
O F
Mr. LOCKE, &c.

CHAP. I.

The only true Foundation of Civil Government, according to Mr. LOCKE *and his Disciples:—All Governments whatever being so many Encroachments on, and Violations of, the unalienable Rights of Mankind, if not founded on this Hypothesis.*

IN order to shorten this Controversy as much as possible, and to strike every Thing out of it foreign to the Subject, I shall first shew wherein I agree with Mr. LOCKE and his Followers, and 2dly wherein I differ from them.

FIRST then I agree with him, and his Disciples, that there is a Sense, in which it may be said, that no Man is born the *political* Subject of another. Infants the Moment they are born,

are

are the natural Subjects of their Parents : They are alfo entitled by the Law of Nature, as well as by human Laws, to the Protection and Guardianfhip of that State, within whofe Jurifdiction they are born [nay, indeed they are entitled to Protection whilft in Embrio] though they neither did, nor could enter into any Contract with the State for that Purpofe. Therefore in this Senfe, they are juftly deemed the *natural-born* Subjects of fuch a Country. This is the Language of all Laws, and of every Government. But in a *metaphyfical* Senfe, a Man cannot be a Subject before he is a Moral Agent; for it is Moral Agency alone, which renders him amenable, or fubject to any Law, or Government. However, as he is born with the Inftincts and Difpofitions of a focial Creature, he necef-farily becomes a Member of fome Society or other, as foon as he has an Opportunity, by the very Impulfe of his Nature, if there are any human Beings within his Reach to affociate with. But whether this Affociation muft always be formed by Means of an *exprefs mutual Compact*, Engagement, and Stipulation, or whether it *cannot* be formed [I mean *juftly* and *rightly* formed] any other Way, is the important Queftion now to be determined.

2*dly*. LET the Mode of entering into this Society be what it may, whether by exprefs Co-

venant,

venant, or otherwife, I perfeƈtly agree with Mr. Locke and his Difciples, that the Government and Direƈtion of fuch a Society is a Matter of public *Truft*, and not of private *Property* : — a Truft to be executed for the Good of the whole, and not for the private Advantage of the Governors and Direƈtors ; — any otherwife, than as they themfelves will find their own Account in promoting the Profperity of the Community.

3*dly*. I very readily allow, that if thefe Truftees fhould fo far forget the Nature of their Office, as to aƈt direƈtly contrary thereunto in the general Tenor of their Adminiftration ; — and if neither humble Petition, nor decent Remonftrance can reclaim, and bring them to a Senfe of their Dnty ; — then Recourfe muft be had to the only Expedient ftill remaining, *Force of Arms* : — And I add further, that the critical Moment for the Application of fuch a defperate Remedy, feems to be, — when the Evils fuffered are grown fo great and intolerable, without any reafonable Profpeƈt of Amendment, that, according to the moft impartial Calculation, they evidently over-balance thofe which would be brought on by refifting fuch evil Governors.

All thefe Points being previoufly fettled, there can be no Controverfy between Mr. Locke's Difciples and me about the patriarchal
Scheme

Scheme in any of its Branches, or indeed about any Sort of an indefeafible hereditary Right whatever :—Much lefs about unlimited paffive Obedience, and Non-refiftance. For I think we are all perfectly agreed, that neither Kings, nor Senators, neither Patrician-Republics, nor Plebean-Republics, neither hereditary, nor elective Governors can, in the Words of the great Poet,

Have any Right *divine* to govern *wrong.*

And if Sovereigns have no Right to do wrong, the Subjects muft certainly have a Right to prevent them from doing it. For it is clear, that in fuch a Cafe the People cannot offend againft the righteous Laws of God, or the juft Laws of Man, in defending their own Rights.

THE Queftion, therefore, the *fole* Queftion now to be decided, is fimply this, " Whether " THAT Government is to be juftly deemed an " USURPATION, which is not founded on the " *exprefs* mutual Compact of all the Parties in- " terefted therein, or belonging thereunto ?" *Ufurpation* is a Word of a moft odious Sound ; and Ufurpations and Robberies are Things fo deteftably bad, that no honeft, or good Man can wifh them Profperity, or even Exiftence. It is therefore to be hoped for the Honour of human Nature, and the Good of Mankind, that fome Governments or other, befides thofe of

Mr.

Mr. Locke's modelling, or approving, may be found in the World, which deserve a better Fate, than that which is *due* to Robberies and Usurpations.

But let us now hear the Opinion of this great Man himself, and of the most eminent of his Followers, concerning the Origin, and only true Foundation, of Civil Government, according to their System.

QUOTATIONS *from* Mr. Locke.

Mr. Locke, in his 2d. Treatise concerning Government, Chap. viii. *of the Beginning of political Societies*, delivers himself in these Words:

" § 95. Men being, as hath been said, [in the former Chapters] all free, equal, and independent, — *no one can be put out of this Estate, and* subjected to the political Power of another, *without his own Consent.* The only Way, whereby any one divests himself of his natural Liberty, and puts on the Bonds of Civil Society, is by *agreeing* with other Men to join and unite in a Community, for their comfortable, safe, and peaceable Living one among another, in a secure Enjoyment of their Properties, and a greater Security against any that are not of it. This any Number of Men may do, because it injures not the Freedom of the rest: They are

left

left as they were, in the *Liberty* of a *State* of *Nature.* When any Number of Men have fo confented to make one Community, or Government, they are thereby prefently *incorporated,* and made one Body politic, wherein the *Majority have a Right to act.*

" § 98. AND thus, that which begins, and actually concludes any political Society, is nothing but the Confent of a Number of *free* Men, capable of a Majority to unite, and incorporate into fuch a Society. And this is that and *that only,* which did, or COULD give Beginning to *any lawful* Government in the World.

" § 116. 'TIS true, that whatever Engagements or Promifes any one has made for himfelf, he is under the Obligation of them, but cannot by any Compact whatever *bind* his *Children,* or *Pofterity.* For his Son, when a Man, being altogether as free as the Father, any Act of the Father can no more give away the Liberty of the Son, than it can of any Body elfe. He may indeed annex fuch Conditions to the *Land* he *enjoyed,* as a Subject of any Common-Wealth, as may oblige his Son to be of that Community, if he will enjoy thofe Poffeffions, which were his Father's :—Becaufe that Eftate being his Father's Property, he may *difpofe,* or *fettle* it as he pleafes.

" § 119.

" § 119. EVERY Man being, as hath been fhewn, naturally free, and nothing being able to put him into Subjection to any earthly Power, but his *own Confent*, it is to be confidered, what fhall be underftood to be a fufficient Declaration of a Man's Confent to make him fubject to the Laws of any Government. There is a common Diftinction of an *exprefs*, and a *tacit* Confent, which will concern our prefent Cafe. Nobody doubts, but an exprefs Confent of any Man entering into any Society, makes him a perfect Member of that Society, a Subject of that Government. The Difficulty is, what ought to be looked upon as a *tacit Confent*, and how far it binds ; *i. e.* how far any one fhall be looked on to have confented, and thereby fubmitted to any Government, where he has made no Expreffions of it at all. And to this I fay, that every Man, that hath any Poffeffion or Enjoyment of any Part of the Dominions of any Government, doth thereby give his tacit Confent, and is as far forth obliged to Obedience to the Laws of that Government, during fuch Enjoyment, as any one under it, whether this his Poffeffion be of Land to him, and his Heirs for ever;---or a Lodging only for a Week, or whether it be barely travelling freely on the High Way : And it in Effect reaches as far as the very being of any one within the Territories of that Government.

" § 120

" § 120. To underſtand this the better ;---
Whoſoever therefore from thenceforth by Inheritance, Purchaſe, Permiſſion, or other-ways,
enjoys any Part of the Land ſo annexed to, and
under the Government of that Common-Wealth,
muſt take it with the Condition it is under ; that
is, of ſubmitting to the Government of the Common-Wealth, under whoſe Juriſdiction it is, as
far forth as any Subject of it.

" § 121. But ſince the Government has a
direct Juriſdiction *only* over the Land, and
reaches the Poſſeſſor of it (before he has *actually*
incorporated himſelf in the Society) *only* as he
dwells upon, and enjoys that, the Obligation any
one is under by Virtue of ſuch Enjoyment, to
ſubmit to the Government, begins and ends with
the Enjoyment : So that whenever the Owner,
who has given nothing but ſuch *tacit* Conſent to
the Government, will by Donation, Sale, or
otherways quit the ſaid Poſſeſſion, he is at Liberty to go, and incorporate himſelf into any
other Common-Wealth, or to agree with others,
to begin a new one in *vacuis locis*, in any Part of
the World they can find free, and unpoſſeſſed.

" § 122. But *ſubmitting* to the Laws of any
Country, living *quietly*, and enjoying *Privileges*
and *Protection* under them, ☞ makes not a Man
a Member of that Society :— Nothing can make

a

a Man fo, but his ☞ actually entering into it by *pofitive* Engagements, and *exprefs* Promife and Compact.

CHAP. IX. *Of the Ends of Political Society and Government.*

" § 123. IF Man in a State of Nature be fo free, as hath been faid: If he be *abfolute Lord* of his own *Perfon* and Poffeffions, *equal* to the greateft, and SUBJECT TO NO BODY, why will he part with his Freedom, why will he give up this Empire, and fubject himfelf to the Dominion and Controul of any other Power? To which it is obvious to anfwer, that tho' in the State of Nature he hath fuch a Right, yet the Enjoyment of it is very uncertain, and conftantly expofed to the Invafion of others. For all being Kings as much as he, every Man his equal, and the greater Part no ftrict Obfervers of Equity and Juftice, the Enjoyment of the Property he has in this State is very unfafe, very infecure. ☞ This makes him willing to quit his Condition; which however free, is full of Fears, and continual Dangers.

" § 127. THUS Mankind, notwithftanding all the Privileges of the State of Nature, being but in an ill Condition, while they remain in it, are quickly *driven* into Society.

CHAP.

CHAP. XI. *Of the Extent of the Legiſlative Power.*

" § 138. THE ſupreme Power [the Legiſlature] cannot [lawfully, or rightly] take from *any Man* any Part of his Property without his own Conſent.

" § 140. 'TIS true, Governments cannot be ſupported without great Charge ; and 'tis fit every one who enjoys his Share of the Protection, ſhould pay out of his Eſtate his Proportion for the Main-, tenance of it. But ſtill it. muſt be with his own Conſent, *i. e.* with the Conſent of the Majority, giving it either by themſelves, or by their Repreſentatives *choſen* by them.

CHAP. XVII. *Of Uſurpation.*

" § 198. WHOEVER gets into the Exerciſe of any Part of the Power [of governing] by other Ways than what the Laws of the Community have preſcribed, hath no Right to be obeyed, tho' the Form of the Common-Wealth be ſtill preſerved: Since he is not the Perſon the Laws have appointed, and conſequently not the Perſon the People have conſented to. Nor can ſuch an Uſurper, or *any* deriving from him, EVER have a Title 'till the People are both at Liberty to conſent, and have actually conſented to allow, and confirm him in the Power he hath till then *uſurped.*" *Extracts*

Extracts from Mr. MOLYNEUX's *Cafe of* Ireland *being bound by Acts of Parliament in* England. Dublin, *printed* 1698, *and dedicated to King* WILLIAM : *And lately reprinted by Mr.* AL- MON, *with a long Preface, exciting the* Irish *to rebel, and promiſing full Liberty, and Security to the Papiſts, if they will join in this good Work.*

" *Page* 18. IF a Villain with a Piſtol at my Breaſt, makes me convey my Eſtate to him, no one will ſay, that this gives him any Right. And yet juſt ſuch a Title as this has an unjuſt Conqueror, who with a Sword at my Throat forces me into Submiſſion ; that is, forces me to part with my natural Eſtate and Birth-right, of being governed *only* by Laws, to which I give my *Conſent,* and not by his Will, — or the Will of any other.

" *P.* 26 *and* 27. FROM what has been ſaid, I preſume it pretty clearly appears, that an unjuſt Conqueſt gives no Title at all ; — that a juſt Con- queſt gives Power only over the *Lives,* and *Li- berties* of the actual Oppoſers,---but not over their *Poſterity* and *Eſtates* ;---and not at all over thoſe that did *not concur* in the Oppoſition.

" THEY that deſire a more full Diſquiſition of this Matter, may find it at large in an INCOM- PARABLE

PARABLE Treatife concerning the true Original,
Extent, and End of Civil Government, Chap. xvi.
This Difcourfe is faid to be written by my ex-
cellent Friend JOHN LOCKE, Efq.

" *Page* 113. I fhall venture to affert, that the
Right of being fubject ONLY to fuch Laws, to
which Men give their *own* Confent, is fo *inherent*
in *all* Mankind, and founded on fuch *immutable*
Laws of Nature and Reafon, that 'tis not to be
aliened, or given up by any Body of Men whatever.

" *Page* 150. ALL Men are by Nature in a
State of Equality, in refpect of Jurifdiction or Dominion.---On this Equality of Nature is founded
that Right, which ALL Men claim of being free
from *all* Subjection to pofitive Laws, 'till by
their *own Confent*, they give up their Freedom
by entering into Civil Societies for the common
Benefit of all the Members thereof. ☞ And
on this Confent depends the Obligation of all
human Laws.

" *Page* 169. I HAVE no other Notion of
Slavery; but being bound by a Law, to which I
do not confent.

" *Page* 170. IF *one* Law may be impofed without Confent, *any other Law whatever* may be
impofed on us without our Confent.   This will
naturally

naturally introduce taxing us without our Confent. And this as neceſſarily deſtroys our Property. I have no other Notion of Property,
but a Power of difpofing of my Goods *as I pleafe*,
and not as another fhall command. Whatever
another may *rightly* take from me, I have certainly no Property in. To *tax* me without
Confent is little better, if at all, than down-right
robbing me.

Extracts from Dr. PRIESTLY'S *Effay on the firft
Principles of Government. Second Edition.*
London, *printed for* J. JOHNSON, 1771.

SECTION I. *Of the firft Principles of Government,
and the different Kinds of Liberty.*

" *Page* 6. To begin with firſt Principles,
we muſt for the Sake of gaining clear Ideas on
the Subject, do what almoſt all political Writers
have done before us, that is, We muſt fuppofe
a Number of People exiſting, who experience
the Inconvenience of living independent and
unconnected : Who are expofed without Redrefs,
to Infults and Wrongs of every Kind, and are
too weak to procure to themfelves many of the
Advantages, *which they are fenfible might eafily be
compaffed by united Strength.* Thefe People, if
they would engage the Protection of the whole
Body, and join their Forces in Enterprizes and
Un-

Undertakings calculated for their common Good, muſt voluntarily refign fome Part of their natural Liberty, and fubmit their Conduct to the Direction of the Community : For without thefe Conceſſions, fuch an Alliance, attended with fuch Advantages, could not be formed.

" Were thefe People few in Number and living within a fmall Diſtance of one another, it might be eafy for them to aſſemble upon every Occafion, in which the whole Body was concerned ; and every thing might be determined by the Votes of the Majority. ☞ Provided they had *previoufly* agreed that the Votes of a Majority fhould be decifive. But were the Society numerous, their Habitations remote, and the Occafions on which the whole Body muſt interpofe frequent, it would be abfolutely impoffible that all the Members of the State fhould aſſemble, or give their Attention to public Bufinefs. In this Cafe, though, with Rousseau, *it being a giving up of their Liberty,* there muſt be Deputies or Public Officers appointed to act in the Name of the whole Body : And in a State of very great Extent, where all the People could never be aſſembled, the whole Power of the Community muſt neceſſarily, and almoſt irreverfibly, be lodged in the Hands of thefe Deputies. In *England*, the King, the hereditary Lords, and the Electors of the Houfe of Commons

Commons are thefe *ftanding* Deputies: And the Members of the Houfe of Commons are again the *temporary* Deputies of this laft Order of the 'State.

Section II. *Of Political Liberty.*

" 11. In Countries, where every Member of the Society enjoys an equal Power of arriving at the fupreme Offices, and confequently of directing the Strength and the Sentiments of the whole Community, there is a State of the moft perfect political Liberty. On the other Hand, in Countries where a Man is, by his Birth or Fortune, excluded from thefe Offices, or from a Power of voting for proper Perfons to fill them; that Man, whatever be the Form of the Government, or whatever Civil Liberty, or Power over his own Actions he may have, has no Power over thofe of another; he has no Share in the Government, and therefore has *no political Liberty at all.* Nay his own Conduct, as far as the Society does interfere, is, in all Cafes, directed by others.

" It may be faid, that no Society on Earth was ever formed in the Manner reprefented above. I anfwer, it is true; becaufe all Governments whatever have been, in fome Meafure, compulfory, tyrannical, and oppreffive in their Origin.

Origin. But the Method I have defcribed muft be allowed to be the ONLY equitable and fair Method of forming a Society. And fince every Man retains, and can never be deprived of, his natural Right (founded on a Regard to the general Good) of relieving himfelf from all Oppreffion, that is, ☞ from every Thing that has been impofed upon him without his own Confent, this muft be the only true and proper Foundation of all the Governments fubfifting in the World, and that to which the People who compofe them ☞ have an unalienable Right to bring them back.

" *Page* 40. THE Sum of what hath been advanced upon this Head, is a Maxim, than which nothing is more true, that every Government, in its original Principles, and antecedent to its prefent Form, is an *equal Republic* ; and confequently, that *every* Man, when he comes to be fenfible of his natural Rights, and to feel his own Importance, will confider himfelf as fully equal to any other Perfon whatever. The Confideration of Riches and Power, however acquired, muft be entirely fet afide, when we come to thefe firft Principles. The very Idea of Property, or Right of *any Kind*, is founded upon a Regard to the general Good of the Society, under whofe Protection it is enjoyed ; and nothing is properly a *Man's own*, but what general Rules, which have

have for their Object the Good of the whole,
give to him. To whomsoever the Society delegates its Power, it is delegated to them for the
more easy Management of public Affairs, and
in order to make the more effectual Provision
for the Happiness of the whole. Whosoever
enjoys Property, or Riches in the State, enjoys
them for the Good of the State, as well as for
himself: And whenever those Powers, Riches,
or Rights of *any Kind* are abused to the Injury
of the whole, that awful and ultimate Tribunal,
in which every Citizen hath an equal Voice, may
demand the Resignation of them: And in Cir-
cumstances, where *regular Commissions* from this
abused Public cannot be had, EVERY MAN,
who has Power, and who is actuated with the
Sentiments of the Public, may *assume a public
Character*, and bravely redress public Wrongs.
In such dismal and critical Circumstances, the
stifled Voice of an oppressed Country is a loud
Call upon every Man, possessed with a Spirit of
Patriotism, to exert himself. And whenever
that Voice shall be at Liberty, it will ratify and
applaud the Action, which it could not formally
authorise.

Extracts

Extracts from Dr. Price's *famous Treatise, Ob-*
servations on the Nature of Civil Liberty, &c.
a new Edition, 12mo. *corrected by the Author,*
Price Three-Pence, or One Guinea per Hundred.

Preface *to the* Fifth Edition.

" The Principles on which I have argued.
form the Foundation of every State, as *far as it
is free;* and are the fame with thofe taught by
Mr. Locke.

" *Page* 1. Our Colonies in *North-America*
appear to be now determined to rifque, and fuffer
every Thing, under the Perfuafion, that *Great-
Britain* is attempting to *rob* them of that Liberty,
to which *every Member* of Society, and all civil
Communities, have a *natural,* and an unalienable Right.

Section I. *Of the Nature of Liberty in general.*

" *Page* 1. In order to obtain a more diftinct
and accurate View of the Nature of Liberty as
fuch, it will be ufeful to confider it under the
four following general Divifions.

[It is hard to fay, what could have been the
Doctor's Motive for dividing Human Liberty into
four

four Parts; for, in reality, there are either not
fo many Sorts of Liberty, or a great many
more. " Phyfical Liberty, which is the Foun-
" dation of the reft, is, as the Doctor well ob-
" ferves, that Principle of *Spontaneity*, or *Self-*
" *Determination*, which conftitutes us *Agents*; or
" which gives us a Command over our Actions,
" rendering them properly *ours*, and not Effects
" of the Operation of any *foreign* Caufe."
Therefore poffeffing, or enjoying this Power
within ourfelves, we apply it to various Purpofes, according as *Duty*, *Intereft*, or *Inclination*
call it forth: Confequeptly if every diftinct, or
poffible Application of it is to be confidered as
the Exertion of a diftinct Species of Liberty,
we may be faid to have Sorts without Number.
But the Doctor himfelf, as will be feen below,
joins Religious and Civil Liberty in the fame
Clafs. And he alfo obferves, that there is one
general Idea that runs through them all, the
Idea of Self-Direction, or Self-Government.]

" First, Phyfical Liberty,— Secondly, Moral Liberty,—Thirdly, Religious Liberty,— and,
Fourthly, Civil Liberty.

" *Page* 3. As far as in any Inftance, the
Operation of any Power comes in to reftrain the
Power of Self-Government, fo far *Slavery* is introduced: Nor do I think that a precifer Idea
than this of *Liberty*, and *Slavery*, can be given.

SECTION

SECTION II. *Of Civil Liberty, and the Principles of Government.*

" *Page* 4. IN every free State *every Man* is his *own Legiflator.*—All Taxes are *free Gifts* for public Services.—All Laws are particular Provifions or Regulations eftablifhed by COMMON CONSENT for gaining Protection and Safety.

" FROM hence it is obvious, that Civil Liberty, in its *moft perfect* Degree, can be enjoyed only in *fmall States*, where every Member is capable of giving his Suffrage in *Perfon*; and of being chofen into public Offices. When a State becomes fo numerous, or when the different Parts of it are removed to fuch Diftances from one another, as to render this impracticable, a *Diminution* of Liberty neceffarily arifes.—— Though all the Members of a State fhould not be capable of giving their Suffrages on public Meafures *individually* and *perf nally*, they may do this by the Appointment of *Subftitutes* or *Reprefentatives.*

" *Page* 7. IN general, to be *free* is to be guided by one's own Will; and to be guided by the Will of another is the Characteriftic of Servitude. This is particularly applicable to political Liberty.

SECTION

SECTION III. *Of the Authority of one Country over another.*

" *Page* 15. As no People [either individually, or collectively] can lawfully furrender their re-ligious Liberty, by giving up their Right of *judging* for themfelves in Religion, or by allow-ing any human Being to *prefcribe* to them, what *Faith* they fhall *embrace* or what *Mode* of *Worfhip* they fhall *practice*; fo neither can any civil Societies [* either individually, or collectively] lawfully furrender their civil Liberty, by giving up to any extraneous Jurifdiction their Power of legiflating for themfelves, and difpofing of their Property. Such a Ceffion, being inconfiftent with the unalienable Rights of Human Nature, would either not bind at all, or bind only the Individuals who made it. This is a Bleffing, which no Generation of Men can give up for another ; and which, when loft, a People have always *a Right to refume.*

---

* I have added the Words *individually, or collectively*, as being Terms abfolutely neceffary for making the Cafes of Religious, and Civil Liberty to tally with each other, according to the Doctor's Syftem. In the Concerns of Religion, every Man muft act for himfelf, and not by a Deputy: He has a Confcience *of his own*, which he cannot delegate to, or entruft with any Proxy or Reprefentative whatfoever. If therefore the Cafes are parallel, as the Doctor fuppofes them, there can be no fuch Thing allowed as *Reprefentatives* in Parliament; but every Voter muft attend in Perfon.---This is an important Point; therefore more of this hereafter.

OBSER-

OBSERVATIONS *on the foregoing* EXTRACTS.

THUS I have finifhed my Extracts from Mr.
LOCKE, and fome of the moft *eminent* of his
Difciples ; — Men, whofe Writings, (we charitably hope, not intentionally, or malicioufly ; —
though *actually*) have laid a Foundation for
fuch Difturbances and Diffentions, fuch mutual
Jealoufies and Animofities, as Ages to come
will not be able to fettle, or compofe. Many
more Paffages might have been added from other
celebrated Writers on the fame Side. ; but
furely thefe are full enough to explain their Meaning.   And therefore from the following may
be collected.

I. THAT Mankind do not fpontaneoufly,
and, as it were, *imperceptibly* flide into a Diftinction of Orders, and a Difference of Ranks,
by living and converfing together, as Neighbours
and focial Beings : — But on the contrary, that
they naturally fhew an Averfion, and a Repug-
nance to every Kind of Subordination, 'till dire
Neceffity compells them to enter into a folemn
Compact, and to join their Forces together for
the Sake of Self-Prefervation.   Dr. PRIESTLY,
the faireft, the moft open, and ingenuous of all
Mr. LOCKE's Difciples, excepting honeft, undiffembling ROUSSEAU, has expreffed himfelf

fo clearly and fully on this Head, that I fhall
beg Leave to quote his Words again, tho' I had
mentioned them before.

" To begin with firſt Principles, we muſt,
" for the Sake of gaining clear Ideas on the
" Subjeƈt, do what almoſt all political Writers
" have done before us, that is, we muſt fuppofe
" a Number of People exiſting, who *experience*
" the Inconvenience of living independent and
" unconneƈed; who are expofed without Re-
" drefs, to Infults and Wrongs of *every Kind*,
" and are too weak to procure to themfelves
" many of the Advantages, which they are *fen-*
" *fible* might eafily be compaſſed by united
" Strength. Thefe People, if they would en-
" gage the Proteƈtion of the whole Body, and
" join their Forces in Enterprizes and Under-
" takings calculated for their common Good,
" muſt *voluntarily refign* fome Part of their na-
" tural Liberty, and fubmit their Conduƈt to
" the Direƈtion of the Community: For with-
" out thefe *Conceſſions*, an Alliance cannot be
" formed."

HERE it is very obfervable, that the Author
fuppofes Government to be fo entirely the Work
of *Art*, that *Nature* had no Share at all in forming it; or rather in *predifpofing* and *inclining*
Mankind to form it. The Inſtinƈts of Nature,
it feems, had nothing to do in fuch a complicated

cated Bufinefs of Chicane and Artifice, where every Man was for driving the beft Bargain he could; and where all in general, both the future Governors and Governed, were to be on the catch as much as poffible. For this Author plainly fuppofes, that his firft Race of Men had not any innate Propenfity to have lived otherwife, than as fo many *independent, unconnected* Beings, if they could have lived with tolerable Safety in fuch a State: In fhort, they did not feel any Inftincts within themfelves kindly leading them towards affociating, or incorporating with each other; though (what is rather ftrange) Providence had ordained, that this Way of Life was to be fo effentially neceffary towards their Happinefs, that they muft be miferable without it:—Nay, they were driven by Neceffity, and not drawn by In-clination to feek for *any Sort* of Civil Govern-ment whatever. And what is ftranger ftill, it feems they were fenfible, that this Kind of Infti-tution, called Government, to which they had no natural Inclination, but rather an Averfion, and whofe good or bad Effects they had *not* expe-rienced, might eafily procure Advantages which they then wanted, and protect them from many Dangers, to which they were continually expofed, in their independent, unconnected State. All thefe Things, I own, are ftrange Paradoxes to me: I cannot comprehend them. However, fact it is, that almoft all the Writers on the re-

publican

publican Side of the Queſtion, with Mr. LOCKE
at the Head of them, ſeem to repreſent Civil
Government at the beſt, rather as a *neceſſary*
Evil, than a *poſitive* Good ;—an Evil to which
Mankind are obliged to ſubmit, in order to avoid
a greater.

BUT if Mr. LOCKE and his Followers have not
granted much to human Nature in one Reſpect,
they have reſolved to make abundant Amends
for this Deficiency in another. For tho' they
have not allowed human Nature to have any innate Propenſities towards the firſt Formation of
civil Society ;---yet they do moſt ſtrenuouſly in-
ſiſt, that *every Man*, every Individual of the
human Species hath an unalienable Right to
chuſe, or refuſe, whether he will be a Member
of this, or that particular Government, or of
none at all.

THIS was to be my ſecond Obſervation : And
a material one it is. For Mr. LOCKE and his
Followers have extended the Privilege of voting,
or of giving *actual* Conſent, in all the Affairs of
Government and Legiſlation, beyond what was
ever dreamt of before in this, or in any other
civilized Country ;—Nay, according to their
leading Principles, it ought to be extended ſtill
much farther, than even they themſelves have
done.

BEFORE

BEFORE this new Syftem had made its Appearance among us, the Right of voting was not fuppofed to be an unalienable Right, which belonged to *all* Mankind *indifcriminately*: But it was confidered as a Privilege, which was confined to thofe few Perfons who were in Poffeffion of a certain Quantity of Land, to Perfons enjoying certain Franchifes, (of which there are various Kinds) and to Perfons of a certain Condition, Age, and Sex. Perhaps all thefe Numbers put together may make about the Fortieth *Part* of the Inhabitants of *Great-Britain:* They certainly cannot make much more, if an actual Survey and Enumeration were to be made. Whereas the great Mafs of the People, who do not come within this Defcription, are,* and ever have been, excluded by the *Englifh* Conftitution from voting at Elections for Members of Parliament, &c. &c. And heavy Penalties are to be levied on them, if they fhould attempt to vote. Now, according to the Principles of Mr. LOCKE and his Followers, all this is totally wrong; for the Right of voting is not annexed to Land, or Franchifes, to Condition, Age, or Sex; but to human Nature

---

* See an exprefs Differtation towards the Clofe of this Work on the three Orders of Men formerly in *England*, Slaves,--- Tradefmen,---and Gentlemen.

itfelf,

itfelf, and to moral Agency: Therefore, whereever human Nature, and moral Agency do exift
together, be the Subjeƈt rich or poor, old or
young, male or female, it muft follow from
thefe Principles, that the Right of voting muft
exift with it : For whofoever is a moral Agent is a
Perfon ; and *Perfonality* is the only Foundation of
the Right of voting. To *fuppofe* the contrary, we
have been lately told by a Right Reverend Edi-
tor of Mr. LOCKE, is *grofs Ignorance,* or fomething worfe : And to *aƈt on* fuch reftraining
Principles, by depriving the Mafs of the People
of their Birth-Rights, is downright Robbery and
Ufurpation.

III. IF all Mankind indifcriminately have a
Right to vote in any Society, they have, for the
very fame Reafon, a Right to rejeƈt the Proceedings
of the Government of that Society to which they
belong, and to feparate from it, whenever they
fhall think fit. For it has been inculcated into
us over and over, that every Man's Confent
ought firft to be obtained, before any Law whatever can be deemed to be valid, and of full
Force.---We have been alfo affured, that all,
and every Kind of Taxes are merely *Free-Gifts :*
Which therefore no Individual Giver is obliged
to pay, unlefs he has previoufly confented to
the Payment of it. From thefe Premifes it undoubtedly follows, that every individual Member

ber of the State is at full Liberty either to submit, or to refuse Submission to any, and to every Regulation of it, according as he had pre-determined in his own Mind. For being his own Legiflator, his own Governor, and Director in every Thing, no Man has a Right to prefcribe to him, what he ought to do. Others may ad-vife, but he alone is to dictate, refpecting his own Actions. For in fhort, he is to obey no other Will *but his own.*

THESE are furely very ftrange Pofitions; and yet they are evidently deduceable, and do na-turally refult from the Extracts given in this Chapter. Nay, there are feveral others equally paradoxical, and equally repugnant to every Species of Government, which hath ever yet exifted in the World. Such Paradoxes therefore deferve a diftinct and particular difcuffion.

CHAP.

C H A P II.

Several very grofs Errors and Abfurdities charge-
able on the Lockian Syftem.

The firft Species of Error, with its Subdivifions.

THAT Species of falfe Reafoning, which the
Logicians term *a dicto fecundum quid ad
dictum fimpliciter*, or that which proceeds from
a few Particulars to general Conclufions is fo
common in Practice, and fteals into the Mind fo
imperceptibly, that Men can hardly be too much
on their Guard againft it.—Confidered in its
own Nature, nothing can be more obvious than
that a Propofition, which may be true in a particular Inftance, may not be fo invariably: And
that therefore two fuch Propofitions fhould never
be confounded together, as if they were fynoni-
mous.—Yet the Identity of Words and Sounds
often leads Men to fuppofe, unlefs they are very
watchful, that there is alfo an Identity of Senfe.
Many Cafes might be given to corroborate and
illuftrate this Obfervation; but perhaps there is
no Inftance whatever, which confirms it more
ftrongly than that now before us, the Lockian
Principle of the indefeafible Right of private
Judgment.

MR.

MR. LOCKE in his early Days was a Witnefs to grievous Perfecutions inflicted on the Score of Religion. He faw the Rights of private Judgment expofed to continual Vexations; and he faw likewife, that the Interefts of the State were not at all concerned in maintaining that rigid, univerfal Conformity in Religion, for which the Bigots of thofe Times fo fiercely contended; — nay, that the Principles of Humanity, Juftice, and Truth, as well as the Suggeftions of found Policy, plainly required a more extended Plan of religious Liberty: All this he clearly faw: And hence he inferred, and very juftly, that every Man had a Right not only to think, but even to act for himfelf, in all fuch religious Matters as did not oppofe, or clafh with the Interefts of civil Society. And had he ftopt there, and gone no farther, all would have been right; nay, he would have truly deferved the Thanks of Mankind for pleading their Caufe fo well.

BUT, alas! he extended thofe Ideas, which were true only in what concerns Religion, to Matters of a mere civil Nature, and even to the Origin of civil Government itfelf;---as if there had been the fame Plea for Liberty of Confcience in difobeying the civil Laws of one's Country, as for not conforming to a Church Eftablifhment, or an Ecclefiaftical Inftitution;---and that the

Rights

Rights of private Judgment [I mean the open and public Exercise of thofe Rights] were equally unalienable and indefeafible in both Refpects. Indeed it muft be confeffed, that, had the Cafes been truly parallel, a Non-conformift in the one Cafe ought to have been tolerated equally with a Non-conformift in the other: And I will add, that the whole Merits of the Queftion depend on the fingle Point, whether the Cafes are parallel, or not.

Thus, for Example, no Man, not even the fupreme Magiftrate, has a Right to moleft me for worfhipping God according to the Dictates of my own Confcience, provided I do nothing in that Refpect, which can *fairly* be conftrued to hurt the Property of another Man, or difturb the Peace of Society. Therefore I may be a Papift, as well as a Proteftant in my fpeculative Opinions, and yet do nothing, which can, when juftly interpreted, be accounted to be injurious to others: Nay I will not fcruple to declare, that I may be a Jew, or a Mahometan, a Gentoo, or a Confucian, and yet be a loyal Subject to my Prince, an honeft Man, and an ufeful Member of the Community. Therefore, if * Toleration were ever to be extended

---

* Matters of ftrict Right are undoubtedly very different from, Matters merely prudential; and in the Reafon of Things a Line

as far as in Reaſon, and Juſtice, and good Policy it ought to go, it ought to be ſo large as to
comprehend every religious Sect whatever,
whoſe Doctrines, or rather whoſe Practice [for
'tis chiefly by Men's Practice that we ought to
determine, whether any Sect deſerves to be
tolerated, or not;---therefore I ſay, whoſe
Practice] proves them worthy to enjoy the Protection of the State. And there is a very particular, and a moſt important Reaſon to be
given, why this Liberty of Conſcience in religious Matters ought to be extended as far as
ever the Safety of the State will permit: It is,
becauſe in the Affairs of Conſcience no Man can

---

ought always to be drawn between them. Every peaceable and
uſeful Subject has a Right to the Protection of the State under
which he lives, in order to enjoy the Fruits of his Induſtry:
And it would be an Act of flagrant Injuſtice to debar him of
that Protection either in whole, or in Part. But he cannot
have the ſame juſt Pretenſions to demand to be created a Ma-
giſtrate or Judge, or to be raiſed to Poſts of Honour, Power,
or Profit of any Kind; becauſe theſe Offices do not belong to
him of *Right*, in the mere Capacity of a Subject. Therefore as
they are Matters of a prudential Nature, they muſt be diſpoſed
of according to the Diſcretion of the ruling Powers in every
State, and not according to the Ambition, or Expectation of
the Candidates. There may be many Things, in reſpect of
Capacity, Education, outward Circumſtances, Party-Attach-
ments, &c. &c. which may diſqualify from certain Offices
thoſe, who, in other Reſpects, are uſeful Subjects, and therefore entitled to Protection. It belongs ultimately to the Prudence of the Legiſlature to ſettle the Boundaries.

act,

act, or be fuppofed to act as Proxy for another ;
no Man can be a Deputy, Subftitute, or Reprefentative in fuch a Cafe ; but every Man
muft think, and act perfonally for himfelf. This
is the Fact ; and in this Senfe it is very
true, that the Rights of private Judgment
are abfolutely unalienable : — But why unalienable ? — It is becaufe they are *untransferable* : And therefore every Man muft of
Neceffity, after having ufed the beft Lights and
Helps he can obtain, be his own Legiflator, (under God) his own Governor, and his own Director in the Affairs of Religion.

APPLY now thefe Ideas to the Cafe of Civil
Government ; and then fee, what ftrange Confequences will arife.

1. IN the firft Place, if the fame Train of
Reafoning is to be admitted in both Cafes, then
it is evident, that none, no, not Women nor
Children, ought to be excluded from the Right
of voting on every political Queftion that may
occur ; unlefs indeed you can prove beforehand,
that thofe, whom you exclude, have no Confcience
at all, and have no Senfe whatever of Right and
Wrong : — And you muft prove likewife that they
are incapable of judging in this Refpect, not
only to the Satisfaction of others (which perhaps
would not be difficult) but alfo of themfelves ; —
which it is humbly apprehended, will be a moft
arduous

arduous Tafk: Yet, I fay, you muft prove it, otherwife you will exclude thofe from voting, who have juft Caufe to think, on your State of the Cafe, that their Right is as unalienable as your own ; and you will act diametrically oppo-fite to the grand fundamental Principle of your Founder by excluding them. In fhort, to ufe your own Language, you yourfelf will be an Ufurper and a Robber. Therefore draw the Line, if you can, between the promifcuous Ad-miffion, or Exclufion of fuch Voters as thefe, according to the Lockian Syftem.

2*dly.* If the Cafes are parallel, then the un-alienable Rights of private Judgment are not to be fet afide by the Determination of any Ma-jority whatever. For as a Plurality of Votes is no Evidence of Infallibility, a Man's inward Conviction may not be altered by his being overpowered by Numbers. What then is he to do in fuch a Cafe ?. The Anfwer is obvious : He muft follow the Dictates of his own Confcience ; and he has an *unalienable* Right fo to do. Well, but Mr. Locke himfelf acknowledges, that were this to be allowed, that is, were the Minority to be permitted to act contrary to the Senfe of the Majority, civil Government itfelf could not fub-fift. True : He makes fuch an acknowledge-ment : And by fo doing he reduces himfelf to the Dilemma, either of giving up his whole

Syftem

Syſtem, that no Man is bound to obey thoſe Laws, which have been impoſed upon him without his own Conſent;—or he muſt ſhew that a Man doth conſent, and doth not conſent, at the ſame Time, and in the ſame Reſpeſt. Indeed it is evident, that he found himſelf greatly perplexed, when he came to touch on this Point; and that he ſeemed to be like a Man got into a dangerous Paſs, full of Precipices, which he wiſhed not to ſee, in paſſing through, by not looking about him. Dr. PRIESTLY is more open and ingenuous. He did not attempt to ſhun the Difficulty, which he ſaw was unavoidable, but prepared to encounter it, as well as he could.---For after having obſerved [ſee the Quotation, P. 14] that every thing in a ſmall Society might be determined by the *perſonal* Votes of the Majority preſent, he prudently adds, " provided they had *previouſly* agreed, that the Votes of the Majority ſhould be deciſive." Such a Conduſt of the Doſtor's is commendable; though the Argument he made uſe of is weak and trifling: Weak it is, becauſe, 1ſt. It is impoſſible for the Doſtor to prove, that previous Meetings were held in every, or perhaps in any State whatever, in which it had been *unanimouſly* determined, that the Votes of the Majority ſhould be deciſive;---and trifling, becauſe 2dly. were it even poſſible to prove the Faſt, it could be of no Service to

the

the Doctor's Caufe; inafmuch as an *unalienable* Right is of fuch a Nature, that it cannot be furrendred to a Majority: And even if this were attempted, " fuch a Ceffion, (to adopt the Words " of Dr. PRICE,) would either bind not at all, or " bind only the Individuals, who made it." And fo could be of no Continuance. Therefore in every View, it is ftrictly demonftrable, that according to the Lockian Syftem, nothing lefs than *Unanimity* in every Meafure can keep fuch a Society as this from the Danger of breaking to Pieces every Moment; for a fingle *diffentient Voice*, like the VETO's of the republican Tyrants of *Poland*, is fufficient to throw the whole Conftitution of the State into Chaos and Confufion. In fhort, ftrange as it may feem, the unalienable Right of one fingle refractory Member of the Diet deftroys, or annuls the unalienable Rights of the whole: Nor is there any other effectual Remedy to be applied in this defperate Diforder, but that of a Sabre held over the Diffentient's Head, with a Threat of cleaving him down, if he fhould perfift in the Exercife of his unalienable Right. This indeed has been known to have produced *Unanimity*, when other Motives could not prevail. What infatuated Politics are thefe! And to what Mazes of Error, and Abfurdity, do Men run, when they ftray from the Paths of common Senfe! But

Thirdly.

Thirdly. FOR the very fame Reafon, that the Members of a Lockian Republic cannot furrender their unalienable Rights to a Majority, be it fmall or great, they cannot likewife *tranf-fer* their unalienable Right of voting to Deputies or Reprefentatives to aƈt and vote for them. For this in Faƈt comes to the fame Thing with the former. They muft therefore all vote in Perfon or not at all. Now this is a direƈt Inference, which neceffarily follows from the foregoing Premifes. And it is an Inference, which Dr. PRICE is fo far from difavowing, when applied to the Cafe of the *Americans*, that he glories in, and greatly exults upon it. " As no People (fays " he) [fee the Quotation, Page 21] can law-" fully furrender their religious Liberty, by " giving up their Right of judging for themfelves " in Religion, or by allowing any human Being " to prefcribe to them, what Faith they fhall em-" brace, or what Mode of Worfhip they fhall " praƈtice ; fo neither can any civil Societies law-" fully furrender their civil Liberty, by giving " up to any extraneous Jurifdiƈtion their Power " of legiflating for themfelves, and difpofing of " their Property. Such a Ceffion being incon-" fiftent with the *unalienable Rights* of human Na-" ture would either bind not at all, or bind only " the Individuals who made it. This is a Bleffing, " which no Generation of Men can give up for " another ; and which, when loft, a People have " always a *Right to refume.*" THE

THE Doctor's Aim in this Paragraph, we plainly fee, was to defend his beloved *Americans* a-gainft the fuppofed Ufurpation of the *Englifh* over their unalienable Rights. Be it fo: But was he aware, that the very fame Argument holds equally ftrong againft the Appointment of Affemblies of Reprefentatives in *America*, and of an Houfe of Commons in *England*, as againft the *Englifh* Legiflature ruling over the *American*? Was he, I fay, aware of this? And yet nothing can be more evident than that the fame Argument con-cludes equally ftrong in both Cafes, if it concludes at all. For Example, " No People, fays the " Doctor, can lawfully furrender their Religious " Liberty, by giving up their Right of judging " for themfelves in Religion, or by allowing any " human Being to prefcribe to them, what Faith " they fhall embrace, or what Mode of Worfhip " they fhall practice." I agree with him moft heartily on that Head :—But then I add [and I am fure, what I add in this Cafe, Dr. PRICE will readily allow] that no one Individual can depute another to judge for him, what Faith he fhall embrace, or what Mode of Worfhip he fhall practice.—And then what is the Confe-quence? Neceffarily this, That if the Cafes be-tween Religion and Civil Government be fimi-lar, as the Doctor fuppofes them to be, no one Individual can appoint another to judge for him, what Laws fhall be propounded, what Taxes fhall

be

be raifed, or what is to be done at Home or
Abroad, in Peace, or in War:---But every Perfon, who has this indefeafible, this unalienable,
incommunicable, and untransferable Right of
voting, judging, and *fighting*, muft vote, judge,
and *fight* for himfelf.---This I fay is a neceffary
Confequence from the Premifes : And I defy the
acuteft Logician to deduce any other Inference
from the above Hypothefis.

HONEST, undiffembling ROUSSEAU clearly
faw, where the Lockian Hypothefis muft neceffarily end. And as he was a Man who never
boggled at Confequences, however extravagant
or abfurd, he declared with his ufual Franknefs,
that the People could not transfer their indefeafible Right of voting for themfelves to any others ;
and that the very Notion of their choofing Perfons to reprefent them in thefe Refpeﬅs, was a
Species of Contradiﬅion. According to him, a
Transmutation of Perfons could not be a greater
Impoffibility than a Tranflation of thofe Rights,
which were abfolutely incommunicable. And
therefore he adds [See his Social Compaﬅ,
Chap. 15. Of Deputies or Reprefentatives]
" The *Englifh* imagine, they are a free People :
" They are however miftaken : They are only
" fuch during the Eleﬅion of Members of Parlia-
" ment. When thefe are chofen, they become *Slaves*
" again." The Doﬅors PRIESTLY and PRICE do
not indeed abfolutely join ROUSSEAU in condemning

demning the Ufe of national Reprefentatives;
but it is plain, that they admit them with a
very ill Grace, and, with great Reluctance.
Nay, they are fo far confiftent with themfelves
as to declare very freely, that the Admiffion of them is an *Infringement* on Liberty, more or lefs :---even on that Liberty,
which they proclaim aloud, every Man has an
unalienable Right to *refume, as foon as ever he
can*. Moreover, they accord with ROUSSEAU
in another general Pofition; that true, genuine
Liberty can only be enjoyed in a State fo very
fmall, [undoubtedly they muft mean fome paultry Village, confifting of a few thatched
Cottages] that the People can perfonally
attend on all Occafions.---Much more might
have been added: But furely we have now
had enough, and to fpare, of this Kind of
Reafoning *a dicto fecundum quid ad dictum fimpliciter*. And the Upfhot of the whole is this,
That if Men will jumble thofe Ideas together,
which ought to be kept feparate, they muft
fall into palpable Errors, and be guilty of great
Abfurdities in the Courfe of their Reafoning.

The fecond Species of Errors, with its Subdivifions.

THOUGH I have obferved before, yet I muft
repeat again, that according to the Lockian
Syftem, civil Government is not *natural* to
Man.

Man. It feems, the Seeds of it were not originally implanted in our Conftitutions by the Hand
of Providence. For had that been the Cafe, we
might reafonably have expeſted, that they would
have fprouted up, and germinated of their own
Accord, at leaft in fome Degree ; without dating
the Origin of Government from the jealous
Efforts of political Contrivance, mutual Com-
paſts, and reciprocal Stipulations. We might,
I fay, have naturally fuppofed, that Government
and Mankind were, in a Manner, coeval ; and
that they had grown up together from fmall Beginnings, or a Kind of infant State, 'till they had
arrived at a maturer Age ; in regard to which
we might further have fuppofed, that they became
more, or lefs polifhed and improved, according
as they had received different Cultures from human Art and Induftry. All this, I fay, we might
have naturally fuppofed ; but all thefe Suppofi-
tions we muft entirely lay afide, in order to adopt
another Mode of accounting for the Origin of
civil Government. For according to the Lockian
Syftem, Mankind had no natural Inclination towards any Government whatever : But having
found the Evils of Anarchy to be quite intolerable, they refolved at laft to fubmit to the Evil of
Government, as the leffer of the two. But in
order that they might guard againft the Dangers
to be feared on this Side, as well as felt on the
former, they determined not to part with their
precious natural Liberty, 'till Security had been
given,

given, that fuch a Ceffion fhould not be turned to their Difadvantage. Therefore they folemnly ftipulated, that in cafe their new Lords and Mafters fhould not pleafe them, they might return again to their dear State of Nature, and begin the Work of Government *de novo*, if they chofe fo to do, or remain as they were, all equal, all free, and independent. And thus it came to pafs, that they, who were under no Sort of Subjection one Moment, became the Subjects of a regular Government the next: And from being no Ways connected with any Body politic whatever, they were transformed, all on a fudden, by the Magic of the *original* focial Contract into moft profound Politicians. The Lockians have not yet vouchfafed to tell us, where any one fingle Copy of this famous original Contract is to be found,—in what Language it was written,—in whofe Hands depofited,—who were the Witneffes,—nor in what Archives we are to fearch for it. But neverthelefs they have taken Care to fupply us very amply with Inferences and Deductions refulting from it;---as if it had been a Thing, which had been already proved and admitted, and concerning whofe Exiftence no further Queftions ought to be afked. We muft therefore, as we cannot be favoured with a Sight of the Contract itfelf, attend to thofe Inferences and Deductions, which they fay, are derived from it.

THE

The firſt Inference is, that no Man ought to be deemed a Member of a State Politic, 'till he has enrolled himſelf among the Number of its Citizens by ſome expreſs and poſitive Engagement. " For, ſays Mr. Locke, [See the Quo-" tation, Page 9.] ſubmitting to the Laws of " any Country, living quietly, and enjoying Pri-" vileges and Protections under them, makes not " a Man a Member of that Society ;---nothing " can make a Man ſo, but his actually entering " into it by poſitive Engagement, and expreſs Pro-" miſe and Compact." And again : " Whatever " Engagements or Promiſes any one has made " for himſelf, he is under the Obligation of " them, but cannot by any Compact whatever " bind his Children or Poſterity. For his Son, " when a Man, being altogether as free as his " Father, any Act of the Father can no more " give away the Liberty of the Son, than it can " of any Body elſe." [See the Quotation, Page 9.]

All this is certainly agreeable to the Nature of the original Contract here ſuppoſed. For if we can believe the one to have exiſted, and to have been the only Foundation of Civil Government, we muſt allow, that the other ought to have followed. Here therefore let us ſuppoſe a Caſe.---A Man, tho' born in *England*, and of *Engliſh* Parents, yet, it ſeems, is not by Birth an *Engliſhman;* that is, he is not a Subject of
this

this Realm, 'till he has made himself so, by some expreſs Covenant and Stipulation. This methinks appears a little ſtrange: But ſtranger Things will foon follow. For, after having weighed all Circumſtances, and conſidered the Matter pro. and con. he at laſt conſents to become a *Britiſh* Subjeſt, and gets his Name enrolled among the Number of its Citizens. Then he marries, and has a Family; and by living under the Proteſtion of the *Engliſh* Conſtitution, where every Man is ſafe in the Enjoyment of the Fruits of his Induſtry, [not to mention thoſe honourable, and *lucrative* Imployments he obtained under the Government.] He grows rich and wealthy, leaving ſeven Sons behind him, all grown up to Man's Eſtate: To the ſix younger he gives ample Fortunes in moveable Goods and Chattles, and to the eldeſt a large Eſtate in Land. The Queſtion therefore is, Among what Species of political Beings are theſe ſeven Children to be claſſed? And are they the Subjeſts of *Great-Britain*, or are they not, before they have entered into an expreſs Covenant, or Treaty with the State for that Purpoſe?

ACCORDING to Mr. LOCKE's leading Idea, he ought to ſay, that they are the Subjeſts of no Government upon Earth; but that they are all in the original State of Nature, perfeſtly free from any political Laws or Conneſtion whatever,

entire

entire Mafters of themfelves, and abfolutely independent Beings. — Confequently, that they
ought to be allowed to do as they pleafed relative
to *Great-Britain* [*Great-Britain* I fay, which *had
enriched their Father, had nurfed them up, and protected them* from their very Infancy to mature
Eftate] and that if they chofe to forfake her in any
particular Period of her Diftrefs, fhe ought not to
ftop their Emigration, or to hinder them from carrying all their *moveable* Goods and rich Effects with
them [their *Immoveables,* no Thanks to them, they
could not carry] much lefs ought fhe to demand
the Affiftance either of their *Perfons,* or of their
Purfes, as a Matter of *ftrict Right,* if they fhould
not be difpofed to grant it.   This I fay, is the
true Lockian Principle without Exaggeration:
And let the impartial World be the Judge,
whether it be confiftent with common Senfe, or
common Honefty.   Indeed Mr. Locke himfelf
feems to have been aware, that he had carried
this Point too far : For he allows, that one of
thefe Sons, fuppofe the eldeft, that is, the Landholder, might be obliged, by the Nature of his
Tenure, to defend that State, within which his
Lands lay, and to make fome Recompence to it
for the long Protection and many Bleffings he
had enjoyed.   Yet, that he might never lofe
Sight of his darling Ideas of Confent, or Contract,
he calls the Accepting of the Eftate on thefe
Terms, a *tacit Confent*.   And then he adds :
" He [the Father] may indeed annex fuch Conditions

" ditions to the Land he enjoyed, as a Subject of
" any Common-Wealth, as may *oblige* his Son
" to be of that Community, if he will enjoy
" thofe Poffeffions, which were his Father's; be-
" caufe the Eftate being the Father's Property,
" he may difpofe, or fettle it *as he pleafes.*" And
thus Reader, at laft we feem to have gotten one
of thefe Sons, the *Landholder,* back again into
the Service of his Country, in order to defend it
in Times of Danger. But let us not be too
fure: For this Lockian Principle is of fuch a
changeable Nature, and is endowed with fo much
Verfatility, that it will often give us the Slip,
when we think we have the firmeft hold of it.

HERE therefore let it be afked,—If a Man
hath a Right to annex what Conditions he pleafes
to the Poffeffion of his Landed Eftate after his
Deceafe,—By what Law did he acquire that
Right? And who gave him that Authority?
Surely in a *mere State of Nature* he could have
had no fuch Right;---becaufe the Land could be
no longer *his,* than whilft he himfelf was ufing
and occupying it;---which tis plain, he could not
do after he was dead. Granting therefore, that
in a State of Nature he had a Right, during his
Life-Time, to appropriate to himfelf a certain
Portion of Land for his own Suftentation, [which
yet *ROUSSEAU with great Shew of Reafon

Difcours fur la Queftion, propofée par l'Academie de Dijon;
Quelle eft l'Origine de l'Inegalité parmi les Hommes; et fi elle eft
positively

pofitively denies.] Still that Land muft revert to the Public, and become *common* again after his Deceafe. But if it fhould be faid, that he derived the Right of bequething Land, and of annexing various Conditions to the Bequeft, from the pofitive Laws of civil Society (which is the Truth of the Cafe, and which Mr. LOCKE himfelf is obliged to allow, by ftiling this Father, a Subject of fome Commonwealth) Then I afk, Why could not the Commonwealth, if it fo pleafed, exercife the fame Right itfelf, which it had empowered the Father to exercife? Why could not the State oblige the other fix Sons, as well as the eldeft, to perform the feveral Offices, and difcharge the Duties, civil and military, of loyal Subjects, if the Exigencies of the State fhould fo require? Or if there be any effential Difference between the two Cafes of moveable Property, and immoveable, refpecting the Duty and Allegiance due to Government;---fhew the Difference if you can. In fhort, what is it, about which we have been fo long difputing?

---

autorifée par la Loi naturelle?---Second Partie. Le Premier, qui ayant enclos un Terrein, f'avifa dire, *Ceci eft a moi*, et trouva des Gens affez fimples pour le croire, *fut le vrai Fondateur de la Societè civile*. Que de Crimes, de Guerres, de Meutres, que de Miferes, et d'Horreurs n'eut point epargnès au Genre Humain celui qui arrachant les Pieux, ou comblant les Foffé, eut criè a fes femblables; *Gardez vous d'ecouter cet Impofteur. Vous etes perdues, fi vous oubliez, que les Fruits font a tous, et que la terre n'eft a perfonne.*

For

For, after all it is plain to a Demonftration, that we muft allow at laft, what ought to have been allowed at firft; *viz.* That Protection and Allegiance, between Prince and People, are reciprocal Ties, and that the one neceffarily infers the other, without the Formality of an exprefs perfonal Covenant, or pofitive Stipulation; fo that if the Duty of Protection be performed on the one Side, that of Allegiance ought to be obferved on the other, and *vice verfa.* An Author, not inferior to Mr. LOCKE, or any of his Difciples, in the Defence of *true* Liberty, both Civil and Religious, and who is acknowledged to be an excellent Judge of the *Englifh* Conftitution, thus expreffes himfelf on this important Subject. " Natural Allegiance is " founded in the Relation every Man ftandeth " in to the Crown, confidered as the Head of " that Society whereof he is *born a Member*; and " on the peculiar Privileges he deriveth from that " Relation, which are with great Propriety called " his *Birthright.* This Birthright nothing but " his own Demerit can deprive him of; it is *in-* " *defeafible* and *perpetual.* And confequently the " Duty of Allegiance which arifeth out of it, and " is *infeparably* connected with it, is in Con- " fideration of Law likewife *unalienable* and " perpetual." [*See* FOSTER'S *Reports. Introduction to the Difcourfe on High Treafon.*]

2*dly,*

2*dly*. The Affertion, that Taxes are a Free
Gift, and not a Debt due to the Public, is
another ftrange Inference refulting from Mr.
LOCKE's Idea of an original Contract. Indeed
had Government been that vague, unfettled,
and precarious Thing, which the Lockian Syftem
reprefents it to be ; without any better Foundation to reft upon, than the Breath and Caprice of
each Individual; — then it would have been very
true, that thofe, who fupported it by their voluntary Contributions, were the *Givers*, or *Donors*
of their refpective Sums. But doth the Idea of
fuch a Benefaction at all accord with the Idea of
a Tax? Surely no : For a Tax, in the very
Nature of it, implies fomething compulfory, and
not difcretionary ; fomething, which is not in
our own free Choice, but is impofed by an
Authority fuperior to our own : Whereas a mere
Gift, or free-will Offering implies juft the contrary. However, as I faid before, it is not the
Inference itfelf, which is here to blame ; for had
the Premifes been true, the Inference would
have been juft enough ; and therefore we muft
trace the Error higher up. Here then be it
obferved, that it can never be true, that Providence hath left Mankind in a State of fuch total
Indifference refpecting Government, that it
fhould depend on their own Option, whether
they will have any Government, or none at all.
I fay, this can never be true of the Species in
general ; whatever particular Exceptions there
might

might be of here and there a wayward Individual, who ought to be regarded as a Monfter deviating from the common Courfe of Nature. In fact, the Inftincts and Propenfities of Mankind towards focial * Life, are in a Manner fo irrefiftible, that I might almoft fay, Men will as naturally feek to enjoy the Bleflings of Society, as they do to obtain their daily Food. In the one Cafe it is not left to their own Choice, whether they will eat or not eat, drink or not drink (for kind Nature has determined that Point for them); but it is left to themfelves to judge and to choofe, in many Inftances, what Kinds of Food, and of Liquids they will ufe, how they will have them prepared, and whether they will make a proper, or improper Ufe of thefe Deftinations of Providence. Juft fo, or nearly fo, in my Opinion, is the State of human Nature refpecting Government. For Providence feems to have determined for them, that there fhall be *a Government* of fome Sort or other ; and then to have left it, for the moft Part, to themfelves to fix on the Form or Mode, and to regulate the feveral Appendages belonging to it, according to their own good Liking, Judgment, and Difcretion. Now, if this be the Cafe, that is, if there muft be a

---

* It will be diftinctly fhewn in the firft Chapter of the fecond Part, that a focial State among fuch Creatures as *Men* muft neceffarily produce a Government of fome Kind or other.

Government

Government of fome Sort, or in fome Shape or other; it then neceffarily follows, that certain *Means* muft be found out for the Support of fuch an *End*. What, therefore, it may be afked, are thefe Means? And which are the beft, the leaft burthenfome, and the moft unexceptionable? [For in this Refpect likewife, as well as in the former, a great deal is left to the Prudence and Sagacity of Mankind to weigh and confider, and provide for themfelves.] The Anfwer to which Queftion is the following, That there can be devifed but three Ways for the Support of any Government whatever, viz. Perfonal Service, — Crown Lands, — or public Taxes; — and each of thefe Methods (fuch are the Imperfections of human Nature) is attended with Conveniences and Inconveniences not a few.

And (firft) as to *perfonal Service*. — In the Infancy of a very fmall State, and before the Arts of Civilization had fufficiently taken Place, perfonal Service feems to have been the firft, and indeed the only Idea, which would occur. For when Men had nothing elfe to pay, towards that Government which protected them, *they muft have paid that;* — paid it, I mean, as a Matter of Duty, Debt, or Obligation, and not as the Lockians fuppofe, a free-will Offering, or voluntary Service. But it is eafy to fee, that fuch a Tribute as this would foon appear to be very burthenfome for the Subject to difcharge, and

not

not at all convenient for the Prince to receive.
In refpeѐt to the Subjeѐt, were he to be obliged
to leave his own private Affairs, in order to attend
the Public on all Occafions, civil, military,
legiflative, and judicial ;—there would be hardly
any Time left, which he could call his own : His
Fields muft lie negleѐted, his Manufaѐture and
his Shop be deferted, and all Bufinefs, both in
the Way of Agriculture, and of Commerce, by
Land and by Sea, be in a Manner at a Stand.
In refpeѐt to the Prince, the State, or the Public, fuch a promifcuous Attendance of Perfons of
all Ranks, Ages, and Profeffions would be found
to be a very great Nufance, and to be productive of many Evils of various Kinds, without
fufficient Benefits to counter-balance them. Add
to this, that as the Bounds of the State became
extended, the Attendance of Perfons living at a
greaţ Diftance, would become more and more
impraѐticable : So that in every View, this Kind
of Tribute, though the Source of all others, muft
foon be laid afide, and be exchanged for fomething more ufeful, and lefs inconvenient.---Only
thus much of this primeval Idea ought always to
be retained, that in Times of univerfal Danger,
we muft again recur to the original Ufe of perfonal Service. For in fuch a Cafe, the Principle
of Self-Prefervation authorizes every State to
fummon all its Inhabitants capable of bearing
Arms, to be ready to appear in its Defence.
Nor, I trow, would the Lockian Plea of Exemption

emption in fuch a Cafe be regarded in any other Light, than as proceeding either from the Fears of an arrant Coward, or from the Schemes and Confpiracies of a Traitor. In either Light it would certainly meet with its deferved Punifh-ment. Indeed the very Recital of fuch a Plea carries fo ftrong a Confutation in it, that nothing ftronger can be added : " Gentlemen, though I
" was born and bred in this Country, and have
" fubmitted to its Laws, [when that was attended
" with fome Advantage, and no Danger ;] and
" though I have lived quietly, and enjoyed Pri-
" vileges and Protection under them ;---more-
" over, tho' the Invader is making great Strides
" to fubdue you, and HANNIBAL is in a Man-
" ner at the Gates ;---yet I muft at prefent beg
" Leave to be excufed from oppofing him : For
" as I never did actually enter into any pofitive
" Engagement, and exprefs Promife and Com-
" pact to defend this Country, I am not legally
" obliged to defend it. In Fact, I am not a
" Member of your Society, and therefore you
" have no Right to prefs me into its Service."---
Thus much for this Part of the Lockian Scheme, that Taxes, alias perfonal Services, are *free Gifts.* And let all Mankind from the higheft to the loweft, from the greateft to the meaneft Capacities, be the Judges, what Epithets fuch a Scheme deferves.

ONCE

ONCE more; the Cafe of preffing Sailors for the Sea-Service, is a Confirmation of every Thing which hath been advanced concerning the Neceffity of retaining the original Idea of ferving the State in Perfon, and not by Subftitutes. For Sailors are a Body of Men, whofe Service cannot be performed by any but Sailors; and therefore they are, and, from the Nature of Things, ever muft be, liable to ferve in Perfon. Now, were you to call *Preffing* a free Gift, or the voluntary Offer of perfonal Service on the Part of the poor Sailor that is preffed, what would the World think of you, but that you were either *infane* yourfelf, or that you efteemed all others to be mere Ideots? However, your Plea perhaps may be, that tho' the perfonal Service of Sailors at prefent is, generally fpeaking, very far from voluntary;---yet it might have been rendered more defireable, and confequently voluntary [rather *lefs-involuntary*] were a proper Mode adopted for inviting Sailors to inlift of their own Accord. This I will fuppofe is your Plea: And the Meaning of it is,---to recommend a *national Regifter for Seamen.* Great Things have been faid of late Years in Praife of fuch an Inftitution; but they have been chiefly faid by thofe, who leaft underftood what is meant and implied by it. I myfelf once thought it a fine Thing; but ever fince the Year 1748 (when I had the firft Opportunity of examining it on the Spot) I have been thoroughly convinced, that a Regifter doth not

deferve

deferve a tenth Part of the Praifes, which our
modern Patriotic Pamphleteers, and ignorant
News-Writers have beftowed upon it. For it is
a very operofe and intricate Bufinefs, not at all
calculated for the Difpatch of Trade, and Freedom of Navigation ; moreover, it is loaded, in
its Confequences, with fuch an Expence, as renders Freight in *France* * exceffively dear :—
Thefe are the Evils attending it even in Times

---

* This Circumftance of the Dearnefs of the French Freight
[more than 30 per Cent. dearer than the Englifh] renders the
Conduct of the French Court, in fupporting the Independency
of *America*, and granting a Freedom of Navigation (at leaft in
part) between *Old France*, the *French Iflands*, and the *American
Continent*, one of the moft impolitic Meafures that ever that
Nation adopted. For, as the very *Forte* of the *Americans* confifts in the Cheapnefs of their Navigation, and as they are a
People more addicted to Chicane of every Kind, to Quirks
and Quibbles in the Law, and have greater *Invention* that
Way, than any People upon Earth (even according to the
Confeffion of their beft Friends) ; they, with the Affiftance of
their new Allies, the *French* Planters of *Martinico*, *Guadaloupe*,
&c. *all united in one common Intereft*, will evade the reftraining
Laws of *Old France*, in Spite of every Effort of a French Miniftry to the contrary. This, I will venture to predict, will
be the Confequence in Procefs of Time. And then the *Americans* will engrofs almoft the whole of that Carrying-Trade to
themfelves, which ufed to be the beft Nurfery of Seamen for
the *French* Navy. What Infatuation is this ! But I forbear---
The filly groundlefs Notion, that the Seperation of *America*
would be the Ruin of *England*, hath done more to advance the
real Interefts of *England*, than we could, or, at leaft, would
have done for ourfelves. May we profit by thefe Blunders of
others, and fee our own real Interefts, before it be too late !

of

of Peace ; and yet it is of little or no Efficacy in Times of War. For when the Sailors, who have been regiftered, will not appear to their Summons at their refpective Ports, or will not voluntarily furrender themfelves up at the Ports where they may happen to be ;---the laft Refource is *Violence* and *Compulfion*. Now I afk, what is there in this boafted Method, which is a Whit preferable to our own ? For we always begin with *Bounties* and *Invitations* ; and feldom or never have Recourfe to *Preffing*, till the gentler Methods are found to fail. So that, after all, we are much on a Par with the *French* in Times of War, and feel none of the Inconveniencies of their Regifters in Times of Peace. The late ALEXANDER HUME, Efq; Member of Parliament for *Southwark*, fpent many Years in framing a Bill for a national Regifter of Seamen ; and as he was a Man of ftrong natural Parts, and had had long Experience in nautical Affairs, it was natural for him to conclude, that he had fucceeded in correcting the many Evils and Imperfections of the *French* Regifter. This Bill, I think, was once read in the Houfe of Commons, and ordered to be printed. At Mr. HUME's Requeft I got it laid before the Society of Merchant Adventurers in *Briftol*, in order to have their Opinion ; and I received for Anfwer, that, bad as the Mode of preffing was, both Merchants and Seamen, and all Parties concerned, would prefer it to the Cloggs and Shackles, and various reftrictive

reſtrictive Clauſes contained in the regiſtering
Bill of Mr. HUME. It ſeems, the Idea of a Regiſter is revived again ; and great Expectations
are founded on ſome promiſing Scheme of that
Nature. My ſincere Wiſh is, that what has appeared ſo plauſible to ſeveral Gentlemen in
Theory, may become as favourable to Liberty,
as beneficial to Commerce, and as practicable in
Fact as they themſelves expect, or deſire. But
in the mean Time, and 'till that happy Period
ſhall arrive, when a ſufficient Number of Sailors
ſhall be induced by ſome inviting Scheme or
other [call it a Regiſter, or call it what you
pleaſe] to enliſt of their own Accord; the
Mode of Preſſing (there is no Help for it) muſt
be retained. — And need I add, that the Man,
who is preſſed, is not a *Volunteer ?* Need I go
about to prove that he is not his own Legiſlator ?
and that he is neither ſelf-governed, nor ſelf-
directed ?

2*dly.* A ſecond Mode of ſupporting Government is by Crown Lands, or large Domains.
Now this is another Species of perſonal Service,
together with the Addition of ſome Part of the
Produce of ſuch Lands either to be taken in kind,
or to be exchanged for Rent. How ſuch vaſt
Tracts of Country came into the Poſſeſſion of
the reſpective *Regents* in Society (which we know
was antiently the Caſe, at leaſt all over Europe)
is

is a Matter not to be eafily explained. Probably thefe immenfe Eftates were principally owing to two very different Caufes, viz. The patriarchal Rights; – and the Rights of Conqneft. The Patriarchs, or the Progenitors of Nations, it is natural to fuppofe, took Care to fecure vaft Tracts of the moft commodious Land to their own Ufe; – and very probably they divided the Remainder, as Mankind encreafed and multiplied, among the Subaltern Heads of Families; – fubject neverthelefs to fuch Reftrictions and Conditions, and to fuch perfonal Duties and Services, as were judged to be neceffary, whether civil, military, or fervile, in the infant State of Society. The Hiftories of the Beginning of all Clans and Tribes, and Hords of People fprung from the fame Original, feem to confirm this Hypothefis. But it ought to be obferved, that the ftrict, patriarchal Plan could not have obtained here in *Britain,* ever fince the Invafion of the *Saxons, Danes,* and *Normans* (and poffibly of the *Romans*) whatever it might have done in the more antient Times of the *Britons,* the primeval Natives of the Country.

ANOTHER Origin of Domain Lands is, – *That of Conqueft:* For when a Country was conquered by any of the barbarous Nations, the Commander in Chief, and his Subalterns, *alias* his Comites, Earls, Thanes, or Generals, divided the Territory into two Shares or Lots: – The one was referved.

ferved, and generally fpeaking it was a very large
one, for the Ufe of the Commander in Chief, in
order to fupport the Dignity of his Station, to
entertain his numerous Vaffals and Dependants,
and likewife to raife, feed, and cloathe a confiderable Body of Troops at his own Expence,
and out of the Tenants on his own Domain without calling for further Affiftance. The reft of
the Country was divided and fubdivided among
the feveral Chieftains, according to their refpective Ranks and Stations, their military Merit, the
Number of their Followers, the Favour of
the Prince, and other Circumftances. In this
Allotment each Chieftain had, for the moft Part,
the fame Jurifdiction, both civil and military,
over his refpective Tenants, as the Prince had
over thofe on his own Domain ;—each Chieftain
had alfo the fame Right to demand the perfonal
Services of thofe who held under him, whether
military, or fervile, as the Prince himfelf :---But
each Chieftain was likewife obliged to do Suit
and Service at the Court of the Sovereign, and
to attend him in his Wars, in the fame Manner,
and almoft in the fame Form, as his military
Tenants were obliged to do Suit and Service to
him. This, therefore, together with Efcheats
and Forfeitures, Compofitions and Confifcations,
and the Perquifites arifing from Efcuage, Reliefs, Heriots, Alienations, Wards and Liveries,
Pre-emptions, Purveyances, Prifages, Butlerages,
&c. &c. conftituted the main Branches of the
Gothic

Gothic Revenues and Prerogatives. Now I aſk, is there any one Thing in all this Catalogue, which in the leaſt reſembles the Idea of a Free-Gift, and voluntary Donation? On the contrary, is it not evident, that the very beſt, and moſt innocent, of theſe Prerogatives were *compulſory* in ſome Degree, and that the moſt of them were arbitrary and tyrannical in a ſhocking Degree? In Faɛt, there hardly ever was a *civil* Conſtitution more produɛtive of Slavery and Oppreſſion on the one Extreme,---or of Tumults, Inſurreɛtions, and Rebellions on the other, than the Gothic. Indeed it ill deſerved the Name of a *civil* Conſtitution: For it partook much more of a *military*, than of a civil Nature; being little better than the Idea of an Encampment, or rather of a Cantonment of Forces extending far and wide, according to the Dimenſions of the Country; and ſubjeɛt to ſuch Alterations, as theſe great Diſtances and Diſperſions made neceſſary. One Thing is certain, that true civil Liberty was a Stranger to every Country, where the Gothic Conſtitution was introduced;---and that what was called Liberty in thoſe Days, and what our modern Patriots ſo much boaſt of in ours, as the Glory of *Old England*, was the Liberty which one Baron took of making War on, and plundering the Eſtates, and murdering the Vaſſals of another.---and tyrannizing over his own:---And that when Half a Score of theſe petty Tyrants
could

could band together, and make a common Caufe, they were a Match for the King himfelf, who otherwife would have been a Tyrant over them. Now this was the boafted Liberty of the Gothic Conftitution : And becaufe that in *France* and *Spain, Sweden* and *Denmark*, and perhaps in fome other Countries, this Power of the Barons of doing Mifchief, and of being a Plague to each other, to their own Vaffals, and to all around them, has been much curtailed, if not totally abolifhed;---therefore we are told by very great and grave Hiftorians, that thefe Countries have loft their Liberties.* Indeed

---

* Of a like Nature is that other Affertion of our modern Pa-triots, that in former Times, there was no fuch Thing as a Standing-Army ; but that this is a modern Invention, to en-flave Mankind. Indeed, if they meant to fay, that the Term itfelf was not in ufe in former Times, they are right ; for the Word *Standing-Armies* is of modern Date. But if they wifh to propagate a Notion, (which they certainly do) that the Thing itfelf, the *Subftance*, was not in Being 'till very lately, they are guilty of a wilful Mifreprefentation ; for they *do* know, that the Gothic Conftitution neceffarily created a Standing-Army in *Fact*, tho' not in *Name*, in every Kingdom, wherever it pre-vailed. They know alfo, that the effential Difference between antient and modern Standing-Armies confifts in this, that ours are paid in *Money*, and the *Gothic* Troops were paid in *Land :* And that confequently their Forces were much more difperfed, much worfe difciplined, much more fubject to the Wills and Caprice of their refpective Generals and fubaltern Officers, *alias* the Barons, and Lords of Manors ; and, in fhort, in every View much more unfavourable to civil Liberty than ours are.— Not many Miles diftant from the Place where I now write, the

I

I grant, that the Kings of each of thefe Countries have rifen in Power in Proportion as the
Nobles have funk; but neverthelefs I do aver
it for a folemn Truth, that the common People
have been Gainers likewife. For though they
have not *acquired* as much Liberty, as they
ought to have, and what is their Right to have,---
yet they have obtained a much greater Degree
of it every where, *even in Denmark itfelf,* than
ever they enjoyed before.

---

two great Barons, Lord BERKELEY and Lord LISLE, fought
a bloody Battle on *Nibley Common, Anno.* 1470 [*See* ATKYNS's
Hift. Glocefterfhire, Page 577] with 400 Men on a Side, raifed
in lefs than 48 Hours, from among their refpective Vaffals and
Dependants. The famous Battle of *Chevy Chace,* is ftill a more
extraordinary Circumftance, according to the antient Song;
For in that we are told, that Earl PERCY had made a Vow,
that he would be the Aggreffor in breaking the Peace between
the two Kingdoms, by hunting in a Wood that belonged to
the Houfe of DOUGLAS. Yet rafh and unjuftifiable as fuch a
Vow was, the Event fhews, that his Pleafure alone was a fufficient Reafon for the very Flower of his Vaffals and Dependants
to attend him in that frantic bravading Expedition. Now here
I afk, Were any two modern great Men, any two Dukes,
Earls, or Barons, or any two Generals, or Colonels, in the
Army, to have a Quarrel with, and to fend Challenges to each
other (as we are affured was the Cafe between the Lords
BERKELEY and LISLE, and the Earls PERCY and DOUGLAS)
would they be able to prevail on any of their Tenants to take
up Arms in fuch a Quarrel? and could they engage, I do not
fay a Regiment on a Side, but even a fingle Troop, or Company, to draw a Sword, or fire a Mufket in their Defence?
Surely no: Yet we are told, that thefe were the Days in which
our brave Fore-fathers enjoyed that glorious Liberty of thinking
and acting for themfelves, which we, their degenerate Sons,
have loft!

BUT,

But to purfue this Subject no further :---Be it obferved, that the Crown Lands or Royal Domains in antient Times were fo very extenfive, as to contain a fifth Part of the Lands of *England*, and that the feveral Rents, and Profits, and Services arifing from them, and from the other Branches of the feudal Syftem, were judged to be fully fufficient, without further Aid, to anfwer all the common Expences of Government*. Nay, it has been computed, that had all the Lands of antient Demefne borne a Rack-Rent according to the prefent Standard, the Sum total would have been not much fhort of 6,000,000l. Sterling. And what feems to con-

---

* See a very ingenious and inftructive Pamphlet, intituled, The Rights of the *Britifh* Legiflature to tax the *American* Colonies vindicated, printed for T. Becket. I differ from this Author in nothing very materially, but in his Calculation of the prefent Rental of *England*, which he feems to me to have fet a great deal too low. Had he attended to the vaft Improvements in Agriculture throughout *England* and *Wales*, partly by Skill and good Hufbandry, partly by the Enclofure of common Fields, and by the enclofing and cultivating of above a Million of Acres of Commons, Waftes, Forefts, Chafes, Mountains, Moors, Fens, Marfhes, &c. &c. And above all by the prodigious Encreafe of Buildings in *London*, *Briftol*, *Bath*, *Birmingham*, *Liverpool*, *Manchefter*, and in almoft every manufacturing Town and Diftrict whatever, for thefe laft 40 Years: I fay, had he duly attended to the Advance of Rents on thefe, and on other Accounts, he would have found that the Rack-Rental of *England* and *Wales*, independently of *Scotland*, cannot be fo little as 30,000,000l. a Year; a Fifth of which is 6,000,000l.

firm

firm this Calculation is, that it is pretty well known, that the Eftates belonging to what is called the Duchy of *Lancafter* [which were little more than the confifcated Eftates of four great Barons] would not have been much fhort of 1,000,000l. Sterling of annual Rent;---fuppofing, that the feveral Manors, Hundreds, Parifhes, Precinɛts, Streets, and Houfes in *London*, and throughout *England* and *Wales,* which formerly did belong to the Duchy of *Lancafter*; [many of which now claim thofe Privileges, and Exemptions, which the Dukes and Earls of *Lancafter* once granted to their Tenants;]---I fay, fuppofing that all thefe Eftates were at prefent in the Hands of one Perfon, and that he were to receive a Rent for each proportionably to the prefent Standard,---- then, and in that Cafe, it has been computed, that the Amount of the whole would be little lefs than 1,000,000l. Sterling.

But be this Calculation erroneous, or not, the Faɛt is certain, that even as low down as the Reign of EDWARD the Fourth, the Crown-Lands, together with the feudal hereditary Revenue, were judged to be adequate to the common Expences of Government. Indeed, this is not much to be wondered at, when we confider, that the Charges of the Navy, together with the feveral Appendages of Docks, Yards, Magazines, Fortifications, Viɛtualing and Admiralty Offices,

Offices, &c. &c. (fo expenfive at prefent) fcarcely had an Exiftence in thofe Days: and that the military Tenures then fupplied the Place of a ftanding Army. Therefore, as the Crown could fupport itfelf, without the Aid of Parliament, it is obvious to any reflecting Mind, that the real and rational Liberty of the Subject could hardly have been enjoyed during all that long Period :---I fay, the real and rational, to diftinguifh it from the *mad, fanatical* Liberty of a *Polifh* VETO, which our modern Republicans feem to wifh to introduce among us. In fhort, when the hereditary Revenue of the Prince, and his hereditary Prerogatives, were fo exceffively great, as to fet him above Controul, by making him independent of the Parliament, what Remedy was to be applied, in Cafe he abufed his Power?—None that I can think of but that one, which is almoft as bad as the Difeafe, and to the common People it was certainly worfe ;---the Remedy I mean, was that of the great Barons forming a League againft him.----I have not fcrupled to fay, that fuch a Remedy was worfe to the common People than the Difeafe itfelf: For there cannot be a clearer, and a more evident Propofition, than that it is far better to be a Subject under the abfolute Monarchies of *France* or *Denmark*, than to be a Vaffal to a Grandee of *Poland*, or, what is nearly the fame Thing, a Slave to a Planter in *Jamaica*. [But more of this hereafter.]

HOWEVER,

HOWEVER, as Providence is always bringing Good out of Evil, so it happened, that partly thro' the Profusion of our former Princes, and partly through the Contempt which Queen ELIZABETH had entertained of her Succeffor, JAMES the Firft. the Crown-Lands were fo diffipated and alienated (notwithftanding the common Law Maxim of *Nullum Tempus occurrit Regi*) that it was impoffible for Government even with the utmoft Oeconomy, to fubfift on the fmall Pittance of thefe Lands ftill remaining. This was the Cafe when the STUART Family mounted the Throne. And JAMES the Firft, by his thoughtlefs, and childifh Extravagance, foon made bad to become worfe. What then was to be done in fuch a Situation ?---Two Things, and only two, feem to have occurred. The firft was, to *command* the Parliament to fupply the Place of the former Domain by fome Kind of Tax; and in Cafe the Parliament fhould refufe. then to have Recourfe to the Prerogative itfelf for raifing Money without their Confent : The fecond was, to yield to the Times with a good Grace, and to fue for that as a *Favour* which. in a certain Senfe, could not be ftrictly and legally demanded as a *Right*. Unhappily for them. they chofe the former Method. which begat a long civil War. and ended at laft in the total Expulfion of the Family.

Now as this brings us to the Revolution, I will here obferve, that it may likewife fuggeft to our Thoughts, a   3*d.* MODE

3*d*. Mode of fupporting civil Government, viz. by Means of *Taxes*. For tho' Taxes were in Being Ages before, yet the proper Ufes and Advantages of them never began to be underftood 'till after that Period: Nor indeed are they yet underftood fo well, and fo thoroughly, as the Nature of fuch a Subject, and its great Importance really deferve.

Two Ufes may be made of Taxes, a Primary, and a Secondary; — the primary Ufe is to fupport Government, and to defray the feveral Expences military and civil incurred, or to be incurred thereby: The Secondary is to provide for thefe Expences in fuch a Manner, as fhall render the Subjects in general the more induftrious, and confequently the richer, and not the poorer by fuch a Mode of Taxation, And I do aver, that every judicious Tax tends to promote the latter of thefe Ufes, as well as the former; as fhall be diftinctly fhewn in its proper Place. Now as we have already expofed the great Inconveniences, and the many Dangers attending the Allotments of Crown Lands. or public Domains for the Support of Government;—and as we have likewife fufficiently proved, that the requiring of perfonal Services is a ftill greater Hardfhip. and a much forer Infringement on perfonal Liberty; What have we yet left, but *Taxes*, *Duties*, or *Impofitions* to defcant upon? For in Fact we have no other

Choice

Choice remaining : — And therefore if we will, or muſt ſubmit to have Government at all, we muſt ſubmit to have Taxes ; — there being no other Reſource.

But ſay the Lockians, Taxes are the Free-Gift of the People :---Nay, they are the Free-Gift of each Individual among the People : " For even the Supreme Power [the Legiſla-" ture] cannot [lawfully or juſtly] take from " *any* Man any Part of his Property without " his own Conſent." This is Mr. Locke's own Declaration. And Mr. Molineux corrobo-rates it by another ſtill ſtronger, viz. " To tax " me without my own Conſent is little better, if " at all, than down right *robbing* me." In ſhort all the Lockians hold one and the ſame Lan-guage on this Head : And therefore you muſt take their favourite Maxim for *granted*, or you will incur their high Diſpleaſure : " You are an " Advocate for Deſpotiſm, if you do not ac-" quieſce in this Maxim : You attempt to de-" fend what is down-right Robbery ; you are a " miniſterial Hireling, a dirtty Tool, &c. &c."

Now, as there is no anſwering ſuch Argu-ments as theſe, I ſhall very contentedly let them paſs ; in order to proceed to ſome others, which really deſerve to be properly ſtated, and clearly explained.

Therefore

THEREFORE in the firſt Place, we muſt dif-
tinguiſh between *Power* and *Right*: For without
this we do nothing. The People in their
collective, as well as every Individual in his
private Capacity, may have the *Power* of doing
many things, which ought not to be done.
Power therefore doth not in all Caſes confer
Right. This I lay down as a fundamental
Maxim: And if I am wrong in this, I ſhall be
wrong in all the reſt. In the next Place I ob-
ſerve, that a free Gift implies in the very Idea
of it, a Matter of mere *Favour*, and not a
Matter of ſtrict *Right* :—Conſequently the
with-holding of a Favour is not the with-
holding of a Right. Being advanced thus far,
I have yet to add, that Government itſelf may
be conſidered in a two-fold View: 1ſt. As it is
in its own Nature, abſtracted from the Conſideration of this, or that particular Set of Ad-
miniſtrators, or of this, or that particular Mode
or Form of adminiſtering it: And 2dly, as it
comprehends the latter as well as the former,
being relative to ſome certain Perſon or Perſons
preſiding in the State, and to ſome particular
Mode or Form of Government. And then I
do aſſert, that Taxes never ought to be conſidered
as *Free-Gifts*, or Acts of mere Favour, or voluntary Generoſity reſpecting the former;---
becauſe Mankind have no *Right* to ſay, we will
have no Government at all ; and therefore we
will have no Taxes for the Support of it : But
reſpecting the latter, they may have a Right to
ſay,

fay. in certain Cafes, and on particular Emergencies, we will have this, and not that Man to reign over us ;---or we do prefer this Form or Mode of Government and do reject that. Therefore at the *original Settling* of fuch a Conftitution, they may have a Right to confider fuch fpecial Defignations, as particular Free Gifts, or fpontaneous Options.

But left I fhould be mifunderftood by the carelefs and inattentive, or be mifreprefented by the malevolent on this Head, I will endeavour to illuftrate the Subject by a familiar Example, taken from the Cafe of the *Americans* themfelves, and to confute my Opponents by their own Arguments.

Here then I will wave my Opinion, that the *Americans* are, and indeed that they ever were, as far as they dared to fhew themfelves, a moft ungrateful, ungovernable, and rebellious People;—I fay, I will wave this Notion, and for the prefent adopt theirs; viz. That the Cruelties and Oppreffions, the Miferies and Slavery, which the poor, plundered, ruined and famifhed *Americans* had long fuffered under the tyrannical Yoke of the *Englifh*, were at laft become fo many, fo great, and intolerable, that it was high Time to throw off fuch a galling Yoke, and affert their native Freedom. Well: They have thrown off the *Englifh* Yoke, and have fet up

what

what they are pleafed to call *American* Independency. [Would to God they had done fo
fifty Years ago.] But in what Manner did they
fet up this Independence? And what did they
do on this Occafion?---Did they, for Example,
attempt to live in an abfolutely independent
State, without Order, or Controul, or Subordination of any Sort? No: Did they even pretend to fay, that they had a *Right* to live after
that Manner, if they faw fit? No; They did
not. On the contrary, their own Conduct
plainly intimated, that they thought themfelves
bound to have fome Government, or other:---
And therefore, the only Point which they
had to determine [for they did not pretend to
determine any other] was, Who fhould govern,
Americans or *Englifhmen?*---And after what
Manner?---Now their Conduct in this Affair
clears up all the Difficulty at once, by fhewing,
that in one Refpect, Taxes are a Debt due to
the Public for the Support of Government,---
and that in another, they are the free Gifts of
the People towards a particular Set of Men, to
whom they have entrufted the Adminiftration of
the Common-Wealth. For though Government
was to be fupported, and Taxes to be raifed, as
the beft and moft eligible Means of fupporting
it;---yet it did not follow from thence, that
Meffrs. HANCOCK and ADAMS, WASHINGTON
and LAURENS, &c. &c. &c. were, by an unalienable hereditary Right, or indeed by any
legal

legal Right whatever, ['till after they were chofen] to be the Adminiftrators, or Conductors of it. In one Word, from this View of Things, it evidently follows, that Government itfelf, or in its own Nature, is INDEFEASIBLE : Though the feveral Forms of it may undergo various Changes and Alterations, and the old Adminiftrators of it may be fet afide, and others chofen in their Room, according as certain preffing Exigencies, or very great Emergencies fhall require.

AND what has been obferved relative to the prefent Revolution in *America*, is alfo applicable [fuppofing the *Americans* to have *Right*, as well as *Power* on their Side] to the Cafe of the Revolution here in *England*, in 1688. For in that Cafe, as well as in this, there was evidently a Line drawn, and a Diftinction made, between the *Indefectibility* of Government, and the *Defectibility* of the Governors ;—Inafmuch as the Convention-Parliament never prefumed to ftart the Queftion,—Whether there fhould be any Government, or none at all.—Probably becaufe Mr. LOCKE's Syftem, or rather the Confequences of his Syftem, had not then fo far prevailed over the Underftanding of Mankind, as to extinguifh the Feelings of Common Senfe.

BUT neverthelefs, tho' the Lockians are, I fhould think, fairly beaten out of this Hold, which they ufed to confider as one of their
ftrongeft,---

ftrongeft,---they will not, I am perfuaded, give up the Caufe for loft, feeing they have one For- trefs more to retire to, which is built on the ex- prefs Words of all Acts of Parliament, where Taxes are to be laid, and Money to be raifed on the People. The Stile of fuch Act being the following, WE GIVE AND GRANT; or Words of a like Import.

Now in order to go to the Bottom of this Affair, we muft return to the Cafe of Crown Lands, or Royal Domains. For when thefe, together with the feudal, hereditary Revenues, were fufficient to anfwer all the ordinary Ex- pences of Government, what Right or Pretence could the Prince have, in a common Way, to afk for more ?—And if more was granted him, in what Shape, or under what Denomination, could it be granted but as a *Free-Gift?*—that is, as a Matter of *Favour,* and not of *Right?* In- deed the very Ufes, for which thefe public Be- nevolences were afked, and to which they were generally applied, is a plain Proof, that they were not underftood by either the Givers, or the royal Receiver, as intended to defray the ordi- nary Charges of Government, but to make Pro- vifion for fome extraordinary Feftivities or Re- joicings:—fuch as a royal Tilt or Tournament, a Repetition of the Ceremony of Coronation [a favourite Entertainment in thofe Days;] the

making

making of the King's eldeſt Son a Knight, the Marriage of a Daughter; &c. &c.;—all of them Matters of public Feſtivity and Diverſion, in which Spectacles the great Families of the Kingdom bore a principal Part,—and therefore made the leſs Objection againſt ſuch Kinds of Free-Gifts.

HENCE therefore the Propriety of the Expreſſion *give* and *grant*, confidered with a View to ſuch Things as theſe;—or indeed to any others, which are of a ſimilar Nature, where the Parade, and external Grandeur of Government, and not the Vitals or Eſſentials of it, are concerned.

HOWEVER the Language *give* and *grant* being once introduced, continued to be the Stile of Parliament ever after.—So that in fact, it hath come to paſs in this, as well as in many other Caſes, that certain Words and Phraſes, Uſages or Cuſtoms, which owed their Originals to particular Cauſes, have been retained long after the Cauſes themſelves have ceaſed, and been forgotten,—to the great Confuſion of Ideas, and Increaſe of Error.

IN ſhort, if Stile alone is to govern our Opinions, then we muſt conclude, that the King of *Great-Britain*, is alſo King of *France*: An

Inference

Inference this, which I think no Man in his Senfes can make at prefent ; whatever might have been the Cafe formerly.—And if the Stile *give* and *grant*, can revoke at Pleafure the public Faith folemnly pledged, by turning Matters of *ftrict Debt* into Matters of *mere Favour*, then our Lockian Politicians have difcovered a more expeditious Method of difcharging the National Debt, than any of our plodding Projectors had thought of before. For it is only to tell the *public Creditors*, that the Parliament will give and grant *no longer*, and then.—What ?—Then thefe Creditors can have no Right to complain of any Injury or Injuftice done them :—Becaufe they ought to have known, that all Taxes are abfolutely free Gifts : And therefore it was a Matter of mere Indulgence, (for which they ought to have been very thankful) to have thefe Gifts and Grants continued to them as long as they were. This happy Difcovery will, no Doubt, adminifter great Confolation to all the national Creditors, both Foreigners and Natives, who have vefted their Property, on the Security of Parliament. in our public Funds. And therefore I would humbly recommend it to Dr. PRICE, and his Friends, the *American* Congrefs, to try to borrow Money on thefe Terms, towards defraying the Expence of their glorious War.

BUT to purfue fuch Abfurdities no farther, be it obferved in general, that the Root. from which
thefe

thefe Evils fpring, is, that ftrange Notion fo ftiffly maintained by all the *Lockians*,—That the Father's being a Subject to any Government, lays no Sort of Obligation on the Son to be a Subject likewife; notwithftanding that he was born under its Jurifdiction, bred and educated under its Protection, and had enjoyed all its Privileges and Advantages from his helplefs Infancy 'till he arrived at Man's Eftate: Yet, for all this, it feems the State has no Right to confider fuch a Perfon as a *Subject*:—She has no juft Pretenfions to fuppofe, that he is bound in Duty and Confcience to be obedient to her Laws, to affift her with his Perfon, or his Purfe, or to bear any Part of her Burdens.—On the contrary, fhe ought to allow, that he has a juft, and an *unalienable* Right to refufe to contribute a fingle Farthing towards any of thefe Things. unlefs he had actually given his previous Confent thereunto. And if you fhould be curious to know, how fuch an extravagant Notion as this ever came to enter into the Heads of Men of fober Senfe, it is, becaufe they efteem civil Government. even in its beft Eftate, to be a Kind of unnatural Reftraint on the native Freedom of Man:—It is an Evil which he muft bear, becaufe he cannot help himfelf;—but yet which he is continually endeavouring to fhake off, in order to become totally free and independent.

So

So much as to the *primary* Ufe of Taxes : And the Reader muft now determine for himfelf, whether he will confider them,—I mean, in all Cafes *effential* to Government,—to be real Debts due to the Public, as a Compenfation for the Enjoyment of its Benefits and Protection,—or to be mere Free-Gifts and voluntary Donations, which every Man has a Right to chufe, or to refufe to pay, as it feemeth beft.

THE *fecondary* Ufe of Taxes comes next to be fpoken to : But in refpect to this I muft be very brief, partly on account of having been obliged to be fo copious and diffufive in regard to the former Article ; and partly becaufe this is itfelf a Digreffion from the main Subject, tho' an ufeful one. Suffice it therefore for the prefent juft to obferve, that I fet out on the Strength of two Propofitions, which neceffarily infer each other, viz. That the Hand of the diligent maketh rich,—and that the Hand of the idle maketh poor. Therefore all Taxes whatever are to be denominated either good or bad, in Proportion as they promote Induftry, or difcourage it. Now were a Survey to be taken of our prefent Syftem of Taxation, according to this Rule, it would be found, that many of our Taxes are very good ones.—that fome are indifferent. partaking of a Kind of neutral State,— and that very few are really bad ones. Whereas formerly the very Reverfe was the true State of

the

the Cafe; which might eafily be made to appear to the Satisfaction of any reafonable, impartial Man, by comparing the whole Syftem of Taxes, Article by Article, as it ftands in the prefent Year 1780,—and as it ftood at any Period whatever during the Life-Time of Mr. LOCKE,—or during the golden Days of good Queen BESS, including her Monopolies,—or indeed at any Time, or during any Reign, antecedent to the 8th of GEO. 1, C. 15 :—That famous commercial Statute, for which the Authors of it [Sir ROBERT WALPOLE and his Brother] received the moft ungrateful Returns from a Set of Mock-Patriots, and from a deluded commercial Nation.

EXPERIENCE plainly tells us (and therefore we muft ceafe to wonder) that the Generality even of intelligent People, do not reafon at all, or at leaft will not reafon to the Purpofe concerning the Tendency of Taxes: That is, they will not enquire, whether they tend to promote Idlenefs or Induftry, to transform Drones into Bees, or Bees into Drones. In Fact, that which they moftly attend to, is the Quantity of Money, or the Sum Total produced by any given Tax. If the Sum fhould be a great one, then they generally pronounce that they are fadly oppreffed, and moft heavily taxed, and complain moft bitterly of their Rulers: In regard to which, they are fure that Mock-Patriots and feditious News-Writers will echo back their Complaints from every Quarter. But if the

Sum

Sum produced fhould be a very fmall one, then
they think, that they are not quite fo heavily
taxed; and therefore they are not altogether fo
profufe in their Lamentations. Now, nothing
can be more fallacious than fuch Conclufions:
Inafmuch as it is ftrictly demonftrable, that a
Tax, which would hardly produce 100,000l. a
Year to the Revenue, might yet be more oppreffive, more impoverifhing, and a much
greater Stab to Induftry of every Kind, than
others which produce TEN MILLIONS. For the
Nature of Taxes is fuch, that they may be compared to the pruning of Fruit-Trees; an Operation, which all will allow to be not only ufeful,
but in fome Senfe neceffary. Now if this fhould
be judicioufly performed, the Trees will be much
healthier, and bear abundantly the better; but
if ignorantly and unfkilfully done, the Trees will
bear nothing, or next to nothing, and perhaps
will ficken, and die away.

HERE therefore let us put a Cafe :—Suppofe,
that all the numerous Taxes at this Day fubfift-
ing, were to be repealed, and that only one
Tax was to be laid on in their Room, viz. A
Tax of 20l. a Day on every Plow, when at
Work, [or on every Machine performing the
Office of a Plow] and the like Sum on every
Cart, or Waggon, or any other Machine draw-
ing, or carrying Goods, or Merchandize of any
Kind :—And then I afk, What would be the
Confequence ?

Confequence?—Plainly this; That fuch a Tax would produce but a very Trifle to the Revenue; becaufe it would ftop Labour and Induftry to fuch a Degree, that our Farms in the Country would be deferted,—Grafs and Weeds would grow in the Streets of our Towns and Cities;— and the whole Kingdom would in a Manner be- come a Defert.—Yet the few Beggars who were left in fuch a defolate Country, would have it to fay, that they paid but one fingle Tax; nay, that they could get drunk on Spirituous Liquors [as fmall Stills would be fet up every where, be- ing light of Carriage, and paying no Tax] Therefore they would have it to fay, that they could get drunk for a Halfpenny, and perhaps dead-drunk for a Penny. Happy Times thefe! whereas their enflaved, op- preffed, exhaufted, and impoverifhed Fore- fathers in the Year 1780, paid feveral Hundred different Taxes! And, what was harder ftill, they could not enjoy the Bleffing of getting drunk under the exorbitant Price of 6d.—Such were the Miferies and Calamities, which poor *Old England* then fuffered under the Preffure of a Multitude of Taxes, and of minifterial Excifes!!! And now, Reader, having ended this long Ar- ticle concerning Taxes, I cannot help exclaiming at the Clofe of it, in the Words, which I have heard the late Earl of CHESTERFIELD feveral Times repeat, How much eafier is it to *deceive* Mankind, than to *undeceive* them! But to re- turn. A

A third capital Error chargeable on the Lockian Sect, (and to be ranked under this Clafs of Errors) is that dreadful Notion, propagated by them with a Kind of enthufiaftic Ardor. that *their Syftem* of Government is the only true one, in the Nature of Things : —And that all others, not built on this Foundation, are, in Deed and Truth, fo many deteftable Robberies. and bare-faced Ufurpations of the unalienable Rights of Mankind. Now this is in Fact proclaiming War againft all the Governments upon Earth, and exciting their Subjects to rebel. And indeed thefe new-fangled Republicans do not appear to be fhocked at the Imputation of fuch horrid Con-fequences, but on the contrary, they admit them with a Kind of Pleafure, and feem to glory in fuch Deeds. The Extracts from their Writings already given, are fo decifive on this head. that there can be no Need of any further Proof, or Illuftration.

But that which feems the moft unaccountable in this whole Proceeding is, that they have adopt-ed almoft every Thing into their own Syftem, which is exceptionable in Sir ROBERT FILMER'S, and againft which they have raifed fuch tragical Exclamations.

Thus for Example, Sir ROBERT, and all the Patrons of an indefeafible, hereditary Right, de-clare with one Voice, that no Length of Time

can

can bar the Title of the right Heir. For when-ever he fhall fee a fit Opportunity of fetting up his Claim, every Subjeĉt is bound in Duty and Confcience to renounce their Allegiance to the reigning Prince, and to refort to the Standard of the Lord's Anointed :—Juft fo, *mutatis mutandis,* is the Stile and Declaration of the Lockians : The People are the only right Heirs ; or rather, they are the only Perfons who have a *Right* to appoint right Heirs; and no Length of Prefcription can bar their Title. For every Settlement of a State, monarchical, or even republican, whofe Title is not derived from a popular Eleĉtion, or doth not exift at prefent by Virtue of fome exprefs, and previous Contraĉt, is a manifeft Ufurpation of their unalienable Rights ; and therefore ought to be fubverted and deftroyed as foon as poffible;— moreover the Authors of fo daring an Attempt on the Liberties of a free People deferve to be pu-niflied with exemplary Vengeance, and to have their Goods and Eftates confifcated for the Benefit of the Public, alias, to reward the Patriots. Now if any one flhould aflk, what that is, which con-ftitutes the People in this Cafe ? or who are thofe Perfons that are invefted, *jure divino,* with thefe extraordinary Powers, thefe King-creating, and King-depofing Prerogatives?—The Anfwer I own, in Point of Theory, is attended with very per-plexing Difficulties :—But in refpeĉt to *Praĉtice,* and as referring to a *Matter of Faĉt,* it is the eafi-eft Thing imaginable. For the Perfons, or the

People

People in this Cafe, are no other than the firft
Mob that can be got together, provided they are
ftrong enough to undertake, and execute the
work ; if not, the next Mob, or the next to
that, and fo on, *ad infinitum*. For this is a Subject, which, it feems, ought never to be loft
Sight of by a true-born Patriot : Though he may
allow that the Efforts of the People for regaining
their native Rights, may be delayed for a while,
or may be *diffembled*, and poftponed till he and
his Friends fhall find a more convenient Seafon
for executing their laudable Defigns.

Again : The Notion of Kings de *Facto*, and
Kings de *Jure*, that Opprobrium of the Jacobites, is alfo revived by the Lockians. For
whofoever dares to reign without, or in Oppofition to the Lockian Title, is only a King *de Facto*:
—The rightful King, or the King *de Jure*, being yet in *petto*, and not to be brought forth, 'till
the People can affemble together to affert, and
exercife their *unalienable* Rights with Safety.

Moreover the perfecuting and intolerant
Spirit of the Syftem of Sir ROBERT FILMER,
and of the Jacobites, is another very juft Reproach to it : And none inveighed more bitterly,
or more juftly againft it on this Account, than
Mr. LOCKE himfelf, and his Difciples.—Yet fuch
is the Inconfiftency of thefe Men ;—that they tell
us fo plainly, that we cannot miftake their meaning,

ing, that they would allow no Government on the Face of the Earth to fubfift on any other Title, but their own, had they a *Power* equal to their *Will* in thefe Cafes. For fays Dr. PRIESTLY, [and all the Reft join in the fame Sentiments] " This [the Lockian, or popular Title] muft be " the *only* true and proper Foundation of *all* Go- " vernments fubfifting in the World; and *that to* " *which the People have an unalienable Right to bring* " *them back.*"—" This is a Bleffing, fays Dr. " PRICE, which no Generation of Men can give " up for another ; and which, when loft, the *Peo-* " *ple have always a Right to refume.*" So that nothing lefs will content thefe Men than the univerfal Eftablifhment of their own Principles, and the Renunciation or Abjuration of all others. Yet thefe are the Champions who ftand up for Liberty of Confcience, and are the only Friends to reconciling Meafures, to univerfal Toleration, to Peace on Earth, and Good-Will among Men.

ONCE more: All Laws made, or to be made by the Authority of *Ufurpers*, alias of Kings *de Facto*, are, according to the Doctrine of Sir Robert FILMER and the Jacobites, abfolutely null and void; 'till they fhall have received the Sanction and Confirmation of the rightful King. And fo fay the Lockians in refpect to *their fole* rightful King,—the People. For here again they have told us fo often that we cannot forget it, that no Law can be valid, unlefs the people have authorized the making of it :—Nay, they have

gone

gone fo far as to declare, that the very Effence of Slavery doth confift in being governed by Laws, to which the Governed have not previoufly confented. This being the Cafe, you fee plainly, that the Confideration, whether the Law be good or bad in itfelf; whether it is a Law that is wanted or not wanted ; and whether it tends to promote the Liberty of the Subject, or to reftrain it, is at prefent entirely befide the Queftion :—For the fole Point here to be determined, is fimply this.—Had the Makers of fuch a Law any *Right* to make it, according to the Lockian Ideas of *Right* and *Wrong* ? If they had no fuch Right, they muft be pronounced to be *Ufurpers*, be the Law in itfelf whatever it may ; and therefore as they are Ufurpers, their Doom is fixed ; inafmuch as they cannot expect Mercy for their daring Attempts to alienate the unalienable Rights of Mankind.

BEFORE this Lockian Syftem had been broached, or at leaft before it had made many Profelytes among us, it ufed to be confidered as no bad Maxim in Politics,—" Not to be very in-" quifitive concerning the *original Title* of the " reigning Powers." For if the State was actually at Peace, and if every Man fat, or might fit under his own Vine, and his own Fig-Tree ; or in plainer Englifh, if the effential Ends of Government were anfwered both by the Protection of good Subjects, and by the
Punifhment

Punishment of bad ones, and also by the Defence of the Community from external Violence ; — then it was thought, that this was a sufficient Reason for considering such Powers as ordained of God.—And if ordained of God, the People ought to obey them, under Peril of Damnation.—But now it seems, the World is grown much wiser: For the first Question to be asked is, What is your Title, to be the Governor, or Chief Magistrate of this Country? And what Proofs do you bring that you have received your Authority from the People, without Fraud on the one Hand, or Violence on the other? Answer me this, before you can expect, that I should submit to obey you.

FEW Governors, I believe, would like to be catechized after this Manner by their Subjects: And fewer still would be able to answer these Questions to the Satisfaction of a Lockian Patriot.—Nay, we have been expresly told by one of the chief among them, Dr. PRIESTLY, that there is not a Government on the Face of the Globe, which can stand the Test of such an Enquiry. " For, says he, all " Governments *whatever* have been, in some " Measure, compulsory, tyrannical, and op- " pressive in their Origin." Now this being the Case, why will not these benevolent, political Philosophers, erect a Government of their

own,

own, for the Good of Mankind ;—a Government on their own Plan, and perfectly agreeable to the Lockian Principles; which shall therefore be a Pattern for the Rest of the World to copy after? Nay, why are they always sowing Discords and Dissentions among *us*, instead of establishing a free, and equal, and *harmonious* Republic among *themselves*? Most certainly *Great-Britain* is not the proper Spot for exhibiting Specimens of this Sort: Because, to say the Truth, we have had, and we have felt, too many of these political Experiments already, during the last Century, to wish to have them revived again. — But *America !* — Yes, the interior Parts of *America* is the Country of all others, the fittest for putting every fond Imagination of their Hearts in Practice. For if Fame says true, and if Mr. LOCKE himself is to be credited, there is as yet no Government at all in the inland Parts of those immense Regions : Nor have even the Congress extended their *gentle Sway* beyond the Lakes *Erie* and *Ontario*, if they have gone so far. Thither, therefore, let all our Republican Patriots speedily repair : Time is precious, and the Cause invites : A Passport will undoubtedly be granted them, as soon as applied for : And ample Leave will be obtained to exchange the Slavery of this Country for the Freedom of *America.* Thi-

ther

ther, therefore, let them all retire : For there they will live (according to the Prediction of Dr. PRICE) undisturbed by Bishops, Nobles, or Kings; and there likewise they will enjoy all the Blessings which can attend that happy State, where every Member of Society will be his own Law-giver, his own Governor, Judge, and Director,

CHAP.

C H A P. III.

An Enquiry how far either the Revolution in Eng-
land,—or the Reduction of Ireland,—or the
present Proceedings of the Congress in America,
can or may be justified according to the leading
Principles of Mr. Locke, *and his Followers.*

I. *Of the* Revolution *in* England.

IT is allowed on all Hands, and it has been the
continual Boaft of the Friends and Admirers
of Mr. Locke, that he wrote his Effay on Government with a View to juftify the Revolution.
We have therefore a Right to expect, that his
fundamental, political Maxims tend immediately
and directly to vindicate this neceffary Meafure.
How great therefore will be our Difappointment,
if the quite contrary fhould appear!

The grand Objections againft King James
the Second were, that his Government was tyrannical, and his Proceedings illegal;— that he
affumed Powers which the Conftitution had exprefsly denied him;—that he had repeatedly
broken his folemn Coronation-Oath, and forfeited his Royal Word;—and that, in fhort, his
Actions

Actions proved him to be an Enemy both to Civil Liberty, and to the Proteftant Religion.

Now grant thefe Objections to be well founded (which I think no Man at this Day, even the warmeft Friend of the STUART Family, will pretend to deny;) and the Inference is plain, that fuch a Prince deferved to be depofed, and that the Nation did very right in depofing him. — So far therefore we are all agreed: For Mr. LOCKE's Principles ferve admirably well for the Purpofes of *Demolition* in any Cafe whatever, as far as mere Demolition is concerned. But alas! after we have pulled down, how are we to build up? For fomething of this Kind muft certainly be done. and that fpeedily. The Nation was then in a State of Anarchy and Confufion, without Law, or Government: The Legiflative Power could not affemble, according to the prefcribed antient Forms of the Conftitution: Nor could the Executive legally act for want of being authorifed fo to do. In fuch a Situation the Principle of Self-Defence would naturally fuggeft to a Nation in general, and to every reafonable Man in particular, — *to do the beft they could without Lofs of Time,* and not to ftand upon mere *legal Punctilios,* where the *Effentials* of the Conftitution, and the Happinefs of Millions were at Stake: Moreover common Prudence and found Policy would likewife fuggeft, that as few Innovations of the antient Forms of Government

fhould

fhould be introduced, and as many of its Laws and Ordinances be retained, as the Good of the whole, and the public Safety would permit. This, I fay, feems to be a fair, and honeft, and upright Mode of Proceedure ;—a Mode which all impartial Men would allow to be reafonable, and every Lover of his Country would approve and juftify :—And in fhort, this was the very Proceedure adopted at the Revolution.

Now, let us fee, what Methods ought to have been taken according to the Syftem of Mr. Locke ;—and whether his Plan, and the Revolution Plan, co-incide with each other.

By the Defertion, or Abdication, or Forfeiture, or Depofition of King James [take which Term you pleafe] the Government was diffolved, and no new one was yet appointed. So far we are again agreed. But fays a Lockian (if he will reafon confiftently with his own Principles) this Diffolution of Government fet the Nation free from all Ties and Obligations: So that they were no longer the *Subjects* of a Government, which itfelf did not exift :— And if they were not the Subjects of an annihilated Government, they could be under no Obligation to any other. They were therefore actually returned back to a State of Nature ;— that happy State, wherein there is a perfect Equality of Rights of all Kinds whatever; and
where

where no one Man can pretend to have a better Claim than another either to Lands, or Legiflations, to Power or Pre-eminence of any Kind. Admirable! CATALINE himfelf could not have wifhed for a more ample Scope,— not only for paying all his own Debts, and thofe of his Followers,—but alfo for coming in for a confiderable Share in the general Scramble, on a new Divifion of Property. Nay, his Speech in Salluft feems to indicate, as if he had fome fuch Notion in his Head, had his Genius been fertile enough to have drawn it out into Form, and to have methodized it into a Syftem.

But evidently as thefe Conclufions flow from Mr. LOCKE's fundamental Maxims, I do by no Means allow myfelf to fuppofe, that either he or any of his Followers, with whom I have now Concern, would grant, that thefe Conclufions are juftly and fairly drawn. On the contrary, I do verily believe, that they thought they were ferving the Caufe of *rational* Liberty, when they were advancing fuch Pofitions, as, if carried into Execution, would unavoidably introduce the moft fhocking Scenes of Defpotifm on the one Hand, and of Slavery on the other. [Juft as a rank Antinomian wildly imagines, that he is confulting the Glory of God and the Good of Mankind, whilft he is inftilling fuch Doctrines, as neceffarily derogate from the Supreme Being,

by

by making him the Author of Sin; and as neceffarily turn human Creatures into ravenous
Beafts to bite and devour one another, by deftroying all moral Obligation.]

THEREFORE I obferve, that though all thefe
fhocking Confequences are juftly chargeable on
the *Principles* of a Lockian, yet I do not charge
the *Man*, the Individual, with the Guilt of
them, provided he declare his Abhorrence of
fuch Inferences. Now, taking it for granted
that he would difavow them, were the Queftion
afked, I will charitably fuppofe, that if Mr.
LOCKE and his Followers, had the Management
of an Event fimilar to that of the Revolution in
1688, they would not diffolve the Bands of
Society any farther, than was juft neceffary for
compaffing their Ends of a free and general
Election, according to their peculiar Ideas of
Freedom, and of the *unalienable* Right of human
Nature. I will therefore fuppofe alfo, that they
would permit Men to enjoy unmolefted their
hereditary Honours and hereditary Eftates, and
Property of all Kinds, notwithftanding that
their Principles neceffarily tend to level every
thing without Diftinction, and to bring us back
to a State of Nature: Nay, I will fuppofe,
that they would admit a Majority of the Voters
prefent to include not only the Minority prefent, but alfo the great Majority, who might

happen

happen to be abfent:—Though the Lockian
Principles have in themfelves a very different
Tendency; as I have fully made to appear
in the preceding Chapter. However, granting
all this with a liberal Hand; and granting
alfo for Argument's Sake, that it is confiftent
with this modern Syftem of *unalienable* Rights,
to exclude every Male under twenty-one Years
of Age, and Females of every Age, from the
unalienable Right of voting:—And then we
have ftill remaining all the Males in *England* of
twenty-one Years of Age and upwards, to
compofe an Affembly of Legiflators, Electors,
and Directors, according to the Lockian Syftem.
A goodly Number truly! All Voters by the
unalienable Rights of Nature! All equal, free,
and independent! This being the Cafe, the firft
Step to be taken is, to fummon all thefe adult
male Voters throughout the Kingdom to meet
at fome certain Place, in order to confult about
erecting a new Government, after pulling down
the old one: Here therefore I make a Paufe;—
and afk a Queftion, Was this done at the Revolution? No. Was it attempted to be done?
No. Were there any Meetings appointed in
different Parts of the Kingdom, from whence
Deputies could be fent up to reprefent thefe
Meetings, and to act in their Name? No. Was
there then, [tho' that at beft is a very prepofterous Mode of Reprefentation, according to Mr.
LOCKE, yet] was there a previous general
Election

Election of Members of Parliament, in order that there might be at leaſt a new Parliament to elect a new King ? No, not even that, according to any legal, or conſtitutional Forms.—What then was that great NATIONAL VOTE which eſtabliſhed the Revolution ?—A few Scores of Noblemen, and a few Hundreds of Gentlemen, together with ſome of the Aldermen and Common Council of *London*, met at *Weſtminſter*, [but without any Commiſſion from the Body of the People authoriſing them to meet] and requeſted (thereby empowering) the Prince and Princeſs of *Orange* to aſſume the Royal Prerogative, and to ſummon a new Parliament. They ſummoned one accordingly, which was called the Convention Parliament : This Aſſembly put the Crown on their Heads [the Power of which they had exerciſed before] The Crown, I ſay, not only of *England*, but alſo of *Ireland*, and of all the *Engliſh* Dominions throughout every Part of the Globe, and this too, not only without aſking the Conſent, but even without acquainting the People of thoſe other Countries with their Intentions. Now if this Tranſaction can be ſaid to be carried on agreeably to Mr. LOCKE's Plan, or if it can be juſtified by his Principles, I own myſelf the worſt Judge of Reaſon and Argument, and of a plain Matter of Fact, that ever ſcribbled on Paper. Nay, I appeal to all the World, whether the whole Buſineſs of this famous Revolution, from whence nevertheleſs we have derived

rived so many national Bleffings, ought not to be
looked upon as a vile Ufurpation, and be chargeable with the Guilt of robbing the good People
of *England*, of *Ireland*, and of all the Colonies
of their unalienable Rights, if Mr. LOCKE's Principles of Government are the only *true* and *juft*
ones. But I afk further, Was the Convention itfelf
unanimous in its Decifions ? No, very far from
it. On the contrary, it is a well-known Fact,
that the Members of it [I mean a Majority of
the Members] would never have voted the
Crown to the Prince of *Orange*, had it not been
for his threatening Meffage, that he would leave
them to the Refentment of King JAMES, unlefs
they complied with fuch a Demand. So that
even a Majority of this very Convention would
have acted otherwife than they did, had they remained *unawed*, and *uninfluenced*. And thus,
Reader, it is demonftrated to thee, that this famous Convention [and in them the whole Na-
tion] was felf-governed, and felf-directed, according to the Lockian Principle, in eftablifhi
the glorious Revolution!

II. *The* REDUCTION *of Ireland.*

THE Reduction of *Ireland* about the Year
1690 is another capital Affair, which is to receive
Sentence either of Juftification, or Condemnation, at Mr. LOCKE's Tribunal. For if *Ireland*

was

was reduced, and the Conftitution thereof peaceably fettled according to the Lockian Plan, the Founder of this Sect and his Followers have certainly a good deal to glory in. But if the very Reverfe fhould prove to have been the Cafe, what fhall we fay ?—And with what Front could Mr. MOLINEUX, the Friend of Mr. LOCKE, dedicate his Book on the Independency of *Ireland* to King WILLIAM, if King WILLIAM's own Conduct in the Reduction of that Kingdom was altogether repugnant to the Principles of his Book ? Now it unfortunately happens, that all the *Lockians* have precluded themfelves from making Ufe of the very beft Arguments, which could be brought in Juftification of this memorable Event : -- I fay, they have precluded themfelves, by chufing to reft the Merits of their Caufe on one fingle Point, *The Univerfality of Confent ;* — that is to fay, the Confent of the People.-- at leaft of the major Part of them, *exprefsly* obtained, and *freely given.* For they have folemnly declared over and over, and do continue to declare, that no Title whatever in the reigning Powers can be *valid*, if this be wanting. Mr. MOLINEUX's own Words will beft fpeak his Sentiments. and thofe of his Party on this Occafion; which therefore I fhall beg Leave to repeat.

" I fhall venture to affert, that the Right of
" being fubject *only* to fuch Laws, to which Men
" give

" give their *own* Confent, is fo inherent in *all*
" Mankind, and founded on fuch *immutable*
" Laws of Nature and Reafon, that 'tis not to
" be *aliened*, or given up by any Body of Men
" whatever." And a little lower: " I have no
" Notion of *Slavery*, but being bound by a Law,
" to which I do not confent.—If one Law may
" be impofed without Confent, any other Law
" whatever may be impofed on us without our
" Confent. This will naturally introduce *Tax-*
" *ing* us without our Confent. And this as
" neceffarily deftroys our *Property*. I have no
" other Notion of Property, but a Power of
" difpofing of my Goods, *as I pleafe*, and not as
" another fhall command. Whatever another
" may *rightfully* take from me, I have certainly
" no Property in. To tax me without Confent
" is little better, if at all, than down-right *rob-*
" *bing me*."

AND now, Reader, having juft obfervcd, that
this Mr. MOLINEUX of *Ireland* was to all In-
tents and Purpofes, the Precurfor of the Congrefs of *America*, let us confider what Right had
King WILLIAM to invade *Ireland* at firft, and
what Pretenfions could he have afterwards for
eftablifhing a Proteftant Conftitution in that
Popifh Country, according to the Principles of
Meffrs. LOCKE and MOLINEUX.

KING

KING JAMES the Second fled from *England*, and, after having made fome Stay in *France*, landed in *Ireland*, and was received by the whole Body of the *Irifh* Nation with open Arms. A few Proteftants in the North made fome Oppofition; and at laft, being driven to Defpair, they made a moft furprizing Refiftance, under the Conduct of the Rev. Mr WALKER, Governor of *Londonderry*. But it is their *Number*, as having an unalienable Right to *vote*,—and not their *Courage* or Valour, as *Heroes*, which is the fubject Matter of our prefent Inquiry. Now in refpect to this, the Proteftants were vaftly the Minority of the Natives, and are fo ftill, according to every Mode of Computation. Why therefore if the Votes or Confents of a Majority are to decide the Queftion,—Why, I fay, did thefe few Proteftants refift at all?—Or if a Lockian will not fubmit to be governed by this Rule of a Majority concluding the Minority [for fometimes he will, and at other Times he will not] Why did not the Handful of Proteftants defire Leave to retire peaceably into fome other Country, inftead of committing Hoftilities in *that?* Nay more, why did they fend to *England* for Succours, to drive out King JAMES, and eftablifh King WILLIAM? For furely according to the Lockian Hypothefis, that every Man ought to be governed *only* by Laws of his own appointing,—the great Majority of

the

the *Irish* Nation had at leaft as good a Right to refufe Obedience to King WILLIAM, as the Minority had to refufe it to King JAMES. But notwithftanding all this, King WILLIAM failed with a large Reinforcemement of Troops to *Ireland*; he landed, and he conquered; and in a fhort Space of Time the Peace of the Country was fettled by the Capitulation and Treaty of *Limeric*.

Now in order to reconcile the Reduction of *Ireland* to the Lockian Standard of Right and Wrong, of juft Government, and of Ufurpation, we muft believe firft of all, that this Handful of Proteftants, who appeared in Arms at *Innifkillen* and *Londonderry*, were the great Majority of the *Irish* Nation: And when we have digefted this Pill, we muft believe further that all Things were quite inverted, or in other Words, That the *few* Natives of *Ireland*, who were Papifts [not more perhaps than ten to one Proteftant] we muft believe, I fay, that thefe *few* Papifts all voluntarily confented to be governed by the many, who were Proteftants: And having proceeded thus far in our Credulity, we muft not hefitate at fwallowing the reft, viz. That the Papifts of *Ireland* fent an Embaffy to invite King WILLIAM to come over, and offered to fwear Fealty and Allegiance to him at the Battle of the *Boyne*;—yea, and that all the Laws fucceffively made afterwards for difarming them,

for

for taking their Eftates from them, for banifhing them, for exciting their own Children to rebel againft them, and for fubjecting them to Fines and Imprifonments, and to Pains and Penalties in Thoufands of Inftances;—we muft believe, I fay, that all thefe Laws were made with the whole Affent, and Confent, Will, and Agreement of the Papifts of *Ireland*. O Genius of Popifh Legends, confefs thou art fairly outdone by Proteftant Patriots! O Purgatory of St. PATRICK, hide thy diminifhed Head!

III. *The Cafe of the prefent* CONGRESS *in America.*

IT has been obferved at the Beginning of this Treatife, that the Lockian Syftem is an univerfal Demolifher of all Civil Governments, but not the Builder of any. And it has been diftinctly fhewn, that this Obfervation has been found to be remarkably verified in two memorable Inftances, [thofe very Inftances which were pretended to correfpond the moft with the Plan of Mr. LOCKE] the Revolution in *England*, and the Reduction of *Ireland*. Come we now therefore to a 3d Inftance, the Revolt of the Colonies in *North America*.

WHEN it is ferioufly enquired, what were the chief *Grievances* which the Colonies had to complain

plain of againft the Mother Country, the Anfwer is, and muft be, that fhe governed, or attempted to govern them, in fuch a Manner as was not agreeable to the Lockian Syftem. For the impofing Laws on them of any Kind, whether good or bad in themfelves, and whether for the Purpofes of Taxation, or for other Purpofes, without their own Confent, is, according to this hypothefis, a moft intolerable Grievance! a Robbery! and an Ufurpation on the unalienable Rights of Mankind. Nay, we are repeatedly told, that the very Effence of Slavery confifts in the being obliged to fubmit to be governed by fuch Laws as thefe. Therefore if you want to know the very Root and Foundation of the prefent *American* Rebellion, it is this very Principle: And the Fact is fo far from being denied, that it is gloried in by Dr. PRICE, and others their warmeft Advocates. In fhort, the brave *Americans* were refolved not to be Slaves; but Slaves, it feems, they muft have been (according to the Lockian Idea) had they acknowledged the Right of the Mother Country, even in a fingle Inftance, to make Laws to bind them without their Confent:—I fay, even in a *fingle* Inftance; for the Lockian Mode of Reafoning is, that there is no Difference between being vefted with difcretionary Power, and with defpotic Power. " In- " afmuch as, if a Government has any Right to " rule me without my Confent in *fome* Cafes,

it

" it has a Right to rule me in *every* Cafe ; confe-
" quently it has a Right to levy every Kind of
" Tax, good or bad, reafonable, or exorbitant
" upon me, and to inflict all Sorts of Punifh-
" ments whatever."

But Dr. Price himfelf, the great Champion
of the *Americans,* has fo exprefsly applied this
Train of Reafoning to the *American* Caufe, that
I think myfelf happy in co-inciding with him in
Sentiments on this Occafion. " Our Colonies
" in *North America,* faith the Doctor, appear to
" be now * determined to rifque, and fuffer every
" Thing under the Perfuafion, that *Great-Britain*
" is attempting to *rob* them of that Liberty, to
" which *every Member* of Society, and all civil
" Communities have a natural, and unalienable
" Right."

Here therefore the Cafe is plain : For every
Member of Society, as well as the Community
at large, hath, according to Dr. Price, not
only a natural, but an *unalienable* Right to be

---

* Happy would it have been for *Great Britain,* had the Colonies come to this Determination 50 or 60 Years ago ; for then
we fhould have avoided two moft expenfive and bloody Wars,
and, to fpeak the honeft Truth, very *unjuft* ones, entered into
for their Sakes. But better late, than never. *America* ever
was a Mill-Stone hanging on the Neck of this Country ; and
as we would not caft it off, the *Americans* have done it for us.

self-governed, and self-directed. Be it so: And
then comes the important Queſtion, " Is this
" the Caſe at preſent with every Member of So-
" ciety in *North-America*, now groaning under
" the Dominion of the Congreſs?" And as Dr.
Price has taken ſuch Pains to extoll the *American* Mode of Government to the Skies,—a moſt
happy Mode, without Biſhops, without Nobles,
without Kings! I wiſh he would return a plain
Anſwer to the plain Queſtion here propounded.
In Honour and Conſcience he is certainly called
upon ſo to do. But tho' the Doctor loves to ſet
Controverſies on Foot, we learn from his own
Words, that he loves his Eaſe too well, to clear
up the Objections ariſing from them. Conſequently being deprived of the Doctor's Aſſiſtance,
unleſs he ſhould think proper to change his declared Reſolution, we muſt do the beſt we can
without him.

Here therefore be it obſerved, that without
taking any Advantage from the Arguments that
may be deduced from the tarring and feathering
of their numerous Mobs; and without inſiſting
on the burning and plundering of the Houſes,
and deſtroying the Property of the Loyaliſts by
the *American* Republicans, even before they had
openly thrown off the Maſque, and ſet up for Independence ;—I ſay, without bringing theſe Inſtances as Proofs that they would not grant that
Liberty to others, for which they ſo ſtrenuouſly
con-

contended for themfelves;—let us come to that very Period, when they had eftablifhed various Civil Governments in their refpeƈtive Provinces, and had new-modelled their feveral Conftitutions according to their own good Liking:—I afk therefore, Was any one of thefe Civil Governments at firft formed, or is it now adminiftered, and conduƈted according to the Lockian Plan? And did, or doth any of their Congreffes, general or provincial, admit of that fundamental Maxim of Mr. LOCKE, that every Man has an *unalienable* Right to obey no other Laws, but thofe of his own making? No; no;—fo far from it, that there are dreadful Fines and Confifcations, Imprifonments, and even Death made ufe of, as the only effeƈtual Means for obtaining that Unanimity of Sentiment fo much boafted of by thefe new-fangled Republicans, and fo little praƈticed. In one Word, let the impartial World be the Judge, whether the *Americans*, in all their Contefts for Liberty, have even ONCE made ufe of Mr. LOCKE's Syftem for any other Purpofe, but that of *pulling down*, and deftroying; and whether, when they came to ereƈt a new Edifice of their own on the Ruins of the former,—they have not abandoned Meffrs. LOCKE, MOLINEUX, PRIESTLY, and PRICE; with all their vifionary Schemes of univerfal Freedom, and Liberty of Choice.

CHAP.

C H A P. IV.

On the Abuse of Words, and the Perversion of Language, chargeable on the Lockian System.

THE Importance of this Subject requires a distinct Chapter; but it need not be a long one; for the chief Point here to be attended to, is to fix and explain the Meaning of certain Terms and Phrases, and to guard against Misreprefentation or Mistake.

IT is obferveable, that in every Government, from that of a petty Schoolmaster to that of a mighty Monarch, the respective Rulers must be invested with two Sorts of Power;—the one is that which *may be* fixed and limited by written and positive Laws; but the other, being unlimitable in its Nature, must be left to the Discretion of the Agent. The Order and Course of Things require the Use of both these Kinds of Power in every Instance where *Authority*, properly so called, is to be exercifed. In respect to the first of these, it is unnecessary at present to consider it in any separate, or independent View;

becaufe

becaufe it is not the Subject now immediately
before us. But with regard to the fecond, it is
the very Thing here to be attended to ; and by
explaining the Nature of this, we fhall eventually
explain the other.

WHEN the Founder of a School [and the
fame Obfervation, *mutatis mutandis*, would hold
good for Things in a much higher Sphere ;—I
fay therefore] when the Founder of a School is
about to eftablifh Rules and Conftitutions for
the Difcipline, and good Government thereof ;—
he finds himfelf able to eftablifh certain Statutes
and Ordinances in refpect to fome Things, but
unable in refpect to others. He can, for Example, fix the Salary of the Mafter by a pofitive
Law ;—he can limit the Hours of School, and
the Hours of Recreation ; – he can ordain, if he
think proper, what Authors fhall be read in his
School, and may prefcribe likewife a Regimen
of Diet to be obferved by the Youths, who fhall
be maintained on his Foundation ;—with a few
other Things of the like Nature. But much
farther than this he cannot go, were he ever fo
defirous. He cannot, for Inftance, lay down
Rules aforehand, how many Periods or Para-
graphs *each* Youth is to learn at *each* Leffon, or
how many Lines or Verfes he is to get by Heart
on a Repetition Day ; and in Cafes of Neglect,

or Mifdemeanor, he cannot determine the Force
or Momentum, with which the Ferula or Rod
is to fall on the offending Culprit;—nor yet can
he prefcribe, or limit the Tone of Voice, or
Looks, or Geftures of Difpleafure, or Words of
Reprimand, which are to be ufed on fuch Occafions. For as all thefe Affairs are not, and
cannot be fubject to any fixt Regulations, the
Mafter muft be vefted with a *difcretionary*, alias
an *unlimited* Power in refpect to fuch Things.
[Need I add that the very Inftitution of a School
is (according to the Lockian Syftem) a Contradiction to the focial Compact? Becaufe, if every
one is to be accounted a Slave, who is obliged to
fubmit to Laws not of his own making,—or to
Governors not of his own chufing, then School-
Boys and Slaves are fynonimou Terms: Hard
Meafures thefe! And what Inroads are the
Doctrines of Paffive Obedience, and Non-Refiftance daily making in our *Englifh* Schools on
Englifh Liberty! But to return] The Powers
of this Magiftrate, [the School-Mafter] being
thus fhewn to be partly circumfcribed, and partly
indefinite;—I here afk, Doth his *indefinite*
Power thereby become *infinite?* Or is he vefted
with arbitrary and defpotic Power, becaufe he
is entrufted with that which is *difcretionary?*
Surely no: And the very putting fuch a Queftion, one would think, is fufficient to confute every Lockian Cavil on this Head.
* Yet

* Yet, ftrange to tell, the whole Weight of their Arguments refts on this fingle Point. For [according to them] if you admit *difcretionary* Power, you muft admit it to be *arbitrary:* If you allow the Power of your Magiftrate to be in any Cafe *indefinite,* you muft allow it to be *infinite.* Now it fo happens, that Experience and common Senfe, no bad Judges to appeal to, entirely confute thefe confident Affertions. For were the Mafter of any School to treat his Scholars with wanton Cruelty, to beat them unmercifully, or to inflict any unneceffary Severity upon them,—all the World would foon diftinguifh fuch Abufes of Power from neceffary Chaftifement, and moderate Correction; and they would not hefitate in giving their Opinion, that fuch a Wretch deferved the fevereft Punifhment. So much eafier it is, to difcern the Ufe of Things from the Abufes of them, after the Fact has happened, than it is to make Laws in *all Cafes* aforehand for the Prevention of Abufes.

THE King and both Houfes of Parliament, that is, the fupreme Legiflature of this Country, have a general, unlimited Right to make Laws for binding the People, in *all Cafes whatfoever.* They have this Right, becaufe it is impoffible

---

* Dr. PRICE and the Congrefs ground all their Outcries againft the declaratory Law, for binding the Colonies in all Cafes whatfoever, on this very Plea, weak and illogical as it is.

to define exactly in what particular Instances) they ought *not* to be entrusted with such a Right, or how far their Power ought to extend in every Case, and every Circumstance, which might occur, and where it ought to be stopped. I say, it is impossible to define these Points before-hand, or to draw the Line between *Trust*, and *Distrust* in these Respects. Yet can any Man in his Senses pretend to say, that the King and the Parliament would be *justifiable*, or even *excusable*, were they to abuse this discretionary Power of *making Laws in all Cases whatsoever ;*—I mean wilfully and designedly abuse it, so as to enslave the People by cruel, unjust, and tyrannical Laws? Surely no: For even Sir ROBERT FILMER, and the Jacobites, do not say that such Rulers are at all *excusable ;*—nay, they expressly say the contrary ; and are as ready at denouncing Hell and Damnation against such *wicked Tyrants,* as the Lockians themselves : — Indeed they protest against any Punishment whatever being inflicted on Tyrants, especially on royal Tyrants, during the present Life, by the Hands of Men : For which ill-judged Tenderness, and mistaken Points of Conscience, they are highly to blame : And therefore their Tenets of *absolute* and *unlimited* Passive Obedience and Non-Resistance are deservedly had in Detestation : But nevertheless they make no wrong Judgment concerning the Nature of, and the Punishment due to, the

Crimes

Crimes of Tyranny ; tho' they are fo weak as to maintain, that this Punifhment ought to be deferred, 'till the Criminals themfelves are removed into another World, when the Punifhment due to fuch Offences can be no Terror to thofe Evil-Doers who furvive, and who therefore ought to be deterred by fuch Examples from attempting to do the like.

CONCLUSION.

CONCLUSION.

UPON the whole, if this new political Syſtem of Mr. Locke and his Followers hath not received a full and ample Confutation in the preceding Sheets, I muſt ingenuouſly acknowledge, that nothing could have prevented it, but the Inability or Incapacity of the Author. For ſurely a more pernicious Set of Opinions than the Lockian —[I mean, with regard to the Peace and Tranquility of the preſent Life] could hardly be broached by Man. And it is but ſmall Conſolation to reflect, that probably the original Author, and ſeveral of his Diſciples never meant to draw Concluſions ſo horrid in their Nature, and ſo full of *wanton* Treaſon and Rebellion, as the Congreſſes have actually drawn from it in *America,* and as the Republican Factions are daily endeavouring to draw from it here in *England,* had they Power equal to their Will.

MOREOVER what greatly aggravates the Crime of every Attempt of this Nature, and renders it utterly inexcuſable, is, that there is no Manner of Need of having Recourſe to ſuch Meaſures, or to ſuch Principles, for the Sake of confuting either

the

the patriarchal Scheme of Sir R. Filmer, or the
absolutely paffive Obedience Creed of the Jacobites ; Infomuch as both thefe erroneous Syftems
may be, at leaft, as fully and effectually confuted
without Mr. Locke's Principles, as with them.
Nay, if the Lockians had been content with their
own Set of Opinions, and had left others undif-
turbed in the quiet Enjoyment of theirs, fomething
might have been pleaded in their Favour. For
though one may eafily fee, that theirs is an im-
practicble Scheme in any Society whatever, great
or fmall; yet, if they think otherwife, and are
firmly perfuaded that the Affair is of fuch Importance as to merit a fair and open Trial ;—Let a
fair Trial be given it ; and let thofe unpeopled
Regions of *America*, thofe *vacua loca*, mentioned
by Mr. Locke, be the Theatre for exhibiting
this curious Phœnomenon, a Lockian Republic ! Where all Taxes are to be *Free-Gifts !* and
every Man is to obey *no farther*, and no *otherwife,*
than he himfelf *chufes* to obey ! In fuch a Cafe,
inconfiderable as I am, I will venture to promife
[or to ufe the Language of an Arch-Patriot, I
will pledge myfelf to the Public] that all the
Sons and Daughters of *genuine* Freedom fhall be
at Liberty to remove thither as foon as they
pleafe ;—and that Thoufands and Tens of Thoufands of their Fellow-Citizens will be heartily
glad of their Departure.

But if not content with this Liberty for themfelves. they will be indefatigable in difturbing the Repofe of others, and will inceffantly excite the Subjects of every State to rebel, under the fhameful Pretence, that their Governors are *Ufurpers* of their *unalienable* Rights ;—they muft expect to have their Sophiftry detected, and themfelves expofed in their proper Colours. Indeed. happy it is for *them* ;—happy it is for *us all* [notwithftanding fome petty Inconveniencies] that we live in fuch an Age, and fuch a Country, where Men may dare to fay and do fuch Things with Impunity. I own the very Contemplation of this Circumftance always gives me Pleafure : For rejoice to find that on every Comparifon between the Liberty pretended to be enjoyed under the patriotic Congrefs in *America*. and the Slavery, which it feems, we daily fuffer here in *England*. every Inftance is a Demonftration that *Englifh* Slavery is infinitely preferable to *American* Liberty : So that in fhort. while I find, that here in *England*, a Man may fay or do, may write or print, a thoufand Things with the utmoft Security, for which his Liberty and Property, and even his Life itfelf would be in the moft imminent Danger, were he to do the like in *America*, I want no other Proofs, that *Englifhmen* are ftill a Nation of *Freemen*, and not of *Slaves*. Sorry I am, that any of my Fellow-Subjects fhould mifapply fo great a Bleffing as Liberty is, both civil and religious : But at the fame Time, I

am

am sincerely glad that they themselves are such undeniable Evidences of the Existence of Liberty among us, by the Security they enjoy in their manifold Abuses of it. May they grow wiser and better every Day; But may we, on our Parts, never attempt to weed out these Tares from among the Wheat, lest by so doing, we should root out the Wheat also.

PART

PART II.

CONTAINING

THE TRUE BASIS

OF

CIVIL GOVERNMENT,

In OPPOSITION to the SYSTEM of

Mr. LOCKE and his FOLLOWERS,

By JOSIAH TUCKER, D. D.

DEAN of GLOCESTER.

THE

PREFACE

TO THE

SECOND PART.

THE Author imagines, that he has confuted the Lockian *System* in the fore-going Part of this Work. And he is *supported* in this Opinion by the *Judgment* of many Persons, not only distinguished for their Learning and good Sense, but also for their zealous Attachment to the Civil, and Religious Liberties of this Country. If this be the Case, that is, if he has really confuted Mr. LOCKE, he may now, he hopes, with some Propriety, venture to submit to Public Consideration, a System of his own; which he is inclined to think, may serve as a Basis for every Species of Civil Government to stand upon.—At the same Time he is well aware, that it doth not follow, that his must be true, because Mr. LOCKE's may have been proved to be false: He is also very sensible, that it is much easier to pull down, than to build up; and that many a Man can demolish the System of another, who cannot defend his own.

FOR

THE PREFACE.

For thefe Reafons he is the more defirous of proceeding with due Referve and Caution; — not expecting,. that this Plan fhould be adopted, as foon as propofed, — nor yet fuppofing, that it will be totally rejected, before it fhall have undergone fome Kind of Examination. In order to give it a fair Trial, he has added a Series of Objections, partly as they occurred to himfelf, in reafoning on the Cafe, and partly as they were fuggefted to him in the Converfation he had with others. In refpect to all which it will be readily allowed, that not one Objection has loft any of it's Force and Weight in paffing through his Hands: And as to their refpective Anfwers, every Reader will judge for himfelf.

He is very willing to allow, that fome Parts of his Syftem are weaker than others : For this muft happen more or lefs, to all human Compofitions. Therefore he doth not pretend to lay before the Public a faultlefs Piece, free from all Objections, but only fuch a Plan for a political Edifice, as may ferve all the good Purpofes of real and rational Liberty, and at the fame Time be more practicable, and better accommodated to the State of Mankind in every Age and Country, than Mr. LOCKE's is confeffed to be.

The Author doth not build much on the Authority of great Names.—not that he rejects human Authority, when it can be properly introduced in Matters of doubtful Difputation; but becaufe he cannot find that the Point was ever brought into Controverfy
till

'till of late, whether the Inclinations of Mankind
are naturally and fpontaneoufly turned towards
Society and the Subordinations of Civil Government,
or towards living in a State of perfect Equality,
and Independence.   Therefore it is in vain to look
for long Argumentations in the Works of political
Writers of former Times, relative to this Queftion,
either pro or con, before the Queftion itfelf was fuppofed to exift.

However, as it may be a Satisfaction to fome Perfons to know, What were the genuine Opinions of
the Sages of Antiquity on this Subject, before the
Arts of Sophiftry, and the Rage of Party-Difputes,
had blinded Men's Eyes, and corrupted their natural
good Senfe ;---fuch Perfons will, I hope, be fufficiently gratified, when they come to perufe the third
Part of the enfuing Treatife.   They will alfo there
find the judicious HOOKER now refcued out of the
difagreeable Company of modern Republicans, with
whom he has been made to affociate for fome Time
paft, much againft his Will, and reftored to his true
Friends both in Church and State.

THE

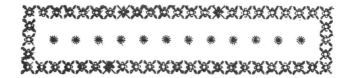

THE
TRUE BASIS
OF
CIVIL GOVERNMENT, &c.

CHAP. I.

Concerning thofe Principles in Human Nature, which may ferve as a Bafis for any Species of Civil Government to ftand upon, without the actual Choice, or perfonal Election of every Member of the Community either towards the firft Erection, or the Continuation of fuch a Government.

AS Mr. LOCKE, and his Followers have ob-jected to our deducing Kingly Govern-ment, or indeed any Kind of Civil Government from the Authority of Parents over their Chil-dren [though the Out-Lines, and firft Rudiments

ments of all Governments had probably no other Origin,] and have taken such Pains to shew the Disparity of the Cases; we will gratify them to their Hearts' Content in this particular: For we will endeavour to shew, that were Numbers of the Human Species to be brought together, (tho' no otherwise connected than by being of the same Species) they would soon fall into some Kind of Subordination among themselves, and consequently into some Kind of Government;—and that too without that personal, and particular Election, for which Mr. LOCKE and his Followers have so strenuously contended.

IN order therefore to keep at a sufficient Distance from the *Patriarchal Syflem*, and the *indefeasible Right Lined Monarchy* of Sir ROBERT FILMER;—Let us suppose, that, instead of one Pair, an Hundred Pair of Men and Women were at first created: And let us contemplate the various Instincts, Qualities, and Propensities (as far as the present Subject is concerned) with which this Tribe of Animals would be found to be endowed;—supposing them to be made of the same Sort of Materials, which we see Mankind to be of, at present.

AND as we are now setting out on our Inquiries, be it carefully remembered, that the *first* Difference between the Lockians, and others
seems

feems to be this ;   The Lockians maintain, that
Mankind have a *Capacity* for becoming Members of a Civil Society ;—but no *natural* Defire,
or Inclination for entering into fuch a State of
Life : [Indeed they do not fay the latter in exprefs Terms, but they do by neceffary Confequences :] Whereas we maintain, that Human
Nature is endowed with both Capacity, and Inclination :—And that the natural *Inſtinct* pre-
cedes the *Capacity*, much in the fame Manner,
tho' not with the fame Strength, or in the fame
Degree, as the innate Inftincts of Individuals
towards Food, or of the Species towards each
other, precede the *Arts* of Cookery, and
Brewery, of Marriage-Ceremonies, and Mar-
riage-Settlements.

THIS therefore being the Queftion, we are
now to endeavour to find out, how far *Nature*
herfelf hath led the Way towards the Formation
of Civil Government by means of various
Inftincts, Biaffes, and Propenfities implanted in
Mankind before *Art* was introduced either to
mend or mar her Handywork.

1. THEREFORE, the firft Thing obfervable in
the Clafs of Animals above-mentioned [the
hundred Pair of adult Men and Women] is,
That they are formed by Nature to be of the
gregarious Kind. For moft certainly the Individuals of the Human Species are fo far from
feeking

feeking Solitude, as their *natural* State, that fuch a Courfe of Life would be one of the foreft Punifhments which could be inflicted on them: And nothing can be a clearer Proof of a contrary Bias in Nature, than the ftrong Defire which not only Children manifeft to affociate together, but which adult Perfons feel, to be acquainted even with Strangers, differing from themfelves in Language, Manners, and in almoft every Thing, excepting their being of the fame Species, *rather than not to enjoy any Company at all.* Now this Difpofition in Human Creatures to affociate with their *Like*, is a leading Step towards Civil Society; becaufe no Animals whatever, but the *gregarious*, can be *fit* to form a Community, or a Common-Wealth.

2. A SECOND Thing obfervable is, That there is a prodigious Variety even in the *natural* Endowments, both of Body and Mind belonging to the feveral Individuals of the human Species: So that probably no two among them are altogether, and in every Refpect alike. Far therefore, very far it is from being true, that all Mankind are naturally equal, or on a *Par*, refpecting their feveral Endowments either mental, or corporeal. Indeed had this been the Cafe, it is hard to fay, how any Kind of Subordination, and confequently Government, could have been introduced among fuch a Tribe of equal, independent, unconnected Beings: Wherefore

3. A

3. A THIRD Obfervation is, that thefe Dif-
ferences of Genius and Talents, thefe feveral
Excellencies and Defects, thefe Capacities and
Incapacities are found, for the moft Part, to be
relative and reciprocal ; fo that wherefoever one
abounds, another is defective, and vice verfa :
By which Means all thefe Animals ftand in Need
of each other's Affiftance in fome Refpect, or in
one Degree or other :—Surely this is another
plain Proof, that they were not framed by Nature for an equal, independent, unconnected
State of Life.

4. A FOURTH Remark is, That *as* thefe Animals mutually want each other's Help and
Affiftance ; *fo* are they naturally endowed with a
Power of making known their Wants to each
other, and their mutual Willingnefs to relieve
them.   Now, as this is a Fact, which cannot be
controverted, it is very immaterial to decide,
whether the Manner of making known fuch mutual Wants, or Intentions, was at firft by Means
of dumb Signs and Geftures, and inarticulate
Sounds, or thro' the Medium of fome primæval
Language infufed in, or communicated to them at
the Time of their Creation.   Therefore be that
as it may, it is more material to obferve in the

5th and laft Place, That each of thefe human
Animals feels, generally fpeaking, a ftrong In-
ftinct to fuccour and relieve the Wants and
Diftreffes

Diftreffes of his Fellow-Creatures :—Inafmuch as, next to providing what is neceffary for his own Prefervation, and removing Pain from his own Perfon, he is prompted and fpurred on to do the like good Offices for others. And he finds, that he receives great Pleafure both in the immediate Gratification of this benevolent, fympathizing Inftinct, and in his fubfequent Reflections on it.

Now from a Contemplation of this Sketch, or Out-line, if I may fpeak, of the Portrait of Human Nature, it is, I think, not very difficult to determine, what would be the probable Refult of an Affemblage of an Hundred Pair of fuch Animals as thefe, after a fhort Acquaintance, refpecting Society and Civil Government. For

1. They would not be long before they endeavoured to gratify the firft, and the quickeft in Succeffion, of all the Calls of Nature, the Appetites of *Hunger* and *Thirft*; and that too without having any diftinct Knowledge, perhaps without the leaft Idea, that fuch a Gratification was neceffary for the Prefervation of the Individual. Nay, it is highly probable, that Nature at the firft Creation of the Human Pairs, proceeded much farther in her inftinctive Inftructions, than fhe need do at prefent. For at the firft, Men were not only impelled by the

Appetites

Appetites of Hunger and Thirst to feek for Meat and Drink, but were alfo taught, either by fome Guardian Angel fent on purpofe to inftruct them, or were led by fome extraordinary Impulfe to difcover and chufe what were proper Eatables and Drinkables in their peculiar Situation.—To fuppofe the contrary, would be to fuppofe, that this Hundred Pair of adult Men and Women, were left to themfelves to make Experiments, as they could, on every thing around them,—by endeavouring to fwallow perhaps Sand or Gravel, inftead of Water, towards quenching Thirft, and to gnaw a Stone, or a Stick, inftead of chewing a Root, a Fruit, or a Berry for appeafing Hunger. It cannot therefore reafonably be doubted, but that the firft Race of Men were taught by Nature, or rather by Nature's God, to diftinguifh, without the tedious Procefs of uncertain Experiments, the proper from the improper, the wholefome from the unwholefome in fuch a Situation.

[As to the Inftinct between the Sexes for the Renovation of the Species (as the former was for the Prefervation of the Individual) fuffice it juft to put the Reader in Mind, that as we have fuppofed the Creation to have been made in *Conjugal Pairs*, we have thereby avoided, at leaft for the prefent, all the Difficulties, that might otherwife have arifen in the Choice and Preference of Objects;—only this much is neceffary

neceffary to obferve on this Head, as well as on the former, that 'till they had been taught by Experience, it was impoffible for the wifeft of them to have gueffed what would have been the Confequence, at the Expiration of a certain Term, of fuch an Intercourfe of one Sex with the other.]

2dly. THESE human Animals, when herding together, and beginning to eat and drink, would foon difcover a vaft Superiority, and Inferiority of *Talents* among themfelves, in refpect of making Provifion for fatisfying the Cravings of Thirft and Hunger. For fome would be found to be much more ingenious, and perhaps more induftrious and provident than others, either in the gathering of Viands, and the procuring and portage of drinkable Liquids;—or in ftoring them up, and preferving them fweet and wholefome. This Man would excel either in turning the Ground in fearch after Roots, or in climbing Trees for Fruit;—another in fwimming and diving for Fifh, or in the Purfuit of Game;--a third in the taming certain Beafts and Birds for domeftic Ufe, or in the planting of fuch Vegetables, as were found to be good for Food, and fo quick of Growth as foon to come to Maturity; —whilft a fourth perhaps would difplay a Dexterity and Genius in the Preparation of feveral Kinds of Victuals, and in the firft Rudiments of the Arts of Cookery. Now in all thefe Cafes, it is obvious to conceive, That the lefs ingenious,

or

or adventurous, the lefs provident and frugal would naturally become, without any formal Contraƈt, dependent on, and fubfervient to their Inftruƈtors and Benefaƈtors, in one Degree or other.

3dly. THE like Superiority of Parts and Talents would neceffarily appear, tho' at fomewhat a later Period, in the Cafes of procuring Rayment, and of conftruƈting Habitations. For no Man can pretend that all the Human Species are endowed with equal Powers, or equal Capacities in thefe Refpeƈts. And therefore in Proportion as the lefs adroit, or lefs provident, felt themfelves incommoded by the Extremes either of Heat, or of Cold, and wifhed to free themfelves from their Evils;—in nearly the fame Proportion would they become the Minifters of thofe, who could, and would relieve them from their Diftreffes. For here it muft be remembered once for all, that in fuch a Situation as we are now defcribing, and before Commerce and Money were introduced, the Perfon who felt himfelf inferior in any of thefe Refpeƈts, could make no other Compenfation to his Superior, but by fome Kind of *perfonal Service.*

4th. THE Advantage arifing from a peculiar Genius to abridge Labour by Means of Machines.

chines, —or to divide, and fubdivide it into diftinct Parts, or Po tions for the Sake of greater Eafe, Expertnefs, and Ex edition, is another Caufe, why fome Men muft rife in Society, without any Compact, or Election, and others as naturally fink;—and confequently, why Subordination at firft, and Government afterwards, muft take Place. For had there been no Difference of natural Genius between Man and Man;—and no Diftinction of Talents and Powers both mental, and corporeal, between Males and Females,—it is hardly poffible to conceive, how there could have exifted any Diftinction of Trades, or Diverfity of Employments. And without them a regular Plan of Government cannot be fupported.

To illuftrate this Matter, be it obferved, that tho' Horfes, and horned Cattle naturally herd together, as well as Men, being all of the *gregarious* Kind; yet as none of thefe Individuals difplay any Genius either to abridge Labour, or to divide it into feparate Parts or Portions,—fo there is nothing approaching towards a Diftinction of Trades, or a Diverfity of Imployments to be found among them;—confequently they are total Strangers to any Forms of Government, Republican, or Monarchical; and they know nothing of the Rules of Juftice or Equity or of any Laws, but thofe of brutal Force. Whereas Bees, Ants, and Beavers, who

are

are remarkable for dividing the Labour of the *Whole* into diſtinct Portions, aſſigning to each Individual a proper Share, become of Courſe a regular Community among themſelves, wherein ſome preſide, and others muſt obey. All Authors, who have favoured us with the natural Hiſtory of theſe three Tribes of Animals, ſpeak with Raptures of their admirable Police, Diſcipline, and Œconomy. Yet not one Writer, that I know of, hath once ſuggeſted the moſt diſtant Thought, that theſe Things are owing to any ſocial Compact, or popular Form of Government : — No, not one hath hitherto dared to maintain, that each Bee, Ant, or Beaver is his own Law-giver, Governor, and Director.

[THERE are other Cauſes which might be mentioned, as greatly contributing towards the firſt Formation of Government, without any explicit Compact, or mutual Stipulation. And theſe are the *Power of Language*,—and the *Power of ſaving*, or *protecting* from impending Dangers. In regard to Language, ſome ſtriking Obſervations might have been made, had we the Time, and Abilities to have done Juſtice to the Subject : —Suffice it for the preſent juſt to declare my Opinion, That at the firſt Creation of the human Kind, the Adams and Eves, ſpoke ſome certain Language (whatever it was) by mere *Inſtinct*, without any previous Teaching (excepting the
inſtantaneous

inftantaneous Teaching of Nature) and without Education, or Inftruction. I know indeed, that the contrary is the prevailing Opinion, That all Words, and the Meaning of all Words were originally fettled by mutual Confent, and at fome certain Congrefs held for that Purpofe. But here I fhould be glad to know, what particular Language was fpoken by Adam and Eve, and their Sons and Daughters, or by this hundred Pair of Adams and Eves, *before* they met in Congrefs ?—In what Language or Dialect were they fummoned to meet?—And even after they had met, how came they to underftand one another fo readily before they had learnt to fpeak ? – And how came they to fpeak at all, to define, and to agree about the Meaning of certain Words, before thefe, or any Words whatever had been known among them? ––– Away therefore with this abfurd Notion : And let us believe, as we ought to do, that Nature was more benevolent to her Children at their firft Appearance on the Theatre of the World, than this and fuch like Schemes' reprefent her to be. She certainly *infufed* the firft Rudiments of Language, fhe *inftilled* the firft Knowledge of Things proper for Meats and Drinks,—and fhe *implanted* the conftituent Principles of Government into Mankind, without any previous Care or Thought on their Parts. But having done this, fhe left the reft to themfelves ; in order that they might cultivate and improve her Gifts and Bleffings in the beft Manner they could.   As

As to the Power of protecting from impending Danger, if that should mean only the Power of refcuing, or preferving from the Injuries of the Weather, from the Attacks of wild Beafts, or from fome other natural Evils, it is included, at leaft in Part. under fome of the former Heads.—But if it is to fignify a Power of protecting the Weak from the intended Violence of the Strong, it will include likewife the Right of Retaliation and Reprifal—and in its Confequences, the Right of Conqueft.   Therefore if this fhould be the Thing meant, I fhall not infift on fuch a Subject at prefent;—becaufe I wifh to fhew, That Government can date its Origin from other Caufes, befides thofe of popular Elections, or popular Defeats;—and becaufe a Government founded on Conqueft, however juftifiable the Occafion of it might have been. is at firft very odious, and requires a Length of Time to reconcile Men to it.]

LASTLY, there is yet another Confideration, which when properly developed, greatly corroborates all the former.   And that is this, That there is found to exift in Human Nature a certain Afcendency in fome, and a Kind of fubmiffive Acquiefcence in others.   The Fact itfelf, however unaccountable, is neverthelefs fo notorious that it is obfervable in all Stations and Ranks of Life, and almoft in every Company. For even in the moft paltry Country Village, there

there is, generally fpeaking, what the French very expreffively term, *Le Coque de Village* ;— A Man, who takes the Lead, and becomes a Kind of Dictator to the reft. Now, whether this arifes from a Confcioufnefs of greater Courage, or Capacity,—or from a certain overbearing Temper, which affumes Authority to dictate and command,—or from a greater Addrefs, that is, from a Kind of inftinctive Infight into the Weakneffes, and blind Sides of others,— or from whatever Caufe, or Caufes, it matters not. For the Fact itfelf, as I faid before, is undeniable, however difficult it may be to account for it. And therefore here again is another Inftance of great Inequalities in the original Powers and Faculties of Mankind :—Confequently this natural Subordination (if I may fo fpeak) is another diftinct Proof, that there was a F undation deeply laid in Human Nature for the political Edifices of Government to be built upon ;— without recurring to, what never exifted but in Theory, univerfal, focial Compacts, and unanimous Elections.

HERE therefore I will fix my Foot, and reft the Merits of the Caufe. An hundred Pair of Adams and Eves are fuppofed (for the Sake of Argument in this Debate) to have been created at once, and to have been endowed with the various Inftincts and Inclinations above defcribed, all tending in one Degree or other, to the Forma-

tion

tion of Civil Government.   As foon as they fee eachother they affociate and converfe. [N. B. Infants and Children do ftill the fame in their Way.] The next Step they take, is to gratify thofe Defires and Inclinations towards which * Nature has moft powerfully incited them.   But they find almoft inftantaneoufly, that they are hardly able to fatisfy any one of thefe Defires without the Help and Affiftance of others of their Kind.   And they feel alfo, that in whatfoever Sort of Talents, Geniuffes, or Capacities they are deficient, others are generally abounding, and vice verfa :---They perceive likewife that in receiving good Offices from others, there is a certain pleafing Temper of Mind excited,   now   called *Gratitude*,—and that in conferring good Offices, there is another very pleafing Senfation raifed, now termed *Benevolence*.   And thus it came to pafs, that a mutual Dependence and a mutual Conne&tion were originally made by the wife Creator of all Things to pervade the Whole :—Yet with this remarkable Diverfity, that the Power and Talents of winning and obliging, of influencing, perfuading, or commanding, were imparted to fome in a much greater Degree than they were to others.

---

* The Appetite between the Sexes can have no Place in this Queftion ; becaufe it is not of that Sort, or Kind, which renders Mankind *gregarius*.   Indeed it is obfervable, that the moft folitary Animals, which are not fond of *herding* together, yet, at certain Periods, converfe in *Pairs*.

SURELY

SURELY therefore in fuch Circumftances as thefe, every human Creature would fall into that Rank in Society, and that Station in Life, to which his Talents and his Genius fpontane- oufly led him,—as *naturally*, I had almoft faid, as Water finds its Level. And be it ever remem- bered, that diftinct Ranks and different Stations, would produce a Civil Government, of fome Kind or other, in a *new* World much fooner than they could in an *old* one. —— I faid MUCH SOONER; becaufe in a new World, there could be no Complaints made againft former Mif- managements, no Fears about the Incroachments of Power on the one Hand, or the Intrigues and Declamation of Faction on the other, and confe- quently no *Diftruft* arifing from the Abufes either of former Governors, or of former Demagogues. In fhort, as in fuch a World there could be no Manner of Experience, there could hardly be any fuch Things as Caution and Referve; and therefore all the Difputes of later Times about focial Compacts, Contracts, and Conventions, about pofitive Stipulations, reciprocal Engage- ments, and Refervations of Rights, would have been probably as little underftood at that Junc- ture, as the Terms of Art in Cookery, before Cookery became an Art, or the Orders in Building, before a fingle Building was erected. In fhort, and to fum up all in one Word, where *Nature* alone was the Guide, the Terms of *Art*, and the Additions, or Alterations of fubfequent

Times,

Times, whether for the better, or for the worfe,
muft have been abfolutely unknown, and confequently could not have been attended to, at the
firft Formation of Civil Government.

But after all, perhaps fome will fay, " We
" do not differ from you in real Sentiments,
" tho' we exprefs ourfelves fomewhat differently.
" We mean to fay, that no Part of the human
" Species, has a Right to enflave the other ;
" and we mean no more." Very well, be it fo,
and we are agreed: But let us firft know, what
do you mean by *Slavery* ? And what Ideas do
you include under that Term ?—For if you
mean to fay, that every Man is a *Slave*, who
has not the Power of electing his own Law-
giver, his own Magiftrate, his Colonel, Cap-
tain, or Judge, I deny the Pofition, and call
on you to prove it by better Arguments, than
your own bare Affertion. But if you only
meant to fay, that bad Laws, if any, ought to
be repealed, and good Laws enacted, and faith-
fully and impartially executed ;—and that when
Governors fhall abufe their Power to the Detriment of the People, they ought to be ftopped
in their Career, and even to be called to an
Account for their Mifconduct, in Proportion to
the Detriment received.---If this be all you
meant to fay, when you talked about original,
unalienable Rights, focial Compacts, &c. &c.
                                         we

we are agreed again: But furely, furely, this
is a very odd, and intricate Way of expreffing
the plaineft, and moft obvious Truths imaginable.

MOREOVER, if you intended to fay, that tho'
Government in *general* did not derive its Exiftence from any *perfonal* Contract between
Prince and People, between the Governors and
the Governed;—yet, that it hath fo much of
what a Civilian would term a *Quafi-Contract* in the
Nature of it, that the Duties and Obligations on
both Sides of the Relation, are altogether to the
fame Effect, as if a particular Contract, and a
pofitive Engagement had been entered into;---
If this be your Meaning, we are ready to join
Iffue with you once more;---and this the rather,
becaufe the Ideas of a *Quafi-Contract* contain our
own on this Head, and thofe of every Conftitutional Whig throughout the Kingdom.

HOWEVER, though we are ready to grant you
all thefe Things, yet it is plain, that you meant
a great deal more;—elfe, why do you cavil at
the Phrafes, *implicit Confent, tacit Agreement,
implied Covenant, virtual Reprefentation*, and the
like?—All which naturally and neceffarily imply
the Idea of a *Quafi-Contract*. Moreover why
fo loud in your Exclamations, and bitter in your
Invectives againft fuppofing, that a Government
may be good and lawful in itfelf, tho the People
are

are not reprefented in it, according to your
Mode of Reprefentation? Recollect the feveral
Extracts from Meffrs. Locke, Molineux,
Priestly, and Price, already produced in
the former Part of this Work: And then you
muft maintain, in Conformity to the leading
Principles of your Sect, That throughout this
whole Difpute, your grand Objection lies not fo
much againft the mere Laws themfelves, or
againft any fuppofed Culpability in the Manner
of adminiftering them,—as againft the Right,
Title, or Authority to make, or to execute any
Laws at all, be they in themfelves good, or bad.
In one Word, according to your Doctrine, *that*
Man is a *Slave*, who is obliged to fubmit to the
beft Laws that ever were made, and to the mildeft
Government, that ever exifted, if he did not give
his previous Confent towards eftablifhing the one,
and enacting the other: And that Man is FREE,
who fubmits to no other Government but that
which he himfelf hath chofen, and obeys no
other Laws, but thofe, which he himfelf hath
helped to make ; tho' they fhould be in themfelves as tyrannical and cruel, as unjuft, and unreafonable, as can be conceived. So that the
great Good of political Liberty, and the intolerable Evil of political Slavery, are according to
this bleffed Doctrine, refolved at laft into the
fingle Words—CONSENT, or NOT CONSENT,
What aftonifhing Abfurdities are thefe!—And
yet, alas! how prevalent, and contagious!

THE

The Idea of a *Quasi-Contract*, instead of an *actual* Contract [which never existed] between any Sovereigns, and *all*, or even the *major Part* of their Subjects, would have prevented Men of good Intentions, and honest Minds, from falling into these gross Absurdities, and dangerous Mistakes. Therefore as the Term itself *Quasi-Contract* may be new to some Readers, tho' the Sense is obvious to every one, when properly explained, I will beg Leave to bestow some Words upon it, before I conclude this Chapter.

In all human *Trusts* whatever, from the highest to the lowest, where there is a *Duty* to be performed, which is not actually expressed, specified, or contracted for,---but nevertheless is strongly implied in the Nature of the Trust;--- the Obligation to perform that implied Duty, is of the Nature of a *Quasi-Contract;*---a Contract as binding in the Reason of Things, and in the Court of Conscience, as the most solemn Covenant that was ever made. This I think is a plain Case; at least I cannot make it plainer, and therefore tho' I might illustrate this Matter by appealing to the Proceedings of the Courts of Equity, which are little more than the inforcing of the Performance of *Quasi Contracts*, yet I will confine myself to Subjects, that are altogether political;—because I wish to meet the Lockians on their own Ground, and to confute them by their favourite Principles.

Be

BE it therefore allowed, for Argument's Sake, that there is an *actual*, and not a *Quaſi-Contract*, this Day ſubſiſting in *Great-Britain* between Prince and People. The Queſtion then is, When was this Contract made? And the Anſwer muſt be [for no other can be given] that it was made at his Majeſty's Coronation, when he took a ſolemn Oath to govern his People according to Law; and when they on their Parts expreſſed their Conſent to his Acceſſion to the Throne by loud Huzzas, and Shouts of Joy.—Well: To take no Advantage of one material Omiſſion among many, that the Spectators on this Occaſion were *not a thouſandth* Part of the People of *Great Britain* and *Ireland* [not to ſay a Word about the Colonies.] Let it be granted, that this was a good Contract, fair, valid, and reciprocal.—Yet the difficulty is ſtill to come,— What was the Caſe *before* this Contract was made? And how ſtood Matters during the long Interval, which elaſped between his Acceſſion, and Coronation? Or ſuppoſe, that he had not yet been crowned, Was the Prince in that Caſe, and during theſe nineteen Years of his Reign, not obliged to govern his People according to Law? Or were the People, on their Parts, not obliged to become his dutiful and loyal Subjects, till they had ſhouted and huzzaed at his Coronation? Reſolve this Difficulty, if you can, on the Lockian Principle of an *actual* Contract: But if you will admit of a *Quaſi-Contract*, the

Difficulty

Difficulty vanifhes at once : So that Reafon and Common Senfe, and the *known Laws* of the Land all co-incide in perfeft Harmony : I faid the *known* Laws of the Land, becaufe it is notorious to all the World, that there was not one political Duty incumbent on either Prince, or People, *after* the Solemnity of a Coronation, but was equally incumbent *before* that Ceremony was performed.

AGAIN : The Lockians ftiffly maintain, that every Civil Government muft be an Ufurpation of unalienable Rights, if the People are neither permitted to affemble together in their perfonal Capacities, for the Purpofes of making Laws, for feeing them executed, and the like,---* nor allowed to eleft Deputies to reprefent them, and to aft as their Attornies or Proxies. Well : Be this Pofition admitted for the prefent : — Nay, be it likewife admitted, that whenever the Freeholders or Freemen of any County, City, or Borough do appoint fuch Parliamentary *Attornies*, they have a Right to infift on their renouncing their own private Judgement (at leaft in Praftice) in order to aft in Conformity to the Inftruftions of their Conftituents, and not ac-

---

* The proper Ufe, and great Advantages of Deputies from, or Reprefentatives of the People, will be fet forth at large in the 4th Chapter of the enfuing Work.

cording

cording to the Dictates of their own Consciences. Such a Contract as this [for a Contract it must be of the Lockian Principle, if it be any thing at all] methinks, sounds a little *odd*,—especially when considered as the discriminating Characteristic of the professed Friends of Liberty ! But let it pass at present among other *odd* Things.— And then comes the main Question to be resolved :   What Contract or Covenant have these Electors made with the other Members of Parliament, chosen by other Freemen or Freeholders, and for other Places, where they have no Concern, and no Right to interfere,—who nevertheless make Laws to bind *them* ?—" Laws to bind them !"   Yes to bind them *in all* [reasonable] *Cases whatsoever*, as much as the Members of their own electing.   " Surely this is strange to tell :" And yet not more strange than true.—Therefore I ask again,   What express Covenant or Stipulations have Mess. PRIESTLY, or PRICE, made with the *rest* of the Members of Parliament,—perhaps not so few as 550 in Number, whom they did *not* elect,---and for whom they had *no Votes* to give ?---I ask this Question even on a Supposition, that they had expressly covenanted with their own Members to act agreeably to those Instructions, which from Time to Time they were to have received from them ?---Or do they indeed pretend to have an Authority to instruct *all* the Representatives of the united Kingdom, as well as their own ?

BUT

But to return to the principal Subject. On the whole, and turn which Way you will, the Upshot of the Matter must come to this, that Civil Government is *natural* to Man;— and that at the Beginning, before the Human Heart was corrupted by the Tyranny of Princes, or the Madnefs and Giddinefs of the People, by the Ambition of the Great, or the Crafts and Wiles of fcheming Politicians, Civil Government as naturally took Place among Mankind, according to their refpective Talents and Qualifications, as the Marriage Union between Adam and Eve fo elegantly defcribed by Milton.

In after Times we will readily allow, That the Scenes were greatly changed in both Cafes: —But to argue from the prefent State of Things, occafioned either by the Mal-Adminiftration of Governors on one Side, or by the falfe Preten-fions of Demagogues on the other, or by the ftill greater Evils which the Public fuffers by the Struggles and Conflicts, and Counter-Machina-tions of both;—to argue, I fay, from thefe Cor-ruptions and Adulterations to the Origin of Civil Government in its pure and uncorrupted State, —would be juft as prepofterous, as it would be to maintain, that Adam and Eve did not begin their domeftic Government till the Marriage Portion was fixt and afcertained, till the Mar-riage-Articles were figned and fealed, the Join-

ture,

ture. Dowry, Pin Money, &c. &c. all previoufly fettled, and Truftees appointed for the due
Execution of thefe feveral Contracts.

THEREFORE, to fum up all in one Word, let
a thoufand Revolutions happen in the Forms or
Modes of Government, and ever fo many
Changes take Place in the Perfons or Families
of the Regents of the State, ftill Civil Government itfelf is no other than a PUBLIC TRUST, in
whatever Shape it may appear, or in whofe
Hands foever it may be placed. In fome few
Inftances [very few indeed] the Terms and Conditions of this important Truft may perhaps be
afcertained and fpecified: But in Multitudes of
others they cannot, tho' of the higheft Concern:
Yet wherever they cannot, they are *implied*:
And this Implication may be very juftly termed
a QUASI-CONTRACT.

CHAP.

C H A P. II.

OBJECTIONS ANSWERED.

HAVING in the preceding Chapter humbly submitted to the Confideration of the Public, my own Opinion concerning the Origin of Civil Government, in Oppofition to the Notion of Mr. LOCKE and his Followers, I efteem it my Duty in the next Place to endeavour to anfwer fuch Objections, as feem to militate the ftrongeft againft what has been advanced.

OBJECTION I.

" ACCORDING to the foregoing Hypothefis,
" the higher Powers in every Country fhould be
" Heroes of the firft Magnitude ;—or if not He-
" roes in War, they fhould at leaft be endowed
" with the greateft Genius, the moft diftinguifhed
" and ufeful Talents in the Arts of Peace.   For
" we are told, that it is their Superiority of na-
" tural Endowments, which, like Water finding
" its Level, laid the Foundation of Civil Go-
" vernment.   Whereas, were we to turn from
" this ideal Perfection, to the plain. fimple Fact,
" we fhall find that few of the ruling Powers,
                                      " efpecially

" efpecially crowned Heads, are wifer, or better,
" or braver, or more ufefully employed than
" other Mortals. Moreover, according to the
" foregoing Reprefentation of the Matter it
" fhould alfo follow, That on the Demife of any
" of thefe fuper-eminent, exalted Beings, a
" Kind of Diffolution, or at leaft a Sufpenfion
" of Government ought to enfue, 'till another
" *Non-pareil* could be found out, in order to fill
" [worthily and properly] the vacant Throne."

A N S W E R.

THIS Objection, fmart and plaufible as it may
appear, is wholely grounded on a Miftake,
which being removed, the Objection vanifhes.
The Miftake is this, That what was neceffary, or
expedient at firft, muft continue to be neceffary,
or expedient ever after. Whereas the Courfe
of Nature in almoft every Inftance plainly proves
the contrary.

SIR ISAAC NEWTON and Mr. BOYLE had
moft extraordinary natural Talents and Sagaci-
ties in their refpective Provinces; which they
improved by almoft inceffant Induftry and Application. Their Difcoveries in Aftronomy,
Mathematics, Optics, Natural Philofophy, Mechanics, Chemiftry, &c. &c. &c. are wonder-
fully great and curious. But doth it follow, that
every Man muft have the Genius of a BOYLE,

or

a NEWTON, in order to be benefited, or n-
lightened by their Difcoveries? And now, that
they have led the Way, may not Men of very
moderate Capacities, be able to tread in their
Steps? Nay I will go farther, and even afk,
may not an illiterate Mechanic [illiterate, comparatively fpeaking] by Dint of mere Ufe and
Practice, and by the Advantage of having good
Models before his Eyes; may not even fuch an
one be able to conftruct, or to manage fome of
their moft curious Machines in a much better
Manner than the great Philofophers themfelves
could have done, had they been alive? Surely
he may: For nothing can be more obvious, than
that the Man, who cannot invent, may neverthelefs by Means of daily Ufe, and Habit, be
able to improve on a former Invention, greatly
to his own Advantage, and that of others.

THE Cafe in Politics is much the fame; or
rather it is a ftill ftronger Confirmation of the
foregoing Remark. For tho' it may be neceffary
to have an Hero to found an Empire; or [to
come ftill nearer to the Plan of the preceding
Chapter] tho' it may at firft require fome extraordinary Efforts of an uncommon Genius, to
form an Hundred Pair of independent Savages
into a regular Community. and to bind them together with the Bonds of Civil Society,—yet
when this is once done. and good Order and
Harmony well eftablifhed,—Things will then go
on

on, in a Manner, of their own accord, if common Prudence be not wanting. Nay what is ftill more to our prefent Purpofe, it is obferveable, that great Geniuffes are likely to do more Harm than Good, if there fhould happen to be a Succeffion of them in the fame Government, for two, or three Generations. The active Spirits of fuch Men, and their excentric Difpofitions will not fuffer them to remain in a neutral State; fo that they will certainly be employed either for the better, or for the worfe. And as Ambition, and the Luft of Power are the reigning Vices of the Great, it is therefore but too probable, that they will become bad Neighbours to other States, in Proportion, as they fhall have lefs Occafion for exerting their Abilities at Home: Or if they fhould confine their Attention chiefly to their own Territories;—can it be a Doubt which Courfe they will take, Whether to encreafe, or diminifh the Privileges of their own Subjects ?—In fhort, Woe be to the Country, which happens to be curfed with a fucceffive Race of Heroes: Long Experience hath too fatally confirmed this Obfervation. And the Misfortune is, that the Subjects of thefe victorious Princes, are, generally fpeaking, fo blinded with the Glare of Glory, and fo intoxicated with the Fumes of Conqueft, that they will be content to be enflaved themfelves, provided they fhall be fo happy as to be employed in the glo-

rious

rious Work of enflaving others.—It muft, I think, be allowed, that a ROMULUS was ne-ceffary to found *Rome*, and to bring that Set of Banditti, which he firft drew together, into fome Degree of Order and Regularity, by obliging them to fubmit to the Rules of Juftice among themfelves, and the Laws of Civil Govern-ment.—But after thofe good Ends were in Part accomplifhed, the mild, pacific Difpofition, and the fteady and temperate Conduct of a NUMA, were much fitter to conftitute a Succeffor, than the dangerous Abilities of another ROMULUS.

OBJECTION II.

" THE Account given in the preceding Chap-
" ter of the Origin of Civil, or Political Go-
" vernment, muft be liable to great Exceptions,
" becaufe it confounds thofe Ideas. which ought
" always to be kept diftinct and feparate.   Thus
" for Example, there is a Society, which may
" be called *natural*, and there is another which
" is *political*.   And tho' Man is formed by Na-
" ture to become a Member of both Societies;
" yet it is a very great Miftake to fay, that he
" has the fame Inducement, or that he is influ-
" enced by the fame Motives in both Cafes.   As
" a gregarious Animal, he loves to affociate with
" his like, and to herd with them.   This is
" mere *natural* Society, and cannot be called
political.

" *political.* And even after it had been per-
" ceived, that there are many Inequalities be-
" tween the refpective Powers, Talents, and
" Capacities of the feveral Members which com-
" pofe this Society :—Perhaps indeed fo great
" as would neceffarily introduce fome Kind of
" Difference, or Diftinction among them ; ftill
" it doth not follow, that thefe Diftinctions
" fhould change natural Society into political.
" For no mere Meeting together, or Affemblage
" of the People, no Contiguity of Habitation, or
" Vicinage of Inhabitants ought to be allowed to
" conftitute a State politic, till *Legiflation* hath
" been actually introduced, and *Jurifdiction* ex-
" ercifed among them :— Which it is appre-
" hended, could not be done without common
" Confent, or at leaft the Confent of the major
" Part."

" IN Fact, the Motives for entering into thefe
" two diftinct Societies, the *natural* and the *poli-*
" *tical,* are not only different, but in a Manner
" *oppofite.* For if Men are drawn to herd to-
" gether as gregarious Animals, by a Kind of
" *inftinctive Love ;*--they may be juftly faid to be
" compelled to form political Affociations by a
" Sort of *inftinctive Fear :* That is, dreading
" the Approach of fome alarming Danger, or
" defirous of retaliating fome Injury received ;
" —they collect their fcattered Forces together,
" and put them under the Direction of one Man,

or

" or of one Set of Men, in order to be em-
" ployed for the public Good and Safety.   Now
" this being the proper Caufe or Motive and
" therefore the only true Origin of *political*
" *Union*, it is plain, that the very Defcription of
" it implies both univerfal Caution, and mutual
" Diftruft.   For in this Cafe, every Man acts
" from a Principle of Self-Intereft, or Self-Pre-
" fervation.   And therefore it is *not credible*, that
" any Number of Men, in order to guard againft
" one Danger, would rufh headlong into another:
" It is not, it cannot be fuppofed That rational
" Creatures would furrender up their natural Li-
" berty and Independence, and with it   in fome
" Senfe, their Lives and Fortunes, without de-
" manding any Security for the right Ufe and
" faithful Application of fo great a Truft."

A N S W E R.

WHEN Mr. LOCKE was a very young Man, it
was the Cuftom of the Paftors of his Time to
make the junior Part of their Congregations to
undergo the following ftrange Examination,
" At what Day or Hour did you feel the In-
" fluxes of Saving Grace, and receive the Seal
" of your Election and Juftification?" Something like the fame Queftion is couched under
this Objection, founded on Mr. LOCKE's Syftem,
relating to the [fuppofed] Time of our firft

Entrance

Entrance into a political Union, or Confederacy
with the State, under which we live. For it
feems, there cannot be any fuch Thing as a *na-*
tural-born Subject: It is, according to the Lockian
Doctrine, a Solecifm in Language, and a Contradiction to common Senfe. Surely therefore
we have a Right to afk a Lockian this plain
Queftion : As you fay you are not a *natural-born*
Subject, tho' born and bred here in *England*, be
pleafed to tell us, Are you *now* a Member of
the *Britifh* Conftitution ? Or are you not ?—
And if you are, When ? Or from what Day or
Hour did your Memberfhip commence ? Moreover what Ceremony of Adoption, Admiffion,
Matriculation, or whatever elfe you will pleafe
to call it, was ufed by you, or by others on that
folemn Occafion ? The Anfwer to thefe Queftions, it is apprehended, would be rather em-
barraffing ; and might draw on Confequences,
which a prudent Man would willingly avoid.

INDEED the whole Objection, tho' feemingly
a new one, is nothing more than a Pofition of
Mr. LOCKE and his Followers already confidered
and confuted. However, as it is here revived,
and appears in fomething like a new Drefs, let
us beftow a Remark or two upon it.

" The Incredibility of fliding *infenfibly*, and
" *without any previous Contract*, from that So-
" ciety, which is merely natural, into that which
" is

" is political!" But why, I pray, is this incredible?—" Becaufe [fays a Lockian] the Mo-
" tives, or Inducements are not only different
" in themfelves, but even contradictory. Inaf-
" much as the Inducement to form the one is
" inftinctive Love, but to create the other is
" evidently Caution, Apprehenfion, or the
" Fear of Danger." Now this is taking that
very Thing for granted, which ought to be
proved. And indeed it is one of thofe Arguments, which deftroys itfelf. For if Caution is
fuppofed to operate fo ftrongly as to prevent the
Formation of political Society, till Men had
previoufly fettled the Terms of this intended
Affociation,—and had given, and received Securities for repofing a Truft and Confidence in
each other ;—it ought to operate ftill more
ftrongly for the Prevention of natural Society,
leaft the *ftrongeft*, or the moft *vicious* of thefe
ungoverned Human Animals, when herding together, fhould bite, or kick, fhould feize on his
Prey, and devour the *Weakeft*:—A Circumftance this, which we muft allow, might *poffibly*
happen. Therefore, according to this Syftem,
neither the Society which is called *natural*, nor
that which i, *political* can exift at all, till there
has been a previous Contract entered into for the
Safety and Prefervation of all Parties. And
yet methinks, it is rather difficult to conceive,
how a Connection could be formed, how Terms
could be fettled, and a folemn Contract entered
into,

into, for binding all Parties, before Men had once met together, or indeed before they could *prudently*, or *safely* truft themfelves in the Company of each other for this, or any other Purpofe.

THE Thing to be proved was this, that there muft be fome certain Period in each Perfon's Life, when he or fhe firft commenced a Member of political Society. A Period, when he or fhe furrendered up thofe Liberties, and that Independence which belonged to him or her, in a State of Nature, in order to receive from the Government of the Country, that Protection, and thofe Advantages, which refult from Civil Society. Now fuch a Covenant as this, fo peculiarly marked and circumftanced, could not eafily have been forgotten, if it had ever happened. And therefore we muft call upon the Lockians once more [each to anfwer feparately for him or herfelf] to name the Year, Month, Week, Day, or Hour, when this Contract was made between the Government of *Great-Britain* on the one Part, and A. B. or C. D. or E. F, on the other.

In the mean Time [as they will not be in Hafte to inform us on this Head] let us endeavour to trace this, as well as other dangerous Errors of modern Republicanifm, to their proper Source, in order to put the Friends of real and conftitutional Liberty on their Guard againft fuch Delufions.   THE

THE arguing from particular Exigences to general Practice, and from extraordinary Events to the ufual, and (for the moft Part) uninterrupted Courfe of Things, feems to have been the *Ignis fatuus*, which mifled Mr. LOCKE, and all his Followers. Thus, for Inftance, if there happened at any Time to be fo much Difcord, and fuch a Diffention between Sovereign and Subject, Prince and People, as could not be healed, without the Help of a written Compact, and a formal Treaty between Party and Party: — Then this *excentric* Emergence is urged as a proper Precedent for requiring the conftant Ufe of formal Compacts in all Cafes, and at all Times and Seafons whatfoever. Now this Reafoning is juft as found and judicious, as it would be to maintain, that if a moft violent Remedy was deemed neceffary to be prefcribed in the laft Stage of a moft acute Difeafe, it would be right to prefcribe the fame Remedy in all Cafes, and in every Circumftance that could happen, let a Perfon be fick, or well, and whatever his Complaint might be, or even if he had no Complaint at all.

AGAIN, when any Number of independent Perfons are incorporated into one Society by Means of a parliamentary Law, or of a Royal Charter: it would be a very eafy Matter not only to tell the Year, the Month, and the Day of fuch a *new* Incorporation, but alfo to affign

the

the public Reafons or Motives for eftablifhing
fuch a Body Politic : --Nay more, it is apprehended, that it would be no very difficult Tafk,
even to point out the refpective Views of Self-Intereft and private Advantage, which fome at leaft
of thefe independent Perfons propofed to themfelves, by giving up their natural Independency,
and putting on the Shackles (if they muft be fo
called) of political Concatenation and Dependence. But in the Name of common Senfe,
what have fuch Cafes as thefe to do with Civil
Government at large ? And what Affinity hath
any political Inftitution of this Sort, where the
Act of Incorporation is in a Manner *inftantaneous*,
with that *progreffive* Courfe of Civil Society,
which like the infant State of Man, [*moral* and
intellectual as well as natural] grows up gradually
from fmall Beginnings to Maturity ?—As well
might you pretend to define, where the Night
ends, and the Day begins, as to affign the exact
Period when that Society which is *natural*, puts
on the Drefs and affumes the Form of the *political*.—Befides, if it hath been already fhewn in
the firft Chapter, that Mankind would infenfibly
flide into fome Kind of Subordination or other,
in Confequence of the Difference between their
refpective Talents, Genius, and Capacities ;—
I would here afk, How could they ftop at any
given Point of natural Society, and proceed no
farther ?—How indeed, when 'tis alfo confidered,
that at the firft Creation of the above-mentioned
hundred

hundred Pair of Patriarchs, thofe Members of
natural Society would be entire Strangers to
every Kind of Fear and Jealoufy, and to all that
Apprehenfion of Danger, which the *Experience*
of after Ages hath fuggefted to Mankind.

To make this Matter ftill plainer, if poffible,
I would hear obferve, That in the Infancy of
States and Empires, political Societies were not
formed at once, as Guilds of Trades, or Companies of mercantile Adventurers, or Bodies
Politic are formed at prefent, by Means of Paper, Parchment, and Wax, Signing and Sealing.
But Civil Societies grew up by Degrees from
fmall, and in a Manner, imperceptible Beginnings, according as the Numbers of Mankind
encreafed, or as their Wants and Exigencies required. Nay, it is exceedingly probable, that
neither the firft Governors, nor the firft Governed [or if you pleafe, neither the Men of
of fuperior Qualifications, nor thofe of inferior]
had conceived the whole of the Plan, which
they were afterwards to purfue through the
reft of their Lives. But they were like Men
groping in the dark, and feeling their Way by
little and little. As new Lights broke in upon
them, they ftill advanced : But it is very abfurd
to fuppofe that at firft, they faw clearly into
thofe Confequences or Relations of Things,
which the prefent Science of Politics, raifed on
the

the Experience of Ages, hath difcovered to us.
Indeed, whenever new Cafes did arife, it is natural to fuppofe, that fuch new Powers, both of
Legiflation and Jurifdiction, would be exerted,
as thofe Cafes required: But certainly the Society itfelf had an Exiftence before the Exertion
of thofe Powers, or even before it could be known
that they were wanted. So that in Fact, and in
every View, this fecond Objection muft be
deemed to be as groundlefs as the former.

THAT which the Lockians ought to have faid,
is probably to this Effect, That tho' it be abfurd
to fuppofe, that Civil Government *in general* took
its Rife from previous Conventions, and mutual
Stipulations *actually* entered into between Party
and Party ; — and tho', whenever fuch a Contract
as here fuppofed did take Place, *at fome very extraordinary Conjuncture,*—[a Contract, by the
by, which could only bind the *contracting Parties :*]—Yet as Civil Government in general is in
Reality a *Public Truft*, be the Origin, and the
Form of it whatever they may; there muft be
fome Covenant or other *fuppofed* or *implied* as a
Condition necef. arily annexed to every Degree
of Difcretionary Power, whether expreffed or
not.—Had they faid only this, they would have
faid the *Truth;* and their Doctrine would have exactly coincided with the Ideas of a *Quafi-Contract*
before mentioned. Nay more, they would have
avoided all thofe Paradoxes, which attend their
prefent

prefent Syftem, and render it one of the moft
mifchievous, as well as ridiculous Schemes that
ever difgraced the reafoning Faculties of human
Nature.

OBJECTION III.

" WHATEVER Difficulties in Theory may be
" fuppofed to attend the Idea of a Contract
" *actually* [not *virtually*] fubfifting between
" Prince and People; the Fact itfelf is fo decifive
" in Favour of an *actual Contract*, that the bare
" mentioning of it, with its concomitant Cir-
" cumftances, is enough to filence any Plea, or
" Pretence to the contrary. For Example,—
" even among the moft unenlightened Nations,
" whether ancient, or modern, it is remarkable,
" that the Powers and Prerogatives of their
" Kings and Leaders were very limited, and cir-
" cumfcribed.—Sometimes extending little far-
" ther, than was juft neceffary for the carrying
" on a War, or conducting an Expedition with
" Secrecy and Succefs;—at other Times con-
" fifting of but little more than a bare Sufficiency
" to act the Part of powerful Judges and Medi-
" ators in civil Difputes;—and at all Times, fo
" balanced by counteracting Powers, as never to
" be, in a *legal* Senfe, unlimited, or defpotic.
" The Cafe of the antient *Gauls*, as defcribed by
" CÆSAR, and of the *Germans* by TACITUS,
" ftrongly confirms what is here advanced. To
                                    " which

" which we may add that amazing Uniformity of
" Government fo vifible in the Feudal Syftem of
" the barbarous Nations, which overfpread all
" Europe, and exhibited every where a *limited*
" Conftitution. If we wanted hiftorical Exam-
" ples of this Sort, our own Country might fur-
" nifh enough. For furely the Mode of obtain-
" ing the famous Magna Charta here in *England*,
" and the Hiftory of the Wars between the
" Houfes of STUART and DOUGLASS in *Scotland*,
" afford fuch flagrant Inftances of a limited Mo-
" narchy, and a *conventional Conftitution* (if I
" may ufe the Term) that more could not poffibly
" be defired, or expected."

ANSWER.

THESE Objectors are very unfortunate in appealing to the Example, or Practice of *unenlightened* Nations for Proofs of actual [not vir-
tual] Contracts fubfifting between Prince and
People, if by actual they fuppofe *written* Contracts. For it is hard to conceive, how written
Contracts could have been in Ufe among Barbarians, before they had learnt to read and write.
But if by *actual* the Objectors mean *verbal* Contracts, the Difficulty is indeed removed in one
Refpect, and as much encreafed in another. For
it exceeds even the Powers of Credulity itfelf to
believe, That the Prince of any Country entered
into a *verbal*, and *perfonal* Contract with every

one

one of his Subjects,—or even with the thoufandth Part of them, if his Territories were at all populous and extended. And yet there certainly is fuch a Thing as an *implied* Covenant [I fay implied, not expreffed] between every Prince, and every Subject throughout his Dominions, be the People many, or few in Number, and his Empire great or fmall. For every Truft implies a Covenant, or Condition of fome Kind, or other, according to the Nature of the Cafe; and therefore thefe Trufts may with great Propriety be termed *Quafi Contracts.* So much as to *this* Part of the Objection.—Need any Thing more be added?

The other Part of the Objection is, " That " all the Kingdoms in Europe, erected on the " Bafis of the Feudal Syftem, were limited Mo- " narchies." Granted: For the Fact was really fo.—But what Inference can be deduced from this Circumftance?—Not furely, that thefe Limitations arofe either from *written* Contracts, or from *verbal* Covenants, and *perfonal* Conferences made with each Individual, or even with the Majority of the Individuals of any of thefe States; [becaufe thefe Things have been proved already to be impoffible:]—But they arofe from the ariftocratical Power of the Heads of Tribes, or the Chieftains of Clans and Families, who in their military Expeditions, acted a Part more like that of Allies and Confederates with the Commander

mander in Chief, than as his own proper Subjects: And who therefore, on the Division of the
conquered Country, got so much Territory, and
such Royalties and Jurisdictions to be allotted to
themselves, that they were all a Species of little
Kings, each on his own Domain.

GRANTING therefore to these Objections every
Thing they ask;—nay granting much more,—
granting, I say, that the Heads of Tribes, and
Chiefs of Clans of all the barbarous Nations of
Antiquity, and more especially of *Gaul* and *Germany*, elected their Kings by *unanimous* Consent;
—and that they bound them down to what Terms
they pleased;—still the Question will return,
Who elected these Heads and Chiefs?—And
what Right of *fair* and *unconstrained Delegation*
had they to act for others, as well as for themselves?—— In fact, if the Chiefs of each Tribe,
or Clan were not elected by *unanimous* Consent,
—nay if they were not elected at all, What have
we gained, by proving, That the Heads of these
little Societies took great Care, that they themselves should be the only Tyrants?—Now, there
is, I believe, not the least Vestige either in CÆSAR,
or TACITUS, or any other ancient Author, that the
Individuals of each Tribe, or Clan, met together
for Election of an Head, or Chief, in Case of a
Vacancy.—No; these Chieftains acted on a quite
contrary Principle respecting their own Power;
—inasmuch as they considered, that they had an

in-

inherent and a *natural* Right to rule over their own Tribes, Clans, or Vaffals, tho' none had fuch a Right to rule over them.—Confequently all the Parade about the Reftraints and Limitations laid on the Power of Kings, according to the Gothic Conftitution, and during the Continuance of the Feudal Syftem, ends at laft in this, *That the Kings were bound, but the Nobles were free.* —— A Sample and Illuftration of which Kind of regal Submiffion, and of Ariftocratical Exaltation, we have, or lately had, in the Gothic Conftitution of that fertile but unhappy Kingdom of *Poland*.   Nay more. the Hiftory of Magna-Charta itfelf is a ftriking Proof, and Confirmation of this Point.   For the Barons of *England*, in that Struggle with King JOHN, did not fight in Defence of the general Liberties of the People of *England*, but for the particular Prefervation and Continuance of their own Domination over their Vaffals.   And at the laft, what little was granted to the People in, and by that Charter, [little, I mean, in Comparifon to the Liberties they have fince enjoyed] was obtained by the King himfelf, not only without the Affiftance, but even contrary to the Good-Will and Approbation of his Barons.   For when he faw himfelf in danger of being ftript of fo much feudal Power, which of Courfe would ftrengthen his Enemies in Proportion as it

weakened

weakened himfelf,* he obliged them to part with
fome of their exorbitant Claims, in Favour of
their Vaffals, according as they had compelled
him to do the like in Favour of themfelves. The
Motives of his Action, it muft be confeffed, were
not the pureft, nor the moft patriotic. But neverthelefs the People in general reaped the Benefit.
And thus it came to pafs, that the Mafs of the
People of England, by a lucky Concurrence of
Circumftances, and without any intentional Efforts of their own, got confiderably by that famous Struggle, and thereby laid the happy Foundation of their future Greatnefs.

---

* It was a great Miftake in a late noble Author to affert, That
the Army of the Barons at Running-Mead was an Affembly of
the People, demanding a Reftitution of their Rights from a tyrannical Prince.———No : The Fact was juft the contrary.
For it was this tyrannical Prince, who took the People's Part,
even whilft they themfelves were ignorant of the Matter, in
order to raife a Power towards counter-balancing the Ariftocracy of his great Barons.———I am credibly informed, That
there is a Copy now extant of the very Magna-Charta, which
the Barons intended fhould have paffed, had their Plan fucceeded in all Refpects, in which there are none, or next to
none of thofe great Advantages in Favour of the Bulk of the
People, which the real Magna-Charta now contains. But it
was hardly poffible for them to withftand the Force of that Argument urged by the Royal Party, [and that too in the Prefence
of their own Vaffals, then in Arms for their Sakes,] which
was to this Effect :----" As you, who are the Vaffals of the
" Crown, demand fuch and fuch Conceffions from your Prince,
" you muft grant the like Conceffions to your own Vaffals, to
" be inferted in the fame Magna-Charta."——See particularly
the 69th Claufe of Magna-Charta.

Now

Now after having faid fo much in regard to
England, we may be allowed to be very brief in
refpect to Scotland: For moft undoubtedly,
neither the great Houfe of DOUGLAS, in all their
Civil Wars with the Crown, nor any of the
Lords in the Lowlands, nor Chieftains in the
Highlands harboured fo much as a Wifh to have
their Power abridged over their refpective Clans,
Vaffals, and Dependents, by their Attempts to
abridge the Power of the Crown over themfelves.
As foon therefore fhould I believe that the late
Mr. BECKFORD of famous, and patriotic Memory, in his Vociferation for Liberty, intended
to fet the wretched Slaves on his numerous Plantations in Jamaica free, as I could fuppofe,
that a Gothic Baron meant to part with his Power
over his own Vaffals and Dependents, when he
contended to abridge the regal Power over himfelf, and his Fellow Barons. And were the
Planters in Jamaica to imitate their Brethren on
the Continent, by fetting up an intire Independence [Would to God, that not only they
but all the Leeward-Iflands were to do the like !
---And that England had the Wifdom and good
Senfe to permit them to do it !] Were, I fay,
thefe Planters, to fet up an independent Government, and to elect a King of their own,---there
is no Doubt to be made, but that they would tie
up his Majefty's Hands as much as poffible, and
make him little more than a Cypher ;---at the
fame Time, that they would expect to be at full
Liberty

Liberty themfelves to whip and fcourge, and torture their poor Negroes, according to their own brutal Will and Pleafure. Nay, it is very obfervable, that the moft eminent Republican Writers, fuch as LOCKE, FLETCHER of *Saltown*, and ROUSSEAU himfelf, pretend to juftify the making Slaves of others, whilft they are pleading fo warmly for Liberty for themfelves. And what is ftill more extraordinary, the greateft *American* Champions for the unalienable Right of Mankind, one the Generaliffimo of the Republican Army, and the other lately the Prefident of the Congrefs, have fhewn by their own Example, that they have no Objections againft Slavery, provided they fhall be free themfelves, and have the Power of enflaving others: For Mr. WASHINGTON, I am credibly informed, has feveral Slaves now on his Plantations, and Mr. LAWRENS got his Fortune by acting as a Kind of Broker in the Slave Trade, buying and felling his Fellow-Creatures on Commiffion.

OBJECTION IV.

" ONE plain Matter of Fact is better than a
" thoufand Arguments fpun out of the Cobwebs
" of Metaphyfics. And therefore the fureft
" Way, in all Cafes of Difpute, is to recur to
" the Fountain-Head, if we can; which in the
" prefent Cafe we may eafily do, by appealing
" to an eftablifhed Cuftom among the Savages

of

" of *America.* For it is an hiftorical Fact, uni-
" verfally acknowledged, that the Individuals in
" each of their Tribes live in a State of abfolute
" Freedom and Equality among themfelves, in
" Times of Peace, without Subordination, Jurif-
" diction, or Legiflation of any Kind: And that
" they only act in Concert, and fubmit to fome
" Kind of Authority during a War.   When
" that is over, the Power of their Chief, or Leader
" ceafes of Courfe; and each returns to his ori-
" ginal Equality and Independence.   Here
" therefore we have the fulleft Proof, and the
" cleareft Illuftration of the diftinct Exiftence of
" the two Societies above-mentioned, namely,
" of that natural Society which is founded on the
" Attractions of inftinctive Love, – and of that
" political Union, which arifes from Fear, which
" operates by Confent, and is grounded on *actual*
" Compact."

ANSWER.

Is it fair, juft, or reafonable, That any of
the peculiar Cuftoms of this favage People, [with
whofe Hiftory natural, moral, or political we are
very little acquainted] fhould be urged in the
prefent Debate, as Patterns of, or Examples to,
the reft of Mankind? Before *America* was ever
difcovered, we had the Cuftoms and Manners of
almoft all *Europe, Afia,* and *Africa,* to defcant
upon;—a Field, one would have thought, large
enough

enough for every Theory of Government, and for all poffible Inveftigations of Civil Society, without having Recourfe to another Part of the World, which was difcovered but as Yefterday. And now it is in * Part difcovered, we have the Mortification to find, that the original Natives, far from being the Ornament, are almoft univerfally the Difgrace of Human Nature ; — as having many Defects and Vices peculiar to themfelves, with few, or no Virtues and Excellencies to counterbalance them. Surely then, our modern Patriots, and zealot Republicans might have fpared both themfelves and us the Trouble of going into this Part of the World in Search after *Models* of Government worthy of Imitation.

BUT neverthelefs, as our Adverfaries, after having been defeated every where elfe, have chofen to entrench themfelves on this Spot, and

---

* See Dr. ROBERTSON's excellent and impartial Hiftory of *America*, Vol. I. Book IV. viz. Condition and Character of the *Americans*, Pages 281—409. I myfelf have heard Monf. CONDAMINE at *Paris* confirming almoft all the Particulars mentioned in thefe Pages. He added likewife one Circumftance, which I ought not to omit: Speaking of the Indians in the Empires of *Mexico* and *Peru*, whom the *Spaniards* had converted to Chriftianity for feveral Generations paft. " They " make, fays he, excellent Catholics; for they are charmed " with the Pomp and Ceremonies of Religion, and *never* " *think*. Indeed it appears to me, that they are incapable of " much Thought: For they are Children all their Lives.— " *Toujours Enfans*."

to fet us at Defiance, let us not avoid the Combat even on their own Ground, and let us not defpair of being able to wreft the *Tomahoc*, their favourite Weapon, out of their Hands.

Now all that we know of *America*, relative to the prefent Subject, feems to be this, That the far greater Part of the Native Indians [Indians I mean, as they were formerly, before their Subjection, or thofe at prefent, who are not in Subjection to any European Power] may be divided into three different Ranks, or Claffes, *mere Savages,*—*half Savages*,—and *almoft civilized*. I do not mention thefe Diftinctions, or Claffes, as accurate Definitions, according to logical Rules, but as Defcriptions of Men, and Manners fufficiently exact for our prefent Purpofe.

To begin therefore with thofe in the moft perfect State of *American* Society, whom I call ALMOST CIVILIZED. The Reafon of giving them this Denomination is, becaufe they had a permanent Government, Legiflation, and Jurifdiction of their own before the *Spanifh* Conquefts, and enjoyed many Bleffings to which the reft of the Natives of that vaft Country were almoft Strangers. Thefe were the Subjects of the two great Empires of *Mexico* and *Peru*. The Queftion therefore is, How were thefe Empires formed? Did they arife from the actual and exprefs Confent [I do not fay, each Individual,

Individual, but even of] the Majority of the Individuals, who compofed them? Or were thefe Empires owing to fome other Caufe or Caufes?—The Empire of *Mexico*, it muft be owned, before MONTEZUMA's Ufurpation, was a *limited* Conftitution: and therefore here, if any where, we may expeƈt to find that folemn League and Covenant between the Sovereign and all his Subjeƈts, which we have been fo long fearching after. But alas! here likewife we muft be prepared to meet with a Difappoint- ment. For the Reftraints and Limitations laid upon the Emperors did not arife from any Com- paƈt folemnly entered into between the So- vereign and the People, or the Mafs of the People, or even any Reprefentatives chofen by the People,—but from the Ariftocratical Power of the Nobles, or Princes of the Empire;—who, like the Barons of the *Gothic* Conftitution in *Europe*, chofe to have no other Tyrants than themfelves: And that their *Tyranny was very great is beyond a Doubt. Granting therefore, for Argument's Sake, that fome folemn Conven- tion had paffed between the Emperor and the mighty Princes of his Empire, whereby he was bound to obferve certain Conditions ftipulated

---

* See ROBERTSON's Hiftory of *America*, Vol. I. Book 7, concerning the State of the *Mexican* Empire before the Inva- fion of the *Spaniards*.---See alfo the fame concerning the State of the Empire of *Peru*.

between

between them,—ftill the Queftion returns again,
Who elected thefe Princes, alias great *Mexican*
Barons ? And what *focial Compact* had they to
fhew for exercifing any Authority whatever,
much lefs defpotic Authority, over their refpective Slaves, and numerous Dependents? Or,
are we to fuppofe, that thefe Slaves and Vaffals
firft met to elect their refpective Mafters, and
then told them, " We prefcribe fuch and fuch
" Terms to you; and then you may, if you pleafe,
" prefcribe the like to your Mafter the Emperor?"
Something like this muft certainly be made to
appear, before thefe Cafes can be allowed to be
any Kind of Confirmation of the Lockian Syftem.
In the mean Time, I will bring a Cafe in Point,
which is a decifive Proof of the contrary in fimilar Circumftances. The King of *Bohemia*, for
Example, and the Marquefs of *Brandenburgh* (at
War with each other in the Year 1777) are the
two greateft Electors in the *German* Empire ; the
former of whom was likewife chofen Emperor a
few Years before ; and the latter is better known
by the Stile and Title of the King of *Pruffia*.
Now there are extant Volumes of Imperial Bulls
and Capitulars, which plainly fhew, that the Electors have reduced the Powers and Prerogatives of
the Emperor to little more than a Shadow. But
what Benefits or Advantage can the oppreffed
Subjects of *Brandenburgh*, and of *Bohemia*, derive from thefe Limitations ? And do the poor
Peafants, and other Vaffals of either of thefe
great

great Princes dare to fay, " You have no Right
" to reign over us, but what we voluntarily gave
" you by fuch and fuch Acts of our Affemblies?
" And therefore we will limit your Power over
" us, in the fame Manner, as you limit the Power
" of the Emperor over you?" Dare they fay
thefe Things? Or indeed can they fay with Truth,
that either the *Bohemians*, or the *Brandenburghers*
did ever elect the Houfes of *Auftria*, or *Brandenburgh* to be their refpective Sovereign Lords
and Mafters?

But to return: The great Empire of *Peru*
comes the next under our Confideration. And
we read, that Manco Capac, and his Confort
Mama Ocollo, were the Founders of it, by
making the People believe, that they were the
Children of the Sun: Which illuftrious Pedigree,
and imperial Title, the *Incas*, their Succeffors,
laid Claim to ever after. Now a rank Republican may, if he pleafes, fpy out a focial Compact
even here: For he may affert, with his ufual
Confidence, that the *Peruvians* firft met together
in Congrefs, and after folemn Debate, and impartially fcrutinizing the Matter, allowed the
Proofs to be valid, which Manco and his Confort there exhibited of their lineal Defcent from
that glorious Luminary; and recognized their
Title to the Empire. For my Part, I can difcern
nothing like a focial Contract between equal, and
independent Beings, in the Formation of this
Empire:

Empire : But I can fee plainly enough, that
Manco ufed, what may be called a *pious Fraud*,
as Minos, Numa, and Lycurgus had done
before him, in the like Circumftances. All
which Examples evidently prove, that thefe Legiflators were confcious to themfelves, that their
Plans even of doing Good, and of being of Service to Mankind, would have mifcarried, had
they trufted only to the Confent of the People,
convened together *a la Monfieur* Locke, and had
they not had Recourfe to Meafures of a very different Nature, by availing themfelves of the popular Ignorance and Superftition.

So much as to the firft Clafs of original *A-
mericans*, the *almoft civilized*.

The next is, the *half Savages*. Now thefe
People may be fo termed, becaufe they were in
a Kind of Medium State, between the more
refined Inhabitants of the great Empires of *Mexico*, and *Peru*, and the grofs Savages of the
Woods and Deferts. They had a Property in
Lands and Goods, and confequently fome Sort
of Induftry, together with a Species of Legiflation and Jurifdiction within themfelves. The
Countries, in which they principally dwelt, were
Florida, and along the Banks of *Miffiffipi*, fome
Part of the great Continent, and particularly a
Diftrict called *Bagota*, *Hifpaniola*, *Cuba*, and all
the greater Iflands : Of whom in general one
striking

ſtriking Obſervation may be made; that they had noble Families among them, who enjoyed *hereditary Honours*, and were poſſeſſed of ample Patrimonies, Dignities, and Prerogatives, which they tranſmitted from Father to Son, without any actual Conſent, or Election of the People. Now whether theſe diſtinguiſhed Perſonages [Some of whom claimed alſo to be deſcended from the Sun, like the *Incas* of *Peru*] Whether, I ſay, theſe great Perſonages, and Heads of their reſpective Tribes, Clans, or Vaſſals, ought to be called Chieftains, or Princes, or Kings, is very immaterial, and nothing to the Purpoſe. Evident enough it is, let them be called by what Name you pleaſe, that neither they, nor the People over whom they preſided, ever dreamt of a ſocial Compact, as the Foundation of their hereditary Power and Pre-eminence. Whether therefore their Fore-fathers acquired this Aſcendency, and theſe Prerogatives, by Means of a certain Superiority of natural Endowments [according to the Suppoſition of the foregoing Chapter] which elevated them above the reſt of their Species,—Or whether by Virtue of a patriarchal, regular Deſcent, or by what other unknown Means, is not worth the Inquiry; ſince it is obvious, that the Merits of the Cauſe cannot turn on theſe Points, that all of them are equally repugnant to the Lockian Hypotheſis of Contracts and Conventions.

HOWEVER,

However, we may from hence take Occafion to make one very ufeful Remark, that the Antiquity of fome Families, and the Refpect and Veneration *every where* fhewn them is another diftinct Proof, that Mr. Locke and his Followers had not fufficiently ftudied human Nature, when they afcribed [at leaft their Arguments, and Train of Reafoning tend to afcribe] the general Pre-eminence of fome Families over others to Contracts, Covenants, and Conventions. For it is not confiftent with any Degree of common Senfe to fuppofe, that the Dignity and Elevation of fome Families, and the fervile Condition and mean Eftate of others, ever were, or ever could be fettled by the mutual Confent of all Parties concerned, who met together in Congrefs for that Purpofe;—each of them equal to, and all independent one of another. Moreover, what makes this Affair ftill the more extraordinary is, that fuch Refpect paid to Family-Antiquity is greateft, by far, in thofe Countries, whofe Inhabitants are the leaft removed from the original State of Nature. In rich Countries, for Example, fuch as *England* and *Holland*, the Honour of a long Pedigree is much leffened to what it formerly was, in Proportion as Riches and Opulence have encreafed among the People: In *Scotland* and *Ireland* it ftill retains its Influence in the *poorer* Parts, but is evidently lofing Ground in the *richer*, according as Manufactures and Commerce have begun

to

to spread. In *France*, the Influence of Family is still confiderable; in *Germany* much more, and in *Hungary*, *Poland*, *Mofcovy*, &c. the moft of all.

Now, what fhall we fay to thefe Things? For the Fact is really fo, reafon how you pleafe upon it: And therefore, whether this Notion of *antient Blood* is well, or ill fupported in *particular* Cafes, ftill as it is generally fo prevalent throughout the World, we ought, I think, to conclude, that it hath its Foundation in human Nature; Providence gracioufly intending to ftimulate us to great and good Actions, and to prevent us from doing any Thing bafe and unworthy of our Anceftors. At the fame Time, as fuch a Predilection in Favour of what is not properly our own, is liable to great Abufe, we ought to be the more watchful in guarding againft the Abufes and Perverfions of it.

HAVING faid thus much, I leave it to every Reader to determine, towards which Extreme, that of paying too great,—or too little a Deference to the Antiquity of Family, and the Notions of high Blood, we of this Age and Country are leaning moft at prefent.—For my own Part, I make no Secret of declaring, that had I now the Option, whether I would chufe to obey the Powers that be, or thofe that *wifh to be*, I fhould have a mortal Averfion againft fubmitting

to

to the upstart Sway of an ADAMS, or a LAURENS, or of any other of that Tribe. And Experience hath taught us long ago, that such Sort of newly exalted Beings grow to be the most insolent of Men, and prove the worst of Tyrants.

BUT to return: It is said, that besides these Aristocratical, or Patriarchal Governments in *America*, there were others subsisting [that of the *Thlascallans* in particular] which bore a nearer Resemblance to a Republic, than to any other Form. But even of Republicks, there are so many different Species, that it is hard to say, to which of our *European* Common-Wealths, the *American* could be supposed to bear the nearest Resemblance. Suffice it therefore to observe once for all, that neither in the old, nor in the new world, in antient, or in modern Times, was there ever, as far as appears, any one Republic, which was literally *democratical*, in the Lockian Sense of the Word, For even at *Geneva*, the most popular of all Governments, which I can think of, a Moiety at least of the Male and adult Inhabitants [not to mention Females, and Male Youths] are excluded from giving Suffrages by the Constitution of the Place: —None but *Citizens* being permitted to enjoy that Privilege; mere *Commorantes*, and *Sojourners*, though of ever so long standing, and Natives of the Place, being all excluded. And

were

were we to mount up into high Antiquity, and ranfack the moft celebrated Republics of *Greece*, for Proofs and Illuftrations of this Matter, we fhould find that their Exclufions and Rejeƈtions were ftill greater,

HAVING now, it is to be hoped, had tolerable Succefs in this Part of our *American* Warfare, let us at laft have the Courage to face that fell Monfter himfelf with his Scalping Knife ; the MERE SAVAGE ;—of whom we have heard fo much from Mr. LOCKE, and all his Followers, that in Times of Peace he bravely difdains all Subordination, becaufe he is duly fenfible of of his natural Rights, and (to ufe Dr. PRIESTLY's emphatic Words) feeling his own Importance, he confiders himfelf as fully equal to any other Perfon whatever.

WELL : The Scalping Knife, if you pleafe, we will here lay afide, as having nothing to do with fuch an Inftrument in this Difpute : Nor yet need we defcrbe the canibal Feafts which thefe celebrated, independent Beings ufed to make on their Prifoners, after having roafted them alive. For as Mr. LOCKE and all his Followers not only allow but even infift, that the Savages generally eleƈt a Chief, and fubmit to his Authority during a War but return to their original Equality after it is over,—our Bufinefs is to find out, if we can, how

it

it comes to pafs, that they live in a State of abfolute Independance, and without the Controul
of Authority in Times of Peace ;—thofe very
Times, when the Advantages arifing from Government and Law would have been productive of
the moft Good, and the leaft Evil, both to themfelves, and others.

Now, in order to profecute this Inquiry in
fuch a Manner as would bring us the neareft to
the Truth, we ought to compare thefe human
Beings with others of their Kind, in every Point,
which can give us any Light.   For by fo doing
we have a better Chance of difcovering the real
Caufe of this furprifing Phænomenon, this grand
Omiffion of a Civil Government for Ages upon
Ages ;—after the reft of the World, all Nations,
People, and Languages, had eftâblifhed one
every where, of fome Kind, or other.   If, for
Example, this capital Defect is, in a great Meafure, owing to fome radical Weaknefs, or Im-
becility in the corporeal and mental Powers, or
moral Tempers of this fingular People,—it is a
Difeafe the more difficult to be cured, in Proportion as it proceeds from thofe natural Imperfections, which human Art and Inftruction may
correct in fome Degree, but cannot totally remove.   But then, if this be the Cafe, furely the
LOCKIANS have not dealt very ingenuoufly by
us,

us, in holding forth this defective Race, as a Sample of the Progenitors of other Men in their original State of Nature: And the Inferences and Conclusion, which they draw from this Inftance of the *American* Savages, muft pafs for nothing.

1*ft*. BODILY CONSTITUTIONS: We will begin with thefe, becaufe all Men, as well as ROUSSEAU, are led almoft naturally to fuppofe, that a Savage is a brawny Creature, healthy, vigorous, and long lived. His fimple Diet, his Way of Life, and continual Exercife in the open Air;—and above all his happy Ignorance of the Delicacies, Luxuries, and Debaucheries of populous Towns and Cities, feem to indicate, that he muft have a Conftitution fuch, or nearly fuch as here defcribed. How great therefore is our Difappointment, when we are informed by the united Voice of Hiftory, that the Savages of *America* are in general, a loofe-jointed, and weakly Race of Men, frequently afflicted with various Kinds of Difeafes, and the leaft capable of under-going any Degree of *hard*, and *conftant* Labour, of any Human Creatures upon Earth: And moreover, that they are, in general, very far from being long-lived. Add to this, that their *beardlefs* Faces, and fmooth Skins betray evident Symptoms of a cold Habit, and a lax Frame; inafmuch as they are deftitute of the

ufual

ufual Signs and Characteriftics of Vigour and Ro-
buftnefs in other Men.   All this is furely
ominous at firft fetting out : And yet every Tittle
of it is true.   Multitudes of Authorities might
here be adduced to corroborate thefe Points.
But I fhall content myfelf with two, both of
which for their Singularity, and for the Opening
they give to various Speculations, eclipfe all the
reft.

THE firft is, the total Ineptitude of the Savages in general for Labour and Toil.

EVERY *European* Nation, which in their
Wars with the native *Indians* has taken any of
them Prifoners, hath attempted to make them
work ; but to very little Purpofe.   For after
repeated Trials, and after ufing them fmoothly,
as well as roughly, it has been found, that the
weakly Frame of an *Indian* would fink under
that Portion of Labour, which was no more
than Exercife to another Man.   An old Planter
from *South Carolina* told me about 35 Years
ago, that the *Carolinians* being at War with a
Tribe of *Indians*, had made the Experiment on
fome of their Prifoners ; and found this Obfervation to be ftriɛtly true.   " It appears to me,
" faid he, that the *Indians* have the Agility of a
" Beaft of Prey, but not the Strength of a Beaft of
" Burden.   They are light and nimble, and can
" march

" march at a vaft Rate for two or three Days;
" provided they have no heavy Burdens to
" carry : They can alfo fubfift without Victuals
" for as many Days, and perhaps longer, by
" drawing their Belts clofer and clofer. But
" here ends all their Excellence. For when
" you take them out of this fauntring Life, and
" put them to any Kind of Labour, their Spirits
" droop, and they foon die." Now, this ftrange
Debility of Body was the very Circumftance,
which gave rife to that moft inhuman Cuftom of
making Slaves of the Negroes of *Africa*, in order
to fpare the *Americans*:—of which deteftible
Practice the *Englijh*, thofe profeffed Patrons, and
Guardians of the unalienable Rights of Mankind,
are, alas! more guilty than any Nation under Heaven : For they carry on a greater Slave-
Trade than any others.

Las Casas, the *Dominican* Miffionary, afterwards Bifhop of *Chiapa*, was the firft who began
this Practice. And what is really aftonifhing, he
began it from a good Motive. Shocked at the
prodigious Numbers of native *Americans*, who
were falling Victims to the Cruelty of the *Spaniards* in *Mexico* and *Peru*, by being made to work
beyond their Strength, he conceived a Plan for
hiring robuft Labourers from *Old Spain*. But
the Landed Intereft both of the new, and the old
World violently oppofed this Scheme, through
different

different Motives; — the former, left their Country should be drained of its useful Hands by such prodigious Emigrations; and the latter, left they should be obliged to give up that Power over the Natives, which they had so unjustly usurped, and of which they had made an Use barbarous, and cruel beyond Example. Being therefore defeated in this Project, he conceived another, in which he had none of his former Antagonists to oppose him :—Nay, unhappily for Mankind, he found them ready enough to join him; as soon as they perceived that his Scheme was practicable, and attended with much Profit and Advantage : That was, To purchase Slaves on the Coast of *Africa*, and transport them to *America*. And thus it came to pass, that this misguided Zealot became the Author of that very Slavery, of those innumerable Murders, and Calamities to Millions and Millions of his Fellow-Creatures born on one Part of the Globe, which he was endeavouring to prevent, and exclaiming against, in another. —As if the black Inhabitants of *Africa* had not as good a Title to Life, and Liberty, as the copper-coloured Natives of *America*, or even the Whites of *Europe*.

THE other Thing remarkable is the *sickly Habit* of these *Indians*. Indeed a sickly Habit, and a weak and tender Frame, are very often both the Cause and Effect of each other. But,

to

to pafs over this, let it be obferved, that there were various Diforders to which the Savages were fubject from their Mode of Living. For not having that conftant Supply of Food, which is to be found in a civilized State, by Means of Agriculture, and regular Markets; but depending altogether on the precarious Events of their Fifhing, and Hunting Expeditions, they fome-times abounded, and then they gorged moft voracioufly, eating their Fifh and Meat almoft raw: At other Times they fuffered great Want, and were forced to faft for feveral Days. Hence Palfies, Pleurifies, Confumptions, and all other Difeafes, which date their Origin from Indigeftions, Repletions, and Inanitions, were very rife among them. Not to mention that terrible Malady, which once was peculiar to *America,* but now is diffufed over every Part of the Globe, to the fartheft Part of *Siberia,* and *Tartary.* [See the Abbè CHAPPE's Account of his Journey into *Siberia.*] But what is ftranger ftill, thefe Difeafes, and others of the fame Stock, continued to make Havock among feveral of them, even after they had altered their former Modes of Living (at leaft in Part) by their Converfion to Chriftianity, thro' the indefatigable Zeal of the *Jefuit* Miffionaries of *Paraguay.*

MURATORI

MURATORI * is the Author to whom I appeal on this Occasion: And his Testimony is the more to be depended on, as he is reputed not only a very faithful and exact Historian, but also as he particularly endeavoured in this Treatise, to set forth the Contrast in the strongest Point of Light, between the *Indians* of *Paraguay* in their converted, and unconverted State.   His Words are these: " Hitherto it has been impossible to " moderate their ravenous Appetites.   Custom, " and a craving Stomach, which has a great " Power over them, have *prevailed constantly* " against all the Instructions they have had, with " regard to the Advantages for the Preservation " of Health: And so they continue to eat with- " out Moderation.—This Irregularity is the " Cause of many *Infirmities*, that descend from " Father to Son.   What is worse, the *Indians*, " when indisposed, cannot take the least Care " of themselves.   A Reduction [This is a Name given to a Number of Savages converted to Christianity by the Missionaries, and incorporated in one Politico-Ecclesiastical Community] " of seven or eight Thousand Souls is esteemed " very happy, that has only two Hundred sick " at once, or reduced to keep their Beds."

* MURATORI'S Relation of the Missions of *Paraguay*. The *English* Translation printed for J. MARMADUKE, 1759. P. 101---102.

Now

Now, I fay, this Circumftance is a very ftrange one, and not to be accounted for according to the common Viciffitudes of Health, and Sicknefs here in *Europe*. For even in thofe Sinks of Vice, Debauchery, and Difeafe, *London* and *Paris*, there hardly ever is an Inftance, unlefs during the Violence of fome epidemical Diftemper, that out of a Parifh confifting of feven or eight Thoufand Souls, two Hundred of them, at an Average, are always fick, and obliged to keep their Beds. And were we to compare this *American* Account, with the Bills of Health of our large and populous Parifhes in Country Towns and Villages, we fhould find that there are not fixty Perfons always fick, out of eight Thoufand, taking the whole Year together. Thus much as to the *Bodily Conftitutions* of thefe poor miferable People.

In refpect to the INTELLECTUAL POWERS of thefe Savages,—very narrow and confined they are, according to the Relation of all Hiftorians. MURATORI obferves, " That the Indians, be-
" fore they were taught Chriftianity, had no
" Word to fignify any Number above four: If
" they would fignify five, they held up one
" Hand, if ten, both : To exprefs twenty, they
" pointed to both hands and feet : Any number
" above twenty was expreffed by a generical
" Word, that fignified many. They could not
                                    diftinguifh

" diftinguifh a Number of Years, Perfons, or
" Things, that fhould be told exactly. But now
" they learn Arithmetic from their Infancy.
" Nor is this all : On *Sundays*, after Divine-Ser-
" vice, the Numeration-Table is repeated to the
" People in the Church, that the Indians may
" retain better what they learned in their
" Infancy."—Surely a more convincing Proof
need not be given of a flow and dull Underftanding, than what is here mentioned. Indeed Dr.
ROBERTSON takes Notice, that the very Negroes
confider themfelves as a Race of Men much fuperior to the Indians in Point of mental Endowments ; and therefore treat them with no fmall
Scorn on that Account. In fhort the original
Natives can hardly be faid to difcover either a
fertile Genius, or a folid Judgment, in any thing
they either fay or do :—At the fame Time, that
they are remarkable for Patience, and Perfeve-
rence almoft invincible in profecuting fuch things,
as they have undertaken to accomplifh, be they
what they may. But the worft Part of their
Character is yet to come,—Namely,

1*ft*,—*Their Want of Tendernefs, Sympathy, and
Affection ;*

2*dly*,—*Their aftonifhing Lazinefs and Improvidence ;*

And 3*dly*,—*Their Gloominefs, Sullennefs, and
Taciturnity.*

With

With refpect to the firft Clafs of thefe bad Qualities, all Hiftorians agree, without one Exception, that the Savages in general are very cruel and vindictive, full of Spite and Malice ; and that they have little, or no Fellow-feeling for the Diftreffes even of a Brother of the fame Tribe,— and none at all, no not a Spark of Benevolence towards the diftreffed Members of an hoftile Tribe. But the Miffionaries, to their eternal Praife be it fpoken, have converted thefe bloodthirfty, unfeeling Animals, into a very different Sort of Beings : So that if the Accounts given of them are true, or even near the Truth, there can be hardly a more humane and benevolent People upon Earth, than the *Indian* Converts of *Paraguay*.

But in Regard to the fecond Clafs, namely, Their Indolence, Lazinefs, and aftonifhing Improvidence,- here alas! it may be afked, Can the Ethiopian change his Skin, or the Leopard his Spots ? For with refpect to thefe Evils, the Miffionaries, with all their Zeal and Emulation, with all their Arts of alluring the Paffions, and captivating the Imaginations of an ignorant, and fimple People, have not been able to work a radical Cure ; - if indeed it can be called any Cure at all. Muratori's Obfervations are very ftriking on this Head ; and after him I will refer to others.

" After

" After having affigned, fays he, (Page 141,)
" a Parcel of Land, more than fufficient to main-
" tain each Family, they [the Miffionaries]
" diftribute among them the Quantity of Grain
" that is neceffary to fow their Ground, but on
" this Condition, that after Harveft, they fhall
" bring to the public Stores as much Grain as they
" have received, that the common Fund of Seed-
" Grain may be always kept up. ☞ Without
" this Precaution the Indians would certainly eat
" all their Grain, and leave themfelves even
" without Hopes of another Harveft.

" Every Family has a Pair, or two of Oxen
" lent them for their Hufbandry. ☞ If they
" were the Property of the Indians, the poor
" Animals would foon be paffed all Service. For
" it has often happened, that fome Indians, to fpare
" themfelves the daily Trouble of putting the Yoke
" on their Cattle, never took it off. Others would
" knock them down, and foon eat them up, with-
" out giving any Reafon, but that they were hun-
" gry. Now indeed they are more careful of
" them, as they are obliged at the Expiration of a
" certain Term, to reftore them in good Plight.
" Whatever Care is taken, Provifions are wanted
" by many about the Middle of the Year, either
" through Sicknefs, or fome private Misfortune
" they have fuffered ; or it is owing to their im-
" prudent Profufion,----To fence againft thefe Inconveniencies

" conveniencies, they [the Miffionaries] take
" this Method. Befides the Lands affigned to
" Particulars, there is a confiderable Extent of
" Ground, the beft, and moft fruitful that they
" can find, which the *Indians* call *Tupambae*, that
" is, the *Poffeffion of God.* The Management is
" committed to fome underftanding laborious
" *Indians.* This is cultivated under their Direc-
" tion, by the Children of the Reduction, who
" to the Age of fifteen are employed in this
" Work, and who fupply by their Numbers,
" what they want in Strength—All Grains, Fruit,
" and Cotton gathered from the *Tupambae*, are
" depofited in the public Granaries and Store-
" Houfes, in order to be diftributed in the Courfe
" of the Year to the Sick, the Orphans, the
" Handicraft's Men, who have no Profit from
" their Labour but being fed and maintained at
" the public Coft ; in a Word to all fuch as are
" any Ways *difpenfed* from Tillage by their Im-
" ployment and Bufinefs, and even to thofe, who
" thro' their *own Negligence,* or fome Cafualty
" reach the End of their Provifions before that of
" the Year."

" KEEPING the Indians in Clothes does not
" require lefs Attention. Were this left to them
" [the converted Indians] *they would foon go naked
" like the Savages.*" Pages 143, 144, 145. Thus
far MURATORI : To whom we might add Abundance

dance of other Authorities, were we not appre-
henfive of having been too tedious already. Suffice it therefore, briefly to obferve, from Dr.
ROBERTSON, and other Hiftorians, that this in-
bred Lazinefs, and unaccountable Indolence, fo
vifible throughout all the original Natives of America, do not arife from the Want of *Mementoes* of
every Kind, were this Clafs of Men but wife
enough to take the proper Warning.   Thus for
Example, the *Indians* dwelling in the higher La-
titudes both in *North* and *South America*, feel
the Colds, and Frofts, and Snows of Winter, as
fenfible as any People whatever :   Indeed perhaps more fo, as their fmooth Skins are evident
Symptoms of a cold Conftitution :   Yet all this is
not enough to teach them to get a Stock of *warm
Cloathing* in Readinefs, againft the Approach of
cold Weather.   The fame Obfervations may be
made with refpect to *Dwelling.* For the return of
every Autumn might put them in Mind, that *that*
is the Seafon for them to repair their Cabins, and
to make them ftrong, warm, and comfortable,
before the Rains, and Snows fall, and Froft fets
in ;—yet the lazy Indian puts off thefe neceffary
Repairs from Day to Day, 'till it becomes too
late, or at leaft fo late in the Seafon, that he
cannot do it effectually, if he would.   In fhort,
he feems to be incapable of ufing any Forecaft :
For even the Example of the provident, and induftrious Beaver, in a like Situation, tho' continually

nually before his Eyes, is loft upon him. Laftly, if any Teaching could fuffice, refpecting Food, one would think that the voracious Stomach of an *Indian*, and his frequent Difappointments, might tell him, that it would be much better to culti- vate fome Spots of Ground near his Cabin, and to tame fome Animals for domeftic Ufe (which he might do by Way of Amufement and Recreation) than to depend on the uncertain Events of Fifh- ing and Hunting, which he knows muft ceafe at fome Seafons of the Year, and which fo often fail, that hundreds of *Indians* are annually obliged to live on the bad Food of wild Roots, Plants, and Berries, and even of the moft naufeous Reptiles, for a confiderable Time, till Death itfelf puts an End to their Mifery.— Yet alas! plain, and in- ftructive as this Voice of Nature is, it is ineffectual to work a *practical* Conviction on the Minds of this ftupid, and unthinking People. Nay more; the Miffionaries themfelves, who according to the Faith of the converted *Indians*, are inveft- ed with the Keys both of Heaven and Hell, and can difpenfe either Happinefs or Mifery both in this Life and the next ;—thefe Miffionaries, I fay, who have civilized the Savages, and have wrought great, and happy Changes in them in fe- veral Refpects; who are therefore beloved al- moft to Adoration—yet even they are not able to work any tolerable Reformation refpecting the capital Points of Lazinefs and Improvidence,

fo

fo deeply rooted in the Conftitution of an Indian:
So that the utmoft they can do, is to palliate an
unhappy, hereditary Diforder, inftead of performing a radical Cure.

HENCE therefore it comes to pafs, that when
the Savages in their natural State, are deftitute of
the Benefit of fuch faithful Monitors, fuch wife
and able Governors, as the Miffionaries have
proved themfelves to be, they frequently kill
their infant Children, becaufe they are not provided with the Means of rearing them up. Thus
for Inftance, if a Mother fhould die before her
Child is weaned, the Child muft be deftroyed,
there being no Nurfe for it: And then it is bu-
ried in the fame Grave with its Mother. A like
Circumftance happens, when a Woman is delivered of Twins; for one, or other of thefe In-
nocents muft be put to Death, becaufe fhe cannot rear them both. And as fhe receives no Affiftance from her Confort, or next to none, towards the Support of their common Offspring
[he on the contrary always ufing her as his
Drudge, and expecting, when he kills the Game,
even at the Diftance of feveral Miles from their
Cabin, that his Squaw fhould go to fetch it
Home.] She herfelf frequently procures Abor-
tion, in order to be freed from the exceffive
Fatigue of rearing up Children, and of providing
for their Suftenance by her own Toil. Nay, we

are

are informed, that there have been Inſtances of Mothers having murdered their female Infants, through mere Tendernefs, forefeeing the perpetual Mifery to which they would be expofed, after they were grown up. For this, and for other Reafons it is obfervable, that favage Nations ☞ never increafe, and multiply like other Men. Nay more, MURATORI, and all the Hiftorians agree, that when the Savages have been unfuccefsful in their hunting Expeditions, and are extremely pinched with Hunger, they hunt, kill, and eat one another. See particularly the Lord Biſhop of *Oxford* [SECKER's] Sermon preached before the Society for propagating the Gofpel. A. D. 1740-1. Page 8.

Now, as one Evil follows another, all thefe horrid Confequences, and perhaps many more, derive their Origin from that almoft unconquerable Averfion to Labour, which prevails fo univerfally in this defective Race. For were they but frugal, and induſtrious, even in a moderate Degree, they might not only prevent thofe Calamities, with which they are often fo grievoufly afflicted, but alfo abound in all the Neceffaries, and in many of the Conveniencies, and Elegancies of Life. But alas ! induſtrious, and provident they will not be : Indeed their very Natures feem to be repugnant to it : For we find, that the Miffionaries themfelves would have failed of

Succefs

Succefs, had they urged no other than *rational* Motives to induce the Indians to Labour; and then had they left it to their own Choice, whether they would work, or not, without ufing any Sort of Compulfion.

THIS being the Cafe, can we want a Reafon, why Civil Government is not introduced among the Tribes of Savage *Indians?*—Yea rather, might it not be very properly afked, How can it be introduced among fuch a Sort of People? —that is, How can the Expences of Government be fupported by a Race of Men, who will not work enough to fupport themfelves? Befides; Of what Ufe, would it be to them? For as to * Property, that great Source of Litiga-

---

* The Savage *Indians* occupy no Lands in *feveralty*: Therefore there is neither Tillage, nor Planting among them; except perhaps what their Wives may do in little Spots near their Cabins. In faɛt, as the whole Country lies open before them, in the Nature of a great COMMON, they hunt and fifh whereever they pleafe. But tho' thefe Lands, Woods, and Waters are confidered as common to all the Individuals of the fame Tribe;—yet, in their public Capacity, or as a colleɛtive Body, they claim an *exclufive Right* to vaft Traɛts of Country againft other Tribes. In this refpeɛt they are fo greedy, that perhaps an Extent of *Waftes, Forefts,* and *Deferts* as large as *England,* is hardly judged fufficient for a few Hundreds of thefe Vagabonds to roam about. And it is the Invafion of this [fuppofed] *public Property,* which furnifhes them with Pretences for their frequent, bloody, and fcalping Wars: For the better Management of which, they eleɛt a Chief, or Governor. Hence

tion

tion among other Men. They have nothing to contend about; becaufe they have no Labour, which is the Foundation of Riches: So that they are all equal, becaufe equally poor. Having therefore no fpecial Right to Lands, Woods, or Waters, one more than another, there can be no Difputes concerning them. And as to their Wives and Children, the mere Savages feem to be quite carelefs and indifferent about fuch Sorts of Chattels. In fhort, their general Mode of Life is this: They fifh, and hunt wherever they think it moft likely for them to get Plenty of Fifh, or Game: Then they greedily devour what they have caught: After this they fleep; and when they are hungry, they fifh, or hunt again; giving themfelves little, or no Concern, what is to become of them, or how they are to fubfift, when thefe Refources fhall fail. Now, whilft they remain in this

---

therefore we fee, even from this imperfeâ State of Things, that wherever the Idea of Property prevails, Government muft follow, as a neceffary Confequence for the Prefervation of it. N. B. Since their Commerce with the *Europeans*, the *Indians* have begun to ufe Horfes, not for the Purpofes of Hufbandry, but for their Journies. They treat thefe Creatures with fhocking Inhumanity; and indeed they feem to exhibit very little Fondnefs or Affeâion for any Sort of Beings whatever, but for SELF. In this they are quite the Reverfe of the wild *Arabs*, who are as remarkable for their Kindnefs and Attachment to all their domeftic Animals, and particularly to their Horfes, as the *Indians* are for the contrary.

Situation,

Situation, and follow fuch a Courfe of Life,
Civil Government muft be almoft, if not altogether an *ufelefs Thing :*—In fact, it never can
be of any real Service, unlefs it caufes them to
forfake their favage Manner of living, and to
become civilized.   Then, indeed, notwithftanding the Ravings of ROUSSEAU, it muft be owned
that it would be of fignal Advantage to them,
and a great Blefling.   But in order to accomplifh
thefe good Ends, there are very great Difficulties to be encountered.   For firft, you muft
either change and alter the whole Frame of their
Conftitutions, if I may fo fpeak, in order to
render them fitter for receiving a good and
liberal Plan of Civil Government: Or, 2dly.
You muft oblige them to fubmit to thofe Terms
which you fhall prefcribe, by the mere Dint of
abfolute Power, according to the fundamental
Maxims of the great Empires of *Mexico*, and
Peru : - Or 3dly. You muft win them to co-
operate with your Meafures, by fuch Combinations of Force and Perfuafion, happily
blended together, as the Jefuit Miffionaries have
devifed and practiced in the Countries of *Paraguay*.   The firft of thefe is, I think, beyond
the Reach of any human Power to effect.—The
fecond is certainly no actual Compact, voluntarily entered into between equal and independent Beings;—the Lockians themfelves being
Judges: And as to the third,—If thefe enlightened,

lightened, and benevolent Philofophers will undertake the Province of Miffionaries to *Paraguay*, or to any other *American* Country, now
the *Jeffuits* are expelled, may good Succefs attend them! And may no one detraƈt from the
Merits of their Labours!

In the mean Time, and 'till they fhall have returned from this Expedition, let them learn a
little Modefty here at Home; and not boaft of
Viƈtories, which they never won. Let them in
fhort, be filent for the future, on this Topic:
And let them not din our Ears with the Examples
of the Savages of *America*, as being any Proofs
and Illuftrations of their Hypothefis;—which,
when thoroughly difcuffed, and accurately examined, prove and illuftrate juft the contrary.

Respecting the third Clafs of *bad* Qualities,
their native Sullennefs and Taciturnity;—It
has been frequently obferved by Travellers, that
the Savages of *North-America* are, in general, a
joylefs Race, feldom difcovering any Symptoms
of Gladnefs, unlefs when exulting over a vanquifhed Foe, and contriving to infliƈt fome new
Torture. Moreover, it has been noted, that
they are fuch Strangers to the Pleafantries of Converfation, and fo fparing of Speech, [except,
when haranguing in Public, in order to prepare
for, or to give an Account of, fome hoftile Ex-
pedition]

pedition] that they will fpend whole Days without uttering a Word, contenting themfelves with
dumb Signs and Nods.

SURELY, furely Mr. LOCKE and his Followers either did not know what they were about,
when they ventured to produce thefe unhappy,
defective Beings, as the Prototypes of Mankind
in all other Countries ;—or they muft have acted
a very difingenuous Part, if they knew better,
and yet wifhed to ferve their Caufe at the Expence
of Truth.

CHAP.

C H A P. III.

A Comparison of the different Forms of Govern-
ment with each other,—A Preference given to
the Mixt, and the Reasons why,—The Republics
of Sparta, Athens, *and* Rome, *proved to be*
improper Models for a Commercial State,—The
supposed unalienable Right of each Individual to,
be self-governed in the Affairs of Legislation, ex-
amined, and refuted.

ACCORDING to the Lockian Syftem there
ought to be no other Legiflators but the
People themselves,— or thofe at leaft whom the
People had exprefsly commiffioned for that
Purpofe;—nor ought there to be any Magiftrates, Judges, Juftices of the Peace, civil or
military Officers, or any executive Powers
whatever, but fuch only, as either mediately
or immediately receive their Commiffions from
the People. Every other Species of Legiflation or of Government is, it feems, a manifeft
Ufurpation of the *unalienable* Rights of Mankind,
let the Antiquity of it be ever fo remote, or the
Syftem and Adminiftration of it ever fo produCtive of public Peace and Happinefs.

It

It is to be hoped, that thefe idle Notions have received a full and fatisfactory Confutation in the former Part of this Work. However, though we muft reject the abfurd Doctrine of perfonal Contracts between Prince and People, as a Thing which never exifted in any State, and which never can (except perhaps in a very fmall Village for a few Days, or rather Hours) yet as all Governments whatever are fo many public Trufts for the Good of the Governed;— therefore there is a Contract *implied*, though not expreft, a *quafi*, tho' not an *actual* Contract always fubfifting between all Sovereigns, and every one of their Subjects. The Confequence of which is, as hath been afore obferved, That thefe *Quafi-Contractors* ought to be made refponfible to each other, for the due Performance of their refpective Engagements.

This being the Cafe, we are now to confider which is the beft Method of *obliging* thefe reciprocal Contractors to perform their refpective Duties;— the beft I mean, as being the fafeft and eafieft, as well as the moft effectual.

In refpect to one Side of the Obligation, viz. The Duty and Obedience of the People,—the Rulers themfelves are to enforce this Part of the Covenant, and no others. For as they are to enact the Laws, and as they likewife, or their
Deputies,

Deputies, are to put them in Execution, it is their Duty, as well as their Intereſt, to ſee, that none but good Laws are made, and when made, that they are impartially and univerſally obeyed. Therefore, if they ſhould permit the People wantonly to trample upon legal Authority, and to tranſgreſs with Impunity, the Blame muſt reſt upon themſelves. For Lenity in ſuch a Caſe is only another Name for Timidity; and Timidity and Government, where the public Good is concerned, are inconſiſtent Things. Only let me add, that thoſe Laws are the readieſt obeyed, and therefore the eaſieſt to be executed, which are plain and ſimple, and obviouſly calculated for the general Good,—not to ſerve a preſent Turn, or gratify a Faction. Therefore great Care ſhould be taken to enact ſuch only as will ſtand the Teſt, and bear to be examined by this Rule. For when any of the Laws in being are of ſuch a Nature, that it would be better to connive at their Infraction, than to enforce their Obſervance, it is high Time that ſuch Laws ſhould be repealed. Indeed every Plea or Pretence for their Continuance, is only ſo many Evidences, that Mankind had much rather find out Excuſes to gloſs over that Syſtem, which they know they cannot defend, than ingenuouſly to acknowledge themſelves in the wrong, and alter their Conduct. Thus much as to the *Governing* Part in all Societies, let the Form of the Government be whatever it may. WE

WE are now to turn to the oppofite Side, the Cafe and Circumftance of the *Governed.*—Here therefore we mufl fet out with this Inquiry, How fhall the People receive a *reafonable* Security, that the Powers, wherewith their Governors are entrufted for their Good, both in making Laws, and in executing them, fhall not be mifapplied ? —That there is a Danger of Mifapplication is, alas ! a Cafe too apparent to admit of any Doubt. And therefore the Queftion comes to this ;— Firft, What is to be done, in order to prevent, as far as human Forefight can reach, the Mifapplication of fuch a Truft ? And 2dly. What Methods fhould be taken to cure thofe Evils, or redrefs thofe Abufes, which either were not, or could not be prevented at the firft, fo that Government in general may be reftored to its original Ends and Ufes, the Good of the Governed?

To folve thefe Queftions in any Manner, that can bear fome Proportion to the Importance of the Subject, feveral Points ought to be previoufly confidered :

As 1ft. What are thofe effential Principles, on which every Government mult be founded, and by Virtue of which it doth actually fubfift ?

2dly. WHAT are thofe Forms, or exterior Modes of Adminiftration, which give diftinct Denominations to different Governments ?

AND

AND 3*dly*. Which Form affords the beft, and moft reafonable Security to the People, that they fhall be well and happily governed ?

WITH refpect to the firft Branch of the Inquiry, there muft be *Power*, *Wifdom*, and *Goodnefs*, fubfifting in one Degree or other, in every Government worthy to be fo called, let the exterior Form of it be whatever it may.

FOR Example, without *Power* the very Idea of Government is annihilated; and there are no Traces of it left.

WITHOUT *Wifdom* to conduct this Power towards fome certain End, or Object, the Thing itfelf would not be *Power*, in a *moral* Senfe, but blind Impulfe, or mechanic Force.

AND without *Goodnefs* to influence and incline the Operations both of Wifdom and Power towards fome benevolent Ufes, conducive to public Happinefs, the Efforts of Wifdom would in effect be Knavery, Trick, and Cunning; and the Difplay of Power mere Tyranny and Oppreffion. There muft therefore be a Coalition, or Cooperation of all three, in order to form a Government fit to rule over fuch a Creature as *Man.*

SECONDLY,

SECONDLY, as to the feveral *Forms*, or external Modes of Government, they are almoft as complicated and various, and their Origins as different, as the Degrees of parental Authority may be fuppofed to vary in different Cafes,—or as the Skill and Forefight of difcerning and good Men may be found to be greater or lefs in others, —or as the Caprice and Humour of the giddy Populace,—or laftly, as the Intrigues, Wiles, and Addrefs of popular Leaders, or daring Ufurpers, may happen to prevail. But notwithftanding this great Variety, and thefe different Origins, all Sorts of Governments may be reduced to four Claffes,— the Monarchical,- the Ariftocratical, the Democratical, and the Mixt. Let us therefore endeavour to inveftigate the *Quafi-Contracts* contained or implied in each of thefe Forms, in order to difcover their refpective Excellencies or Imperfections.

Now this very Attempt will ufher in the third grand Inquiry, namely, which of the feveral Modes of Government affords to the People the beft and moft reafonable Security againft the Mifapplication of the Truft repofed in the Governors for the Sake of the Governed.

I. MONARCHY.

OF all the Forms of Government, *Monarchy*, according to all Hiftory facred and profane, is

the

the moſt antient: It is likewiſe the moſt extenſive and univerſal, for a very obvious Reaſon. For as it is neither clogged in its Motions, nor counteracted in its Schemes by rival Factions, it can exert more Power both offenſively and defenſively, and with greater Eaſe and Expedition, than either of the other Forms. Conſequently it would be the very *beſt*, were there a Certainty, that it would be endowed with *Wiſdom* and *Goodneſs* proportionably to the Advantages it receives from united Strength and combined Power. But here, alas! lies the great and incurable Imperfection of all human Monarchies. An earthly Monarch cannot ſee every Thing with his own Eyes, nor hear with his own Ears, even were he ever ſo well diſpoſed to do what is right, and to make his People happy. Moreover he is continually ſubject to ſtrong Temptations to abuſe his Power through various Motives, ſome of them of a pitiable Nature, and others highly blameable. Add to this, That the very Perſons, who ought to inform him better, and diſſuade him from purſuing wrong Courſes, are, generally ſpeaking, the moſt intent in keeping him ignorant of what is right, and to divert his Thoughts from the real Welfare of his People. Hence it is, that they ſtudy his Weakneſſes with a View to flatter his Vanity, gratify his Vices, inflame his Paſſions, and to

inſtigate

inftigate him to divert that very Power towards accomplifhing fome By-ends of their own, which ought to have been confecrated to the Promotion of public Happinefs. For thefe Reafons an abfolute Monarchy in the Hands of fuch a frail, imperfeEt, and peccable Creature as *Man*, is by no Means a defirable Species of Government.

II.   On A R I S T O C R A C Y.

Nor is an *hereditary* Ariftocracy much more preferable than an abfolute Monarchy. For it is fubjeEt to feveral of the fame Inconveniences, without that Glare of Glory, which furrounds a Throne, and which, by amufing the Bulk of Mankind, captivates their Imaginations, and attaches them ftrongly to that Form of Government. However, it muft be allowed, that there are Advantages attending an Ariftocracy, *provided it be a numerous one*, which ferve to mitigate fome of its greateft Evils, and to provide an Antidote againft others. For its very Numbers, which occafion fo much FaEtion and Contention, ferve as a preventive Remedy againft their conniving at each other's Tyranny and Oppreffion: So that out of mere Spite to each other, they become a mutual Check on the ConduEt of Individuals. Likewife they often enflame each other with an Emulation of doing Good : Hence therefore it is, that in Matters of mere civil Concern, where

where the Difputes are only between Man and Man in private Life, there we find, that Juftice is adminiftered under an Ariftocratical Government impartially enough, and that Life, Liberty, and Property, are as well fecured under that Form, as under any other. Indeed it muft be confeffed, that wherever the Ariftocratical Power is fuppofed to interfere with fome particular Branch of the People's Rights, there the whole Body of the *Nobles* will immediately oppofe the Demands or Expeƈtations of the *Commons*, and aƈt as one Man in keeping them ftill in Subjeƈtion. [Moreover, wherever the Lords have fuch a perfonal Jurifdiƈtion over their Vaffals, as is diftinƈt and feparate from the general Jurifdiƈtion of the State (which is ftill the unhappy Cafe in *Poland*) there Defpotifm and Tyranny prevail to a fhocking Degree, without the Hopes of any Thing to counter-balance, mitigate, or correƈt them. And I will add, that there cannot be a worfe Conftitution upon Earth than an Ariftocracy of Barons tyrannifing over their Vaffals;—or, what comes to nearly the fame Thing, of Planters amufing themfelves with the infernal Pleafure of whipping and flafhing their Slaves.]

THEREFORE, were it to be afked in general, what Degree of *Power, Wifdom,* and *Goodnefs,* naturally

naturally belong to an Ariftocratic Government, —I think it would not be difficult to give an Anfwer clear and fatisfaƐory enough.

For as to Power, it is *externally* very weak, even on the *defenſive* Side, where it ought to have been the ftrongeft, being hardly able to proteƐ itſelf againft Invaders. This Weaknefs is owing to its numerous FaƐions and Divifions caballing againft, and thwarting each other :—The fecret Springs of which are more frequently to be afcribed to foreign Gold fuccefsfully applied to the pretended patriotic Leaders of each Party, than to any other Caufe. But *internally* all thofe FaƐions and Divifions ceafe; inafmuch as the poor SubjeƐs are deftitute of the Means of making the like Application. Moreover, as they have no Perfons particularly appointed to reprefent them in this Form of Government, they have none to ftand forth as their Guardians and ProteƐors, being left in a Manner without Defence. Here therefore an Ariftocracy is the ftrongeft : Becaufe the Nobles will of Courfe unite againft the Plebeians, in maintaining, and perhaps extending, the Dignity and *Power* of of their own Order.

As to the *Wiſdom*, which may be fuppofed to be contained in this Inftitution, it has certainly fome Advantages over a Government merely monarchical,

monarchical, or merely popular. For all the Members, of which it is compofed, are by their Education, their Rank in Life, and other Circumftances, better qualified than moft others, to enaƈt Laws with Judgment, with Prudence, and a Knowledge of the Subjeƈt. The Independence of their Station, and Diftance from mercantile Conneƈtions, prevent them from making Laws refpeƈting Trade and Commerce with a View to fome prefent dirty monopolizing Job: And being Sovereigns themfelves, they are not compellable to fubmit to the arbitrary Will of an ignorant or abfurd Tyrant, nor yet to obey the imperious Diƈtates of a foolifh, headftrong, conceited Populace, * who are almoft univerfally bent on gratifying fome prefent deftruƈtive Whim, at the Expence of their future Happinefs. Moreover as to the executive Part of an Ariftocratical State,

that

---

* During an attentive Obfervation, and the Experience of 50 Years, forry I am to fay, but Truth obliges me to do it, that I hardly ever knew an unpopular Meafure to be in itfelf a bad one, or a popular one to be truly falutary. *Internally* the People violently oppofed the beft of all Schemes for a commercial Nation,—That of warehoufing Goods on Importation, and paying the Duties by Degrees. They were alfo as bitterly averfe to the making of Turnpike Roads, to the Ufe of Broadwheel Waggons, to the enclofing and improving of Lands, to the Freedom of Trade in Cities and Towns corporate, to the Introduƈtion of Machines for abridging Labour, and alfo to the Admiffion of induftrious Foreigners to fettle among them. Nay, they very lately were fo abfurd as to raife loud Clamours

againft

that, as I obferved before, is tolerably free from very grofs Abufes;—becaufe it is under little Temptation to act amifs, except in thofe unfortunate Cafes, where the peculiar Interefts, Honour, or Dignity of the Patrician Order happen to interfere with the general Welfare of the People.—There indeed, it is much to be feared, that the *Quafi-Contract*, on the Part of the Nobles, would be made a Sacrifice to their Luft of Power, their Pride, and Ambition.

HAVING faid thus much as to the *Power* and *Wifdom* of an Ariftocracy, the Reader will of his own Accord fuggeft to himfelf every Idea that is neceffary, concerning the *Goodnefs* or *Benevolence* of fuch an Inftitution.

---

againft the Execution of the Act for preferving the public Coin, and their own Property from Debafement and Adulteration. *Externally*, they are perpetually calling out for new Wars (though againft their beft Cuftomers) on the moft frivolous or unjuftifiable Pretences. Moreover, if there was any Convention or Treaty to be broken through or difregarded, (the Obfervance of which would have reftored Peace or prevented Bloodfhed) or if there was any new Colony to be planted in a defart Country, or Conqueft to be undertaken in a populous one, even in the moft diftant Part of the Globe.--- All thefe Meafures, though totally oppofite to a Spirit of Induftry at Home, and though the Bane of a commercial Nation, were fure to receive the Applaufes and Huzzas of the unthinking Multitude. Such was the *Vox Populi* for 50 Years laft paft, which fome Perfons blafphemoufly ftile VOX DEI.

III.

III. *A* MERE DEMOCRACY.

THE third Clafs of Civil Government is the
Democratical.—I mean, a Democracy literally
fuch, unmixt with any other Form: Where
therefore all the adult *Males* [and why the adult
Females fhould be excluded, is impoffible to fay]
are fuppofed to affemble together, whenever
they will, in order to deliberate and vote on all
public Affairs, to change and alter, to pull down,
and build up, without Controul, and as often as
they pleafe.—Confequently, where every adult
Individual is to confider himfelf as his own Legiflator, his own Governor, and Director in every
Thing.—Happily for Mankind, this wild and
vifionary Plan of a *free* and *equal* Republic is
abfolutely impracticable in any Diftrict of larger
Extent than a common Country Parifh! And
happily again, even there it could not fubfift for
any Length of Time, but muft be transformed
either into a petty Sovereignty or Ariftocracy,
or at leaft into an Oligarchy, much after the
fame Manner, and for the fame Reafons, that
the Bufinefs of populous and extenfive Parifhes
here in *England,* devolves at laft into the Hands
of a *few,* and is managed by a *felect* Veftry.

BUT waving all Confiderations refpecting the
feveral Changes it may probably undergo;--let
us, fince fo much Strefs is laid upon it by our modern

dern Republicans,—let us, I fay, confider it in
its own Nature, as either abounding, or deficient
in the three Qualities afore mentioned, of *Power*,
Wifdom, and *Goodnefs* ;— Qualities, fo effential
for the Formation and Eſtabliſhment of all Civil
Governments, that none can fubfiſt without them
in one Degree or other.

AND 1ſt as to *Power ;*—Scanty indeed muſt
the Pittance of Power be, which is to refult from
the Union of 40, 50, or even 100 Savages,
iſſuing forth from their Dens and Caverns, and
aſſembled together *for the firſt Time*, in order
conſtitute a *Body Politic*. We will not now enquire, *Who* among this Herd of equal and independent Sovereigns had the Right of appointing
the Time and Place of Rendezvous for the reſt
of his brother Sovereigns to meet at and *confult*
together : Nor will we prefume fo much as to
aſk, *How* or *Why* fuch a Superiority came to be
veſted in him alone, or how long this extraordinary excluſive Privilege was to laſt :— Or what
corporal Puniſhment [it being to be prefumed
that they could not be *fined* in their *Goods* and
Chattels, before *meum* and *tuum* was eſtabliſhed.]
Therefore, I fay, what *corporal* Puniſhment
was to be inflicted on thofe independent Sovereigns, who either would not, or did not obey
the Summons. But not to boggle at little Matters, let us fuppofe all thefe Difficulties happily

got

got over : — And then the firſt Queſtion at this
firſt Meeting is, What are they to do? And
wherefore were they called together?—Perhaps
the very Appearance of ſuch a Body of Savages
might be ſufficient to fray away a few Eagles, or
Vultures, Wolves, or Tygers, if they were too
near them : But moſt certainly it would not be
adequate to the Purpoſes even of a *defenſive*, not
to ſay an offenſive War, if this *genuine* Republic
ſhould happen to exiſt in the Neighbourhood of
any State, whoſe Union was more perfeĉt, and
conſequently whoſe Skill and Dexterity were ſuperior to their own. Therefore this Infeĉt Common-wealth, this Grub of a free, equal, and Sovereign Republic would be ſwallowed up, as ſoon
as hatched, by ſome devouring political Animal
of a firmer Texture, and ſtronger Stamina ;—
unleſs theſe lately independent Sovereigns would
condeſcend either to fly away to remote Woods
and Deſerts, or to ſubmit to the Terms which
their Conquerors ſhould think fit to impoſe upon
them.

After this Specimen oſ the *Power*, it will be
unneceſſary to ſay a Word about the *Wiſdom* or
Goodneſs of ſuch a reptile, democratical Inſtitution. But here, methinks, ſome of the enthuſi-
aſtic Admirers of Antiquity will be apt to ſay,
" What? Do you compare the famous Repub-
" lics of *Greece* and *Rome* to Infeĉts, Grubs, and
" Reptiles?

" Reptiles ? Do you dare to fay, That either of
" thefe were of fhort Continuance ? Or that
" they were at all remarkable for the Want of
" Power, Wifdom, or Goodnefs ?"

To this fmart Objection I have the following Reply to make:

1ft. THAT neither of the Common Wealths
above mentioned, were pure Democracies in the
Senfe here fet forth:—For they had other Magiftrates, and other Inftitutions befides thofe which
were merely popular ;—and even in refpect to
the moft popular Part of their Government, they
excluded much greater Numbers from enjoying
a Share in the Privileges and governing Part of
the Conftitution than they admitted: So that
this whole Objection falls to the Ground.

2dly. THE Subjects of thefe Republican
Governments were fo far from enjoying greater
Liberty than the Subjects of other States, that
they were known to be more oppreffed, and
more enflaved, than any others: So that no
Proofs can be drawn from hence concerning the
Wifdom and *Goodnefs*, that is, the Juftice and
Benevolence, of fuch Republics, whatever may
be faid of their great Power, and defpotic
Sway.

BUT

BUT 3dly, Granting more than can be re-quired. even granting [what is abfolutely falfe in Fact] that each of thefe Republics were modelled and adminiftered, according to the Heart's Defire of a true Difciple of Mr. LOCKE, had he been then in being.—Still even on this Suppofition, there was nothing fo inviting in the *funda-mental* Maxims, and *diftinguifhing* Practices of either of thefe Inftitutions, to make us fo much in love with it, as to wifh to copy it into our own.

The SPARTAN REPUBLIC.

THE fundamental and diftinguifhing Maxim of SPARTA was, to lead a military Life in the City, as well as in the Camp, and never to enjoy any of thofe Comforts and Conveniences which Peace and Plenty naturally beftow. Confe-quently, the Police of their * Legiflator was,

to

---

* Quere,---Whether this famous Legiflator was not guilty of a grofs Equivocation in the very Act of making his focial Contract with the People of *Lacedemon*? It is faid, that he bound them by an Oath to obferve his Laws and Regulations, till he fhould return from a Voyage to *Crete*, where he then purpofed to go. He went, but never returned: And left they fhould bring back his Bones after his Death, and thereby fup-pofe themfelves-releafed from the Obligation he had laid them under, he ordered his Body to be thrown into the Sea. Few Moralifts, I believe, would judge fuch a fraudulent Contract as this, to be good and valid. And no Court of Equity upon

Earth

to forbid Improvements of every Kind (excepting in the Science of War) to banifh all Trades and Manufactures whatfoever, which related to the Arts of Peace, to prefcribe every Part of a learned and ingenuous Education, and more particularly, and above all the reft, to expel the Ufe of Gold and Silver from the State of *Lacedemon*. But as thefe military Heroes muft eat, as well as fight, it was contrived that they fhould have Slaves [the *Helotes*] for the Purpofes of Agriculture, and other menial Offices, whom they ufed much worfe, and with more *wanton* Cruelty, than the Planters do the Negroes in the *Weft-Indies* :—And that is faying a great deal. Now I afk, are thefe Meafures proper to be adopted in *Great-Britain?* And is this the Plan of a Republic, which fome future patriotic Congrefs is to fet up, in order to correct the Evils of our prefent unhappy Conftitution ?

Earth would pronounce fuch a palpable Deception to be binding in any other Cafe. The learned Reader is requefted to confult XENOPHON's Account of the Policy of the *Lacedemonians* in the Original. He will there find, that many of the Inftitutions of LYCURGUS were very whimfical and abfurd, (notwithftanding XENOPHON's Endeavours to glofs them over) that fome of them were very criminal, others obfcene, that few were worthy to be adopted into that benevolent and liberal Plan of Government, where *true national Liberty* was to be the Bafis.

The

The ATHENIAN REPUBLIC.

THE diftinguifhing Practice of *Athens*, or at leaft, that which made the Conduct of the *Athenians* to appear different from that of moft other States, was the Ufe of the *Oftracifm*. Nothing could have been better calculated for gratifying the Caprice and Licentioufnefs of a Mob, or for indulging the Spleen and Jealoufy of a Rival, or for concealing the Wiles and Intrigues of a pretended Patriot, than this very Project. For by Virtue thereof, any Man, even the beft and moft deferving in the State, was liable to be banifhed for ten Years, whenever the Citizens fhould have a public Affembly (which they often had) confifting of 6000 Suffrages and upwards;—and when any one of this Number fhould write, or caufe to be written on a Shell, or a Leaf, the Name of the Perfon he chofe to doom to deftruction, then this upright, fagacious, and impartial Sentence immediately took Place : And the *accufed* [if that Perfon can be called *accufed*, againft whom no Crime was alledged] was not permitted to fay a Word in his Defence, or to expoftulate on the Hardfhips of his Cafe, but muft go inftantly into Banifhment, there to remain 'till the ten Years were expired.

By Means of a Condemnation of this Sort, ARISTIDES, who had born fome of the higheft Offices

Offices in the Common-wealth, and who had obtained the Surname of the *Juft*, from his great Integrity and inflexible Honour,—even this A r i s t i d e s was banifhed from his native Country, and dearest Connections, and was reduced to fuch abject Poverty, that his only * Daughter was maintained by public Charity after his Death. The Story of this unhappy Victim to democratical Infolence well deferves to be repeated as a Memento to the prefent Times.— On a Day of public Affembly he was accofted by a Citizen, whom he did not know, defiring him to write the Name of A r i s t i d e s on his Shell. A r i s t i d e s, furprized at fuch a Requeft, afked him whether he knew A r i s t i d e s, and whether he had ever offended him ? No, fays the other, I fhould not know him, were I to meet him. But I hear fuch an univerfal good Character of him, that I am refolved to banifh him, if I can, from the A t h e n i a n State. A r i s t i d e s wrote his Name on the Shell as the Patriot had defired: And as there happened to be no other Names than his then propofed to be profcribed, he was banifhed of Courfe, according to the fundamental Law of this celebrated Republic. The Truth

---

* P l u t a r c h doth not mention this Circumftance of the Daughter of A r i s t i d e s, exactly after this Manner, but other Authors do.

is, [and this explains the Matter] ARISTIDES was a remarkably *juſt Man*, by much too honeſt to cajole the Populace, and to gratify their Follies at the Expence of their own Intereſt; therefore he was not popular; as indeed few honeſt Men really are : * Whereas PERICLES, who laid the Foundation of their Ruin, and deſerved Baniſhment an hundred Times, was the Idol of the Athenians.

ANOTHER Inſtance of the great Sagacity of this People as *Politicians*, and Benevolence as *Men*, is obſerveable in the Methods they took for narrowing and contraĉting the Foundations of their Republic, inſtead of making them broader and firmer. For in the *Times of their Proſperity*, they ſhut up every Avenue againſt the rich, or ingenious, the induſtrious, deſerving, or oppreſſed of other Countries, from partaking in the common Rights of Citizens of Athens. No In-

---

* The moſt unpopular Man in all *France* in his Day, was the Duke de SULLY ; the moſt popular the Duke de GUISE : The moſt unpopular Miniſters in *England*, were the Earl of CLARENDON, and Sir ROBERT WALPOLE, during their refpeĉtive Adminiſtrations ; the former a true, a ſteady, and equal Friend to a limitted Monarchy, and the juſt *civil* Rights of the People ; and the latter the beſt commercial Miniſter this Country ever had, and the greateſt Promoter of its real Intereſts :—The moſt popular in their Turns, were Mr. PULTENEY, and Mr. PITT. *Sed Opinionum Commenta delet Dies.*

vitations, or general Naturalizations were fo much
as thought of: But on the contrary, the whole
Tenor of their Laws ran in a different Strain.
[See particularly POTTER's Greek Antiquities,
and TAYLOR on Civil Law] Nay, they contrived to exclude as many as they could, even of
their own natural-born Subjects, from enjoying
the common Rights and Privileges of Citizens.
And as to their Slaves, tho' almoft twenty in number to one free Man, they were excluded of
Courfe. So that in Fact, had this People been
always fuccefsful in their Wars, and had they
made great and extended Conquefts, or had
their State been of very long Duration, their
Republic would have become an *hereditary Arif-*
tocracy, fimilar to that of Venice; for it was
ftrongly verging that Way.

INDEED in Times of univerfal Calamity, when
their Loffes by Sea and Land were fo great, that
they were in Danger of being annihilated, *as a*
People, then they naturalized Foreigners, and
manumitted Slaves. But it was their Neceffity
that compelled them, and not their Benevolence,
Penetration, or Wifdom, which prompted them
to adopt fuch patriotic Meafures.

BUT above all, the Probity and Rectitude of
this celebrated People will be difplayed in the
ftrongeft Light, by fetting before the Reader
their

their Mode of difpenfing Juftice. In order to do this, let us fuppofe a parallel Cafe exifting in our own Times. The prefent Livery-Men of *London* anfwer very nearly, if not altogether, to the Idea of the antient [ANDRES ATHENAIOI] the MEN OF ATHENS. Let us therefore imagine, that thefe felect Citizens, were the only Legiflators in the State ;—not only making Laws for themfelves and for *Great-Britain*, but alfo for *Ireland*, and for all our Colonies and Settlements abroad. This is fomething ; but what is to come, is ftill more extraordinary : For we are to fuppofe farther, That thefe *Law-giving* Liverymen, are alfo the *fupreme Judges* both of Law and Equity, conftituting the *only* fovereign Court of Judicature for all the Provinces of the Britifh State. Hence it becomes neceffary for every Suitor to this High Court of Juftice,—*every Suitor*, I fay, whether *Englifh*, *Scotch*, or *Irifh*, whether *Armenian*, *Weft*, or *Eaft-Indian*, to flatter and cajole all the Members thereof, as much as he can,—bowing and fcraping to the higheft, and *taking the meaneft by the Hand*, as he is entering Guildhall to hear the Caufe, and to pronounce the final Sentence. The Court being now affembled, let us attend alfo to fome of the Pleadings of the Council on fuch an Occafion.

Gentlemen of the Livery,

" My Client is a rich and generous Man. If " you will decree for him, he fhall treat his

Judges

" Judges with fplendid Entertainments at *Rane-*
" *lagh, Vauxhall,* and *Sadler's Wells,* and at other
" Places of Diverfion. Moreover he will give
" you Tickets to go for feveral Nights to both
" the Theatres, &c. &c. &c.

Now what fhall we fay to fuch an Oration ?
The Parallel here fuppofed, is either juft or unjuft in the *principal Features,* for there can be no
Medium. I am therefore content, that the
learned Reader fhould fit in Judgment on me relative to this Point. Only let me add, that I would
have produced the very Paffages from the original Authors, as Vouchers for the general Truth
and Juftnefs of the Parallel, [*mutatis mutandis,*] if
I had had the Convenience of *Greek* Types at the
Place where I am printing. One Thing more, I
muft beg Leave to fuggeft, namely, that every
Man of Learning muft be fenfible, that, fo far
from exaggerating Matters, — I have taken the
Words of Xenephon concerning the *Athenian*
Polity, in the moft advantageous Senfe, of which
they are capable. For I have allowed him to
fay, that the fupreme Court of *Athens* was a
Court of Appeal from inferior Jurifdictions;
whereas his Words, and the Context ftrongly
imply, that the *Athenians* would not fuffer any
Court whatever, to exift in any Part of their Empire but their own. Nay, Xenephon exprefsly
declares, that the Allies of the *Athenians,* or their
Auxiliaries,

Auxiliaries, or Fellow Soldiers, or Colonies, or by whatever Name you will pleafe to call them [SYMMACHOI is the Term in the original] were *enflaved* by the *Athenians* by thefe Means. Many other curious Obfervations might yet be made; and fome of them of Importance to *Great-Britain*, by Way of *Caution*. — But furely enough has been faid already, to give every true Friend to Liberty an Abhorrence of the Idea of an *Athenian* Common-Wealth.

The ROMAN REPUBLIC.

COME we now to the *Roman State*, whofe Citizens were the great Mafters of the World. But here an unlucky Obfervation arifes at firft fetting out, viz. That the *Roman* Citizens, for the moft Part, were not Tradefmen : For Trades of all Kinds were held at *Rome* in fovereign Contempt. Therefore its Tradefmen and Mechanics, its Shop-keepers and Retailers of all Sorts, were almoft all either actual Slaves, or Slaves, lately made free, or the very Scum of the People. This was the original State of Things. But in the Time of CICERO, the Condition of Tradefmen, and the Idea affixed to Trade were a good Deal advanced in Reputation. Yet even he reprefents the Matter in fuch a Light, as would make, I fhould think, thofe confummate Politicians, the learned Liverymen of *London*, not

very

very defirous of feeing a Return of fuch Times.
* CICERO expreffeshimfelf to this Effect : " That
" according to antient Tradition, and as far as he
" can learn, Trades and the Gains thereof may be
" diftinguifhed into the reputable and difreputa-
" ble, after the following Manner. In the firft
" Place, thefe Profeffions muft be reckoned infa-
" mous, which are odious to Mankind, fuch as
G g 2
the

---

* Jam de artificiis & quæftibus, qui *liberales* habendi, qui *fordidi* fint, hæc fere accepimus. Primum improbantur ei quæftus, qui in odia hominum incurrunt ; ut portitorum, ut fœneratorum. Illiberales autem, & fordidi quæftus mercenariorum, omniumque, quorum operæ, non quorum artes emuntur. Eft enim illis ipfa merces auctoramentum Servitutis. Sordidi etiam putandi, qui mercantur a Mercatoribus, quod ftatim vendant ; nihil enim proficiunt, nifi admodum mentiantur. Nec vero quidquam turpius eft Vanitate. Opificesq; omnes in fordida arte verfantur. Nec enim quidquam ingenuum poteft habere officina. Minimæque artes hæ probandæ, quæ miniftræ funt voluptatum, cetarii, lanii, coqui, fartores, pifcatores. Adde huc, fi placet, unguentarios, faltatores, totumque ludum talarium. Quibus autem artibus aut prudentia major ineft, aut non mediocris utilitas quæritur, ut medicina, ut architectura, ut doctrina rerum honeftarum, hæ funt iis, quorum ordini conveniunt, honeftæ. Mercatura autem, fi tenuis eft, *fordida* putanda eft : Sin magna, et copiofa, multa undique apportans, multifque fine Vanitate impartiens, non eft *admodum vituperanda*. Atque etiam fi fatiata quæftu, vel contenta potius, ut fæpe ex alto in portum, fic ex ipfo portu fe in agros, poffeffionefque contulerit, videtur jure optimo poffe laudari. Omnium autem rerum, ex quibus aliquid acquiritur, nihil eft agricultura melius, nihil uberius, nihil dulcius, nihil homine, nihil libero dignius. ―Vide CICERONEM de Officiis, Liber 1. § 42. | In

" the Bufinefs of Toll Gatherers, at the Ports
" and Gates of Cities, alfo of Ufurers, or Pawn-
" Brokers. In the next Place, all thofe Perfons
" fhould be confidered as a bafe and fervile Peo-
" ple who work for Hire, or Wages, becaufe
" they are paid for their *Labour*, and not for
" their Skill or Ingenuity. For the very receiv-

In the above Quotation there fome Things very difficult to
be explained, at leaft I know not how to explain them. I
think I fee the Reafon, why CICERO claffed Fifh-mongers and
Fifhermen among the Number of thofe, who adminiftred to
Luxury ; for in his Time, Fifh was not ufed as a common
Food, but only as an expenfive Dainty for the Tables of the
Great : And as foon as the *Romans* underftood that Oyfters
were to be procured in *Britain*, they fent as far as *Colchefter* to
fetch them. At prefent Fifh, or Bacalao, that is *Newfound-
land* Cod Fifh, is the cheapeft Provifion which the Poor of *Italy*
can purchafe in the Spring of the Year. And while that con-
tinues to be the Cafe, the *Roman Catholics* will eat Fifh in
Lent, but no longer. As to Butchers and Cooks, why they
fhould be profcribed, as peculiarly fubfervient to Luxury at
that Time, furpaffes my Comprehenfion. [De NOORDT has a
Paffage relative to the Subject, but it is not fatisfactory.]
In refpect to Ufurers and Pawn-brokers, a good popular Reafon may be given, why they were fo odious to the Populace.
After the *Romans* had fubdued the World, and robbed it of
its Treafures, the Mafs of the People of *Rome* were fome of
the pooreft and moft wretched Mortals in the State, hardly
ever being able to procure Money at lower Intereft than £12
per Cent. per Annum ; and at the fame Time fo very in-
digent, and perhaps difhoneft, that their Creditors (who had
fevere Laws on their Side) would not truft them but from
Month to Month. Such were the Fruits of a Series of Victories,
and fuch the Difference between Conquefts and Commerce !
This ought to be a Leffon to *Great-Britain.*

ing

" ing of Wages is a Badge of Servitude. Thofe
" alfo who buy of the Merchants to fell again di-
" rectly, muft be ranked in a difhonourable
" Clafs; for they can get nothing thereby unlefs
" they cheat and lye abominably; and nothing
" can be bafer than cheating. Moreover all Ar-
" tificers whatever are a bafe Order of Men: In-
" deed it is hardly poffible, that a Shop and
" Work-Houfe fhould have any Thing of an
" ingenuous Nature belonging to them: And
" leaft of all, are thofe Profeffions to be ap-
" proved of, which are fubfervient to Luxury,
" fuch as the Trades of Fifh-mongers, Butchers,
" Cooks, Paftry-Cooks, and Fifhermen: To
" whom you may add, if you pleafe, Perfumers,
" Dancers, and Tumblers, and the whole Tribe
" of fuch, who adminifter to gaming.

" But thofe Arts, which require much Study
" and Knowledge, or are of great Ufe to Man-
" kind, fuch as Medicine, Architecture, and
" teaching the liberal Sciences, thefe, if exer-
" cifed by Men of a *certain Rank*, [that is under
the Degree of Patricians] do not difhonour
" their Profeffion. As to Merchandize, if in a
" little low Way, it is mean; but if great and
" extenfive, importing Goods from various Coun-
" tries, and dealing them out again to various
" Perfons, without Fraud, *it is not altogether to be*
difcommended. Nay, if the Perfons who follow

" low it, could be fatiated, or rather be con-
" tent with their Profits, *not making long Voyages,*
" but *returning fpeedily to their Farms,* and landed
" Eftates, they would deferve to be rather
" commended. But after all, in Things of this
" Nature, nothing is better, more profitable,
" more pleafant, or more *honourable* than the
" Cultivation of Land."

WHAT a ftrange Jumble of Things is here !
And how little did this great Man underftand the
Nature of the Subject, about which he was writing ! But leaving our City Patriots to cenfure
CICERO, and to fettle the Points of Precedency,
and the Punctilios of Honour between the different Companies of Trades, as they fhall think proper, I haften to obferve

2dly. That there is another effential Difference between the Freemen of *Rome,* and the
Freemen of *London.* For the Freemen of *Rome*
voted very often by Claffes, Tribes, or Companies ; which I am well perfuaded the Freemen or
Livery-men of *London* would confider as a manifeft Infringement of their Rights and Privileges.
And indeed very little can be faid in Defence of
fuch a Practice. For if one Tribe, or Company fhould have 1000 Voices, and the other not
a tenth Part of the Number, it feems very unreafonable, that the larger Tribe fhould be deprived
of

of nine-tenths of its Suffrages, [which it is in
Effect by this Mode of voting] merely becaufe
the fmaller Tribe had not an equal Number.——
However fuch was the Practice of thofe Lords of
the World, the Citizens of *Rome*.

A 3d capital Difference between their Cafe and
ours, confifted in their Method of enacting or
repealing Laws. For when a Law was propounded to the whole Body of the People in their
public Affemblies, to be either confirmed, or
repealed, they had not the Choice of mending,
or altering any Part, by correcting this, or re-
jecting that, by adding any thing to it, or fub-
ftracting from it, but were obliged either to approve all, or refufe all. This was a very great
Defect in the Conftitution of the *Roman* Common-wealth, but it was unavoidable in their Situation. For as the People did not fend Deputies
from certain Diftricts, or particular Claffes, to
reprefent them in the Senate, fimilar to our Members of Parliament, they could no otherwife tran-
fact the Bufinefs of the State, in their numerous
and tumultuous Affemblies [convened together
for a few Hours] than by a fimple Affirmation,
or Negation. Therefore the only Part, which
this Mob of Voters had to act, or could act, in
the grand Affair of Legiflation, wherein the
Majeftas Populi Romani was fo immediately concerned, was to pronouce a fingle YES or NO.
The

[The *sovereign* Council, that is the Body of Citizens, at *Geneva*, do the same at this Day.] A mighty Matter truly, and greatly to be envied by us *Britons!*

But 4thly, and above all, the Propensity of the *Romans* for War, and their Aversion to any lasting Peace, constituted, or ought to constitute the most direct Opposition between their Conduct, and ours. A Nation, whose only Trade was to conquer and subdue, might with some Propriety, or at least with no Inconsistency, seek every Occasion of following their destructive, bloody Occupation. But how a commercial Nation, such as ours, whose continual Aim it should be to increase the Number of its Friends, and to attract Customers from every Part of the Globe, by promoting the mutual Interests of Mankind, and by giving no just Alarms to their Fears and Jealousies :— I say, how such a Nation should entertain that Fondness for War, and should espouse so many Quarrels as the *English* have eagerly done for almost half a Century last past, is, I own, beyond my Comprehension. Nor can I find, even if we had come off Conquerors in every Engagement, which we had, or * wished to have, whether by Sea or Land,

---

* One Time the People were very clamorous for assisting the Queen of *Hungary* ; and nothing else could content them.—
Then

Land, and had triumphed over all the People upon Earth, that thefe fhining Victories would have reduced the Price of our Manufactures, or have rendered them one Jot the better, or cheaper, or fitter to be exported to foreign Markets. In fact, there is fomething fo prepofterous, and indeed fo ridiculous in the Farce, were any Shop-keeper to try to *bully* all his Cuftomers in order to compel them to deal with him againft their own Intereft and Inclination, that one can hardly treat it in a ferious Manner. Yet alas! *mutato nomine de te Fabula narratur.* [See the Cafe of going to War for the Sake of Trade among my *American* Tracts, printed for CADEL.] Moreover our affecting the Dominion of the Ocean, in the Manner we do, greatly prejudices all Mankind againft us. For the Ocean, and all open Seas, are the bountiful Gifts of Providence, like the Winds and Atmofphere, wherein all the World have a COMMON RIGHT; and ought to enjoy it unmolefted.

Then the Tide turned, and they were equally clamorous to affift the King of *Pruffia*. At one Time that miferable Ifland *Corfica* was the favourite Object, at another a Set of Rocks, abfolutely barren, in the midft of a moft inhofpitable Sea, and in a moft wretched Climate, called *Falkland Ifland*, engroffed their Attention. In fhort, any Thing, and every Thing, excepting that one Thing the moft needful for a Commercial State, To *ftudy to be quiet, and do our own Bufinefs.*

I

I HAVE now, I think, cleared off a great deal of thofe vaft Heaps of Rubbifh, which lay in my Way; and therefore might proceed to ereɛt a Super-Struɛture on the Foundation already laid. But there is one Objeɛtion ftill remaining, which though a very falfe one, and fupported by no Proof, is yet of fo popular, and plaufible a Nature, that it muft not be paffed over unnoticed.

The OBJECTION is this:

" The People, that is, every individual moral Agent among the People," [for it muft mean this, if it means any Thing, it being impoffible to admit fome, and refufe others the Right of Voting, with any Face of Juftice, where all have an equal, indefeafible Right: Therefore the Objeɛtion means, that] " every individual " Moral Agent among the People has an *un-* " *alienable Right* to be *felf-governed*, that is to " chufe his own Legiflator, Governor, and Di- " reɛtor. Confequently to take from, or to " deny any of them the free Exercife of this " natural and fundamental Right, is to aɛt the " Tyrant, and to be guilty of the worft Kind of " Robbery that can be committed. It is fuch an " atrocious Violation of the juft Rights of Man- " kind, as will authorife every Man to ufe the " moft fpeedy and efficacious Methods in his
" Power,

" Power, to affert and recover his native Free-
" dom, by redreffing his Wrongs, and *punifhing*
" the Tyrants and Ufurpers."

Now, if the Cafe be really fuch, as is here
fuppofed, all that we have hitherto faid, muft pafs
for nothing. And therefore we muft firft ex-
amine into thefe ftrange Pretenfions of our
modern patriotic Objectors, which tend to un-
hinge all Society, before we can propofe any
Scheme for regulating the Mode of electing
Deputies or Reprefentatives.

THERE are two Kinds of Rights, and only
two belonging to human Nature which are ftrictly
and properly *unalienable*. Thefe are the Functions of Nature, and the Duties of Religion.
And they are in no other Senfe unalienable, but
becaufe they are *infeparable* from the Subject to
which they belong, and cannot be transferred to
another.

A Man, for Inftance, muft perform his animal Functions for himfelf alone; there being
no fuch Thing as Eating and Drinking by Means
of a Proxy, or Deputation. Neither can one
Man difcharge the Duties of Religion in another's
Stead: For thefe are perfonal Acts, which become null and void the Moment that one Man
fhall pretend to give, or another undertake to
execute

execute a Commiffion to act for him. In fhort, no Man can believe for another: Every Man do this for himfelf. And no Man can fubftitute another to repent, or obey in his Stead: For the Repentance and Obedience muft be his own, otherwife it will not be valid. So far the Cafes are clear: Indeed they are felf evident.

But will any Man dare to affirm, that the Affairs of Government and Legiflation, and all the Concerns of Civil Society relative both to Peace and War. are under the fame Predicament, and incapable of being performed by Proxies or Deputations? Surely no: Nothing lefs than Infanity could excufe the uttering of fuch a Paradox. Indeed the Lockians themfelves, to give them their Dues, are confcious that the Cafes are not parallel: They are obliged to make this Confeffion, notwithftanding all their Parade about their unalienable Rights to be *felf-governed* (as Dr. PRICE phrafes it) that is, to elect their own Legiflators, Governors, and Directors. For all of them [except honeft ROUSSEAU, who is generally confiftent, whether in Truth, or Error, and *perhaps* alfo except Dr. PRIESTLY; – I fay, all of them] fcruple not to maintain, that the Minority ought, for the moft Part, to be concluded by the Majority; and that it is their Duty to acquiefce under fuch Determinations, tho' thofe Decrees may happen to be very contrary to their

own

own private Judgments. Now this is a Thing impossible to be complied with in the Functions of Animal Life: For no Man can, even if he would consign over his own Privilege of eating and drinking; or depute another to act in his Stead: In this Respect the Minority cannot compliment the Majority with their unalienable Rights. Moreover as to the Affairs of Religion, and the Performance of moral Duties,—in these Cases also the Rights of Conscience cannot be transferred either from the few to the many, or from the many to the few, by any Covenant or Compact whatsoever: Because they are truly and literally unalienable. Therefore no Majority of Votes can bind in these Cases.—

WHAT then becomes of this boasted Demonstration, this unanswerable Argument, whereby the Lockians have undertaken to prove, That all the Governments and Legiflatures upon Earth are so many Robberies and Usurpations, (yea too, and all their Subjects *Slaves*) such only excepted, if any such there be, as are administered according to the Lockian System?—Why truly, this same Confidence of boasting, when sifted to the Bottom, dwindles into nothing: And the Mountain in Labour is brought forth of a Mouse. However, one Thing must be acknowledged on their Part, That this very Argument of *unalienable Rights*, weak and trifling as it is, may nevertheless

leſs become a formidable Weapon, in the Hands of deſperate *Catalinarian* Men, for eſtabliſhing a real and cruel Tyranny of their own (according to the Example which the *American* Rebels have already ſet) inſtead of that harmleſs, imaginary Tyranny, of which they ſo bitterly complain at preſent.

CHAP.

C H A P.   IV.

*Of a limited Monarchy, and mixt Government. Its
component Parts, Monarchy, Ariſtocracy, and
Democracy. Of the comparative Influence of
each :—On which Side the greateſt Danger is
now to be apprehended.—The Remedy propoſed,
and proper Regulations.*

HAVING at laſt, it is to be hoped, got over
every *material* Difficulty, let us return to
the main Point, from which we have been detained ſo long.—Deputies from, or Repreſentatives of the People, though not *abſolutely* neceſſary to the very Being and Exiſtence of *every le-
gitimate* Government, might nevertheleſs be of
great Uſe and Benefit to them all. For though
we dare not join with that unhappy Principle
which denounces open War, or meditates Con-
ſpiracies and Aſſaſſinations againſt all who ſhould
preſume to govern without an *actual* Election,
Nomination, or Conſent of the People ;—yet
we would by no means derogate from the ſin-
gular Advantage, which might ariſe from a proper Choice of Repreſentatives, to act as their
Truſtees and Guardians. But above all, be it
ever

ever acknowledged, and for ever gloried in, that the Election of Persons to represent the People of *Great-Britain* in Parliament, is a fundamental Part of the *British* Constitution. Here in *Britain*, the important Distinctions, so often mentioned, of actual Contracts and of Quasi-Contracts, enter into the very Essence of our Government. For every Voter or Elector, by giving his Vote, makes himself an *actual* Contractor: And every Non-Voter, whether Male or Female, young or old, by living peaceably and securely amongst us, and enjoying the Protection of the State, is a *Quasi*-Contractor. By means of that actual Contract, which is made between the Representatives in Parliament, and a certain Number of Electors or Voters in *every District*, the Abuse of delegated Power may be in a great Measure guarded against;—perhaps as effectually as can be expected in the present imperfect State of Things. And by means of that Quasi-Contract, which always subsists between the Governing Powers of a State, and the whole Body of the People, and every Individual thereof; the Evils of democratical Anarchy and Confusion are prevented, and Government itself is rendered an useful, practicable Thing, instead of being either a visionary Scheme, or an Engine of the blind Fury of a mad Populace.

TOWARDS

Towards the Beginning of the former Chapter, we set out with the following Enquiry, "How shall the People receive a reasonable Se-"curity, that the Powers wherewith their Go-"vernors are entrusted, both in making Laws, "and in executing them, shall not be misap-"plied?" And in the Progress of the Work, we examined into those constitutional Principles [*Wisdom, Power,* and *Goodness*] on the Ex-exercise of which, in one Degree or other, all moral and civil Governments must depend. -- In the next Place, we took a View of those several Forms, or exterior Modes of Administration, which give distinct Denominations to different Governments, the Monarchical, the Aristo-cratical, and the Democratical. The chief De-fects and Imperfections of each of which were then endeavoured to be pointed out. [And besides this, particular Exceptions were made to the Governments of *Sparta, Athens,* and *Rome,* as being altogether improper for our Case and Cir-cumstances, and indeed very repugnant to that Provision for general Safety, and social Happi-ness, which ought to be the End and Aim of every political Institution.]

From this Survey of Things, it evidently fol-lows, That as neither of the above Forms is de-firable in itself, a Government compounded of all three, and partaking of so much of the Nature

of

of each, as fhall make every Part be a Check
and Counter-balance to the others, [without im-
peding the Motion of the whole] feems to be
the *beft*: It is indeed the fitteft to give a reafonable Security to the People, that they fhall be
well governed. And fuch a Conftitution, Thanks
to kind Providence, is that under which we now
live ;—did we but attend properly to it, by correcting thofe few Errors, which Time has introduced; and did we but improve every Circumftance belonging to it to the moft Advantage.

Now, as the *Britifh* Government is compounded of three diftinct Parts, the Regal, A-
riftocratical, and Popular; the firft Inquiry
fhould be, which of thefe wants rectifying the
moft? Or, in other Words, Which of them
feems to preponderate fo much at prefent, as to
threaten Deftruction to the other two?

It hath been a Practice of many Years ftanding with thofe Gentlemen who chufe the Road
of Oppofition, (inftead of purfuing other Methods) for obtaining Honours, Places, and Pre-
ferments, to alarm and terrify well-meaning
People with inceffant Cries, that the *Conftitution
is in Danger*, through the corrupt Influence of
the Crown:—And that *they* are the only Perfons who can fave a finking State.—This was
the Watch-Word always made ufe of during a
very

very long Conteſt againſt Sir Robert Walpole. But no ſooner were theſe uncorrupt Patriots got into Power, and had gratified their
Ambition and Revenge, than they changed their
Note. They then happily diſcovered, what
was hid from their Eyes before, that each of the
component Parts of a mixt Government, ought
to have a certain Influence on the others;—and
that the Influence of the Regal on the Ariſto-
cratical and Democratical Branches, was neither
more, nor greater than it ought to be. Nay,
theſe new-enlighted quondam Demagogues then
deigned to inſtruct us in their celebrated Treatiſe,
Faction detected by the Evidence of Facts, in how
many ſeveral Reſpects the ancient feudal Prerogative had been abridged and curtailed, and
how much greater Security we enjoy for the
Preſervation of our Liberties, than our Fore-
Fathers had before us. There is no Doubt to
be made, were our preſent Race of Patriots
ever to become victorious, either by the Subverſion of the Miniſtry, or the Subverſion of the
State, and the Erection of a Common-Wealth,
but that they too would wiſh to mimic their
Predeceſſors in diſplaying the vaſt Advantage
which their Country have reaped from their Labours for the public Good. — The plain *Engliſh*
of which is, That *they ought to be well paid.* In
the mean Time, as this Event is perhaps not ſo
near its Accompliſhment as they could wiſh;—

and

and as neither the *Inns* nor the *Outs* are to be relied upon for giving a fair and impartial State of the prefent Influence of the Crown [neither Side being willing to difcover the real Truth:] It is not impoffible but that a Perfon of infinitely lefs Abilities than thofe who have undertaken to give an Account of this Matter, may fucceed better; becaufe he is enlifted under no Man's Banners, has no Party to ferve, has nothing but the Truth in View, none to fear, and none to flatter.

WHAT is generally underftood by the Influence of the Crown, muft arife either from an open and avowed Exertion of fome undoubted Prerogative of the Crown;—or from fome fecret Artifice, not authorifed by Law, and therefore not to be juftified, which the Crown is fuppofed to make ufe of, in order to obtain fome certain End.

IF the former is here meant by the Affertion, that the Influence of the Crown has rapidly encreafed of late Years;—it is faying in other Words, that the legal or conftitutional Prerogative of the Crown has been *extended*, inftead of being curtailed,—has been enlarged inftead of being abridged;—and that the Power of the Prince is more abfolute and unreftrained, and

lefs

lefs confined by Law fince the Revolution, than it was before. Will any Man in his fober Senfes dare to maintain fuch a Paradox?—

But if the Term *Influence* is to be taken in the latter Senfe; that is, if by it is meant fuch clandeftine Practices as the Law condemns, and therefore would punifh, if legally detected;—this is an Accufation, which muft firft be proved before Sentence can be paft on the Offenders. For tho' it is very probable, that the beft of human Governors have, in all Ages, fhewn themfelves not much averfe to the Ufe of bad Means for the attaining fuch Ends as they wifh to accomplifh, and not otherways attainable;—yet it is much to be queftioned, whether the particular Vices of *Bribery* and *Corruption*, [I mean in the grofs Senfe of the Word] have been practiced by the Agents of the Crown, to a greater Extent of late Years than they ufed to be.—— Far therefore from fuggefting a Thought, that our prefent Minifters, any more than their Predeceffors, are perfectly immaculate;—I only fay, that it has not yet appeared, that they are worfe in this Refpect than former Minifters;—much lefs has it been proved, that *Bribery* and *Corruption* have of late Years made fuch a rapid and alarming Progrefs, as to deferve a peculiar Stigma. My Reafons are the following: Firft, in the greateft Electioneering Contefts, which perhaps this Country
try

try ever faw, when every Species of undue Influence was put in Practice, with fhameful Notoriety :—Yet it was not fo much as attempted to be proved, that the public Treafury had been opened to bribe the Electors in any of thofe Difputes.—For the Truth of this, I appeal to thofe, who remember all, or any of the moft violent Contefts which have been raifed within the laft 30 Years ;—particularly the three great ones at *Briftol* within that Period,—the great Conteft in *Oxfordfhire*, at *Northampton*,—in *Cumberland*,— and lately in *Glocefterfhire*. In all which there can hardly be a Sufpicion, much lefs a direct Proof, that the Bribery and Corruption, (but too much practiced) whether in Money, or by other Means, were owing to the Sums iffued from the Treafury. My fecond Reafon is, That by means of that quick Viciffitude of Things, to which perhaps this Country is more fubject than any other, it has often happened, that many of the *Outs* have come *in*, and many of the *Ins* have gone out ;— yet no Side, notwithftanding their mutual Rancour, hath impeached the other, when they had the Books of the Treafury in their own Hands, of having been guilty of thofe Mal-Practices, and of that Bribery and Corruption which are here furmifed.—Now this they moft probably would have done, had any fuch Proofs been upon Record ;—or even could they have brought any Thing fufpicious from the Minutes in the Trea-
fury-

fury-Books, of fuch a Mifapplication of public
Money.—Thirdly, the Sums generally fpent at
fuch contefted Elections, is another ftrong
Evidence, that Place-Men and Penfioners are
not the principal Actors in thefe modern Tragedies.
A Place-Man [or, if you pleafe, a Penfioner]
has perhaps 1000l. or 1500l. or even 2000l. a
Year: This is accounted to be his *Summum Bonum,*
his Confcience, his Country, and his God. Now,
can it be imagined, that fuch a Man, who is thus
characterized to have no Regard to any Thing
but his own Intereft, would fpend, if *he could,*
10,000l.—perhaps 20,000l. nay, 30,000l.—
or even more, for obtaining a Seat in Parliament to fecure his Place, or his Penfion? No:
The Suppofition is foolifh and abfurd: It con-
futes itfelf. Any Book of Calculations may
fuffice to inform us, that fuch *precarious* Things
as Places or Penfions, are not worth a tenth
Part of fuch Purchafe-Money. -- Laftly, in almoft all vehement Electioneering Struggles,
where vaft Sums are expended, the Ground of the
Conteft is feldom or never about any national
Affair :---But about the important Queftion,---
Who fhall be uppermoft?---Whether this great
Family, or that, in fuch a County, or fuch a Borough?---What Party Connection, or Party Colour
fhall have the Afcendent? And whether this Leader,
or that Leader, this Club, or that, in fuch a County,
City, or Borough, fhall poll the moft Votes?—
Points,

Points, which concern the Public, or even the Minifter for the Time being, juft as much as the Big-endians, or Little-endians of the facetious Dean SWIFT.

WELL then; if the great Influence of the Crown, that *dangerous* Influence, which is every Day encreafing, and ought to be diminifhed, doth not arife from fuch Caufes as thefe, at leaft in any confiderable Degree;—from what doth it arife? and how is the Growth of it to be prevented?---The Caufes of this encreafing Influence, are the vaft Territories abroad, and thofe ruinous Wars, and immenfe Expences which they occafion; and ever will occafion whilft we are connected with them, under one Pretence or other. Can any Man make a Doubt of this?—If he doth, let him try, even in Thought and Imagination, to fubftitute a Syftem for the Government, or Reduction of fuch remote Countries, which would ftand clear of thofe Evils, which we now feel, and continually deplore. Suppofe, for Example, a certain Event, which moft probably is approaching with hafty Strides; *viz.* That the *Englifh* fettled in *Bengal.* and in the other Provinces of the Indian Empire, fhould take it into their Heads, that they too have unalienable Rights as well as the *Americans;*---and that, like them, now they are freed from the Apprehenfions of a *French* Domination, they will

no

no longer receive Laws from a little, paultry Spot in *Europe*, diftant by Sea almoft 10,000 Miles. Fired therefore with the glorious Thought of native Freedom, the Birth-right of every *Englifh-man* [though not of other Men ; for by the by, the moft zealous of our *Englifh* Independents, are the leaft inclined to make other Men independent : And therefore I fay] fired with the glorious Thought of their own Independence, and of Self-Government, they bravely defy not only the Gentlemen and * *Ladies* of *Leaden-Hall* Affembly, but alfo the King, Lords, and Commons of *Great-Britain* in Parliament affembled. Now here I afk, How is this Rebellion to be fuppreffed ? And who is to have the Appointment, and the Payment of all the Troops, and of all the Squadrons, Tranfports, &c. ; alfo of the feveral Officers, Commanders, Contractors, Purveyors, Surveyors, Examiners, Store-keepers, Deputies, Clerks, and of numberlefs other Beings to be employed for the Suppreffion of it ? The Crown undoubtedly,— for it is the undoubted Prerogative of the Crown,—as the fupreme executive Power : Otherwife there

---

* The Ladies have Votes at the *Eaft-India Houfe*.—Let the Lockians give a Reafon confiftently with their Principles, if they can,---Why Women are debarred from voting for *Directors* in Parliament, and yet allowed to vote for Directors at the *India Houfe*.

will

will be two Supremes within the fame State ; — a Solecifm this, which even our modern political Refiners have not yet attempted to propofe. This being the Cafe, how will you prevent the Crown from gaining a prodigious Influence by the Creation of fuch a Multitude of new Appointments, and by the annual Expenditure of of the many Millions which will be wanted for the Payment of them ? How will you prevent it, I fay, whilft it has fuch gainful Things to give ;---even fuppofing (which no Man in his Senfes can fuppofe) that not a fingle Place would be created, nor a Farthing expended, beyond what the Nature of the Cafe required ? Yet, even on this Suppofition, and without Jobs or Embezzlements of any Kind, fo many lucrative Places and Employments, [all neceffarily in the Difpofal of the Crown] muft create a Dependence, call it by what Name you pleafe, as long as human Nature fhall continue to be what it has ever been fince Government began. And this is the very Influence which now too much preponderates in our public Councils. Here then the Secret is out at laft. The legal and conftitutional Prerogative of the Crown is not to be blamed : But our diftant, unwieldly Colonies, and our ruinous Wars for their Sakes are the real Caufes of all our Complaints.—It is thefe which involve us in thoufands of Diftreffes, of which we fhould have been happily ignorant, had it not been for fuch Connections.

nections. They therefore, and they only, are
the Authors of our prefent Misfortunes ; and
will involve us in ftill greater, if we fhall ob-
ftinately perfift in retaining thefe remote, un-
manageable Poffeffions :—☞ For the Governing of which, I will be bold to fay, the *Englifh*
Conftitution was not calculated, and *is not fit*.
This is fo plain a Cafe, that no Man of Reafon
will pretend to deny it, or undertake to prove
the contrary.   How then comes it to pafs, that
neither Minifters, nor Anti-Minifters have ever
affigned the true Caufe of thofe Evils, which we
daily feel, and of which we are perpetually
complaining ?—The Reafon is this, Neither
Minifters, nor their Opponents ever meant to
ferve the Public, at the Rifque of their own
Intereft.—The uttering of difagreeable, unpopular Truths might be attended with certain
Confequences to themfelves which they wifh to
avoid : And therefore they defire to be excufed.

Should, for Example, the Minifter for the
Time being, have the Honefty and Sincerity
openly to declare, that extended Commerce,
and extended Territorial Acquifitions are repugnant to each other :   That Induftry, Probity,
and Frugality are much more ferviceable to the
Promotion of Agriculture and Manufactures
than all the Glare of War and military Glory ;—
and that the Boaft of conquering *America* in
Germany,

Germany, or any where elfe, was, an improper, idle, Bravado, fitter to raife the Refentment of other Nations, than to ferve ourfelves. Should, I fay, a Minifter have the Honefty and Sincerity openly to avow thefe unpopular Truths, and venture to declare, that the proper Way of diminifhing *that Influence* of the Crown which is really dangerous, would be to diminifh our Expences,—by renouncing all foreign Poffeffions. and cultivating the Arts of Peace in the two fruitful Iflands of *Great-Britain* and *Ireland :* Should any oftenfible Minifter have the Courage to utter thefe honeft, unwelcome Truths ;—Who would fupport him ?—Who would thank him ?—Who would not perfecute him

Again, Were any of our Demagogues to tell their beft Friends, the Mob, that *Gibraltar* and *Portmahon* are very expenfive, and very ufelefs Things ;—that the Ocean is the great *Common of Nature*, which belongs to no Nation, Language, or People, in any exclufive Senfe ; but ought to be free, like the Air, for the Ufe of all ; and that the keeping up any Pretenfions to the contrary, is as impolitic, as it is unjuft ; ferving no other End, but to irritate all the World againft us :—Alfo fhould he obferve, that Colonies of every Sort or Kind are, and ever were, a *Drain* to, and an *Incumbrance* on the *Mother-Country*. requiring perpetual and expenfive Nurfing in
their

their Infancy;—and becoming headſtrong and ungovernable, in Proportion as they grow up,—and never failing to revolt, as ſoon as they ſhall find that they do not want our Aſſiſtance :—And that even at the beſt, thoſe commercial Advantages, which are vulgarly ſuppoſed to ariſe from them, are more imaginary than real ;—becauſe it is impoſſible to compel diſtant Settlements to trade with the parent State, to any great Degree beyond what their own Intereſt would prompt them to : [And Self-Intereſt needs no Compulſion.]—Moreover, ſhould any Orator of this Stamp proceed to ſhew, that ſince the Laws for governing the Colonies, have from the Beginning proved nugatory and vain, attended with vaſt Expence, and no proportionable Profit;—therefore ſhould he propoſe a total Separation, and recommend the ſhaking them entirely off;—in Conſequence of which Multitudes of Places would be aboliſhed, Jobbs and Contracts effectually prevented, Millions of Money ſaved, univerſal Induſtry encouraged, and the Influence of the Crown reduced to that Mediocrity it ought to have : —— Should, I ſay, any of our modern Demagogues dare to recommend theſe ſalutary Truths, what would his Brother-Demagogues ſay to him ?—Would they aſſiſt him in this good Work ?—No; they would not, —though conſcious to themſelves, that nothing

better

better, or more feafonable, could be recommended.—On the contrary, they would open in full Cry againſt ſuch an *Apoſtate* from the common Caufe,—would perfecute him in every Shape, and excite the Populace to pour forth the bittereſt Execrations againſt him ;—if not to proceed to ſtill greater Extremities.

WHAT Courfe is he then to také? And how is he to act, in order that he may *feem* to aim at a national Reformation, and a Redrefs of Grievances, without intending any Thing real? The public Good requires one Conduct : But Popularity and Party another. Preffed by this Dilemma, it is but too obvious which his Choice would be. Such a Man would warmly recommend a Reform in the K—g's Kitchen, in his Cellar, in his Houfhold Servants, and his Houfhold Furniture;—nay, I had almoſt faid, in his Dog-Kennel.—In ſhort, he would propofe to fave and to retrench in every Article, except that grand one, a Separation from the Colonies, which is worth a thoufand of the reſt. —So that in order to gratify the perverfe Humours of thefe unhappy Times, Majeſty muſt be facrificed to a republican Faction, and the Power of the Prince in the Management of his own private Concerns, be reduced to a Condition much more abject than that of any of his Subjects.

As

As long as the Temper and Intellects of Mankind fhall remain in this wretched and difordered State, nothing truly good is likely to be done. We muft therefore wait with Patience for better Times; hoping, that kind Providence will infpire one Part of the Community with founder Underftandings, and the other with better Hearts.

§. *The Ariftocratical Part of the Conftitution.*

RESPECTING this Branch very little need be faid. For the prefent Ariftocracy is very far from being formidable. Indeed it can hardly be faid to have Weight enough in the political Scale, fo as to maintain a proper Balance between the two other great Powers of the Conftitution.—'Tis true, the Baronage in former Times was a dreadful Engine of Tyranny and Oppreffion. A few great Lords combining together, often fhook the Throne, often trampled on Law and Juftice, and oppreffed the common People at their Pleafure. But thefe Times are no more: A Peer of the Realm has no Jurifdiction annexed to his Barony; he is entitled to no Privilege or Prerogative authorifing him to treat his Tenants, as Slaves and Vaffals; but is as amenable to the regular Courts of Law, as any private Subject. Moreover as to the landed Eftates of Peers, they being as divifible

into

into fmall Shares as the Eftates of Commoners; therefore the Power of the Peerage is fo far from encreafing, that it is greatly on the Decline, if compared with what we find on Record in former Times.

§. *The Democratical Part of the Conftitution ;— wherein the Power of electing Deputies to reprefent the People is particularly confidered.*

THAT Government was ordained for the Good of the People ; and that this is the great Object which ought always to be attended to in every political Inftitution, are Points, which I fhall take for granted. The only Matter worthy our prefent Inquiry is, How fhall this public Good be moft effectually promoted ? And, if divers Means fhould be propofed, which is the beft ?— Deputies from, and Reprefentatives of the People, not only bid the faireft of any others, for this Purpofe ; but are likewife made an effential Branch of the Britifh Conftitution. Therefore the Benefits and Advantages thence arifing, are the Subjects which come next to be confidered.

THE beft of human Inftitutions cannot be fuppofed to be fo abfolutely perfect, as to want no Correction or Amendment. Nay, Time, and an Alteration of Circumftances will introduce

fome

fome Diforders into the beft, and point out Defects, which could not be forefeen at firft. This
is the Cafe with Refpect to the democratical Part
of our Government. Diforders undoubtedly
there are, and Defects not a few, which call
aloud for a Remedy; if any can be found, which
will not increafe the Difeafe, inftead of curing it,
or will not introduce new, and worfe Evils, by
attempting to remove the old ones.

THE Remedies which have been of late
Years moft warmly propofed by thofe Gentle-
men, who glory in the Title of being the
Difciples of Mr. LOCKE, are the following:

1ft, THAT there fhall be a more equal Reprefentation of the People, refpecting their *Numbers*:

2ndly, THAT there fhall be a more equal Reprefentation of them, refpecting their *Property*.

AND 3dly, THAT thefe Reprefentatives fhall
not continue longer than one Year, or at moft
than three Years, without a new Election.

LET us begin with the firft of the Remedies
here propofed for the Cure of our political Diforders. This Notion of the Neceffity of an
equal Reprefentation, is grounded on that
Lockian

Lockian Idea of the *unalienable Right of each Individual to be Self-governed*; Notions, which I hope, have been fufficiently confuted. However, as Truth will bear to be feen in various Lights, and what is wrong never can become right, I will now purfue this Deception, through a new Difguife, and endeavour to prefent the Reader with a fecond Confutation of it.

THEREFORE in Conformity to the Lockian Plan of equal Reprefentation, I will ftate the following Cafe: [A Cafe fufficiently exact for our prefent Purpofe] Let us fuppofe that the Ifland of *Great-Britain* contains feventy Millions of Acres, and feven Millions of Inhabitants;— and that it is propofed by the Lockian Politicians, [fomething fimilar to which is done almoft every Day] That thefe feven Millions of Inhabitants ought to fend nearly feven hundred Deputies to reprefent them in Parliament: So that each Million fhall elect an hundred Reprefentatives. So far the Scheme looks plaufible; but mark the Confequences:—One Million out of the feven are crowded together, inhabiting a fmall Spot, perhaps not more than twenty thoufand Acres; whilft the remaining fix Millions are fcattered over the Face of the Country; alfo feveral Millions of Acres lie wafte, without any Inhabitants at all. Now this *central* Million, as it may be called, [alias *London, Weftminfter, Southwark,*

Southwark, and their Environs] with an hundred Deputies, all of their own electing, and continually under their Influence, and always ready at Hand, will be an over-match for the Reft of the Kingdom in every Conteft, and become every Day more and more predominant.—— Can any Man doubt of this?—He cannot, if he either knows, what human Nature is in general, when armed with Power;—or can reflect the many Monopolies and Exclufions, which *London* in particular hath already obtained both by Sea and Land. For even at prefent, when *London*, *Weftminfter*, and *Southwark*, have but eight Reprefentatives, they have encroached on the Liberties and Trade of their Fellow-Subjects in Hundreds of Inftances, have had the Appropriation of vaft Sums of the public Money, for building of Bridges, &c. &c. and have engroffed feveral Advantages, which ought to have been left common to all. Now, if the Metropolis has the Balance of Power already fo much in its Favour, would you wifh to make it preponderate upwards of twelve Times more than it doth?

AGAIN: All over-grown Cities are formidable in another View, and therefore ought not to be encouraged by new Privileges, to grow ftill more dangerous; for they are, and ever were, the Seats of Faction and Sedition, and the Nurferies of Anarchy and Confufion. A daring, and
desperate

defperate Leader, in any great Metropolis, at the Head of a numerous Mob, is terrible to the Peace of Society, even in the moſt deſpotic Governments :—But in *London*, where the People are the moſt licentious upon Earth,—In *London*, where the Populace are daily taught, that they have an unalienable Right to be ſelf-governed ;—and that their Rulers are no other than their Servants :—In *London*, where nothing is held ſacred, but the Will of the People [blaſphemouſly called, the *Voice of God*] what are you to expeᴄt from an Addition of Priviſege and Power, but an Encreaſe of the moſt daring Outrages, and the Subverſion of Law and Government ? The audacious Villanies recently committed in *June*, 1780, are ſufficient, one would think, to give any Man a Surfeit of the very Idea of adding ſtill greater Influence and Power to a *London* Mob.

Once more, If a Man has any Senſe of Rectitude and good Morals, or has a Spark of Goodneſs and Humanity remaining, he cannot wiſh to entice men into great Cities by freſh Allurements. Such Places are already become the Bane of Mankind in every Senſe, in their Healths, their Fortunes, their Morals, Religigion, &c. &c. &c. And it is obſervable of *London* in particular, that were no freſh Recruits, Male and Female, to come out of the

Country,

Country, to fupply thofe Devaftations which
Vice, Intemperance, Brothels, and the Gal-
lows are continually making, the whole human
Species in that City would be foon exhaufted:
For the Number of Deaths exceed the Births by
at leaft 7000 every Year.—So much as to the
1ft Remedy propofed by the Lockians for the
Cure of our political Diforders.

THE 2d is, That there fhall be a more equal
Reprefentation of the Inhabitants of this Ifland
refpecting their *Property.*

Mr. LOCKE himfelf ftrongly leans towards the
Doctrine of reprefenting *Property;*—and many
of his Followers directly maintain it.—Though
the Notion itfelf is little lefs than a Contradiction
to their favourite grand Principle of unalienable
Rights belonging to each Individual, whether
poor or rich. For if fuch Rights do belong to
any Beings whatever, they muft belong to *Perfon,* not to *Property.* Moreover, according to
this Doctrine, every Man, who has *no Property,*
ought to have *no Vote,* notwithftanding the fuppofed unalienable Rights of his Nature. And a
rich Man, with large and extenfive Property,
ought to have many Votes in Proportion to his
Riches. Confequently the Grand *Turk,* and
every other Defpot, who is the only rich Man,
being the Proprietor and Lord of all, is juftly
entitled

entitled to every Vote within his Dominions :—
Or rather, he is the only rightful Voter, and
therefore reprefents all Property in his own Perfon.   What a Revolution is this!   For hence it
comes to pafs, that the *Ottoman* Empire, the
very Quinteffence of Tyranny, is all of a fudden
transformed into a mild, juft, and equitable Government ; exhibiting a moft perfeÆ Model of
fair Reprefentation.

THE laft Remedy propofed for the Cure of
our political Diforders, is the Frequency of
general EleÆions, which it feems ought to be
triennial,— if not annual : And then all would
be well.   Never did Mountebank DoÆor puff
off his fophifticated Drugs with more rhetorical
Flourifhes, than our State DoÆors háve celebrated the Virtues of their *infallible Noftrum* of
annual or triennial Parliaments.   Nay, they
have affured the Populace in fome of their Harangues, that they have an unalienable Right to
require us to fwallow this Prefcription.—— But
let us enquire a little before we fwallow.—The
firft Benefit, we are told, which is to accrue from
annual General EleÆions, is,   " That we fhall
" be reftored to our antient Conftitution of an-
" nual Parliaments."   What ?   Doth not the
Parliament now meet annually ?   And hath it
ever failed to meet annually fince the Revolution ?   " Oh, no :   " It meets, 'tis true :   But
                                                " it

" it is not a *new* Parliament, [a *new* Houfe of
" Commons] which meets; but only a Continu-
" ation of the old one; whereas there ought to
" have been a new Houfe of Commons every
" Time that there is a new Seffions of Parliament.
" And the People have an unalienable Right to
" demand a Reftoration of their antient Privi-
" leges."—How doth it appear, that annual General Elections ever were an antient Privilege
of the People ?—And what Authority do you
produce in fupport of this extraordinary Affertion ?—" There was a Law made the 4th of ED-
" WARD III. C. 14.—which enacts, that Par-
" liaments fhalll be held once a Year, or more
" often, if need be : This Law was confirmed in
" the 36th Year of the fame Prince, and ftill re-
" mains unrepealed. Therefore"—Therefore
what ?—" Therefore, the holding of a Parlia-
" ment once every Year, or more often if need
" be,—fignifies the fame Thing, [in patriotic
" Language] as that there fhall be a General
" Election of the Houfe of Commons once every
" Year, or oftener.".—Surely the candid and impartial Reader doth not expect a formal Confutation of fo wild an Argument.—Taking therefore for granted, that the holding of a Parliament, and a General Election of the Commons,
are *not fynonymous Terms*, I will endeavour to
employ the Reader's Time and my own to better
Purpofes, by ftating the Fact, from which this

ftrange

ftrange Notion of the conftitutional Right of an-
nual General Election feems to have taken its
Rife.—When the Commons of *England* were
exceffively poor, and when the Members of the
Houfe of Reprefentatives were, almoft to a
Man, either the Tenants of the Crown, or the
Vaffals, Dependents, and Retainers of the great
Barons [there being hardly fuch a Perfon then
exifting, as what we now call an *independent
Country Gentleman*] two Things were deemed great
Favours at that Juncture, which would be looked
upon in thefe Times in a very different Light.
The one was, The excufing of the poorer Bo-
roughs (efpecially the Tenants of the Crown)
from fending Members to Parliament : And
this was fo frequent a Practice, that even the
Sheriffs would fometimes make Returns, that
this or that Borough was in fuch a pauper State,
as not to be able to bear the Expence of fending
Reprefentatives. The other was, That the
Elected themfelves [for fmall Cities and Towns
Corporate] did not confider the Office of a
Member of Parliament in that high and honourable Light in which it ftands at prefent. Men,
who have not much to give, and no Favours to
beftow, and who ftand more in need of the Protection of others, than others do of them, are
not much courted and careffed at any Time.

* Now

* Now this was the very Cafe with the Reprefentatives in Parliament, I mean for fmall Cities
and Borough-Towns, during all the Reigns of
the *Plantagenets*, and the TUDORS; (as fhall be
more fully made to appear in the enfuing Chap-
ter] therefore many, if not moft of fuch Members, thought it a greater Favour to be excufed from ferving a burthenfome Office, than
to be elected to it. As to the Wages they received from their Conftituents, every one muft
know, that at any Time, and according to
the moft frugal Mode of Living, the Sums received could not be fufficient for defraying the

M m   Expences

---

* An Obfervation of the very learned and Hon. DAINES
BARRINGTON, Efq; corroborates what is here advanced. In
his ufeful Annotations on ancient Statutes, Page 417, of 3d.
Edition, he remarks, That " HENRY [the VII.] had the
" Merit either from Reafons of Policy, or perhaps more hu-
" mane Motives, to render the lower Clafs of People lefs de-
" pendent upon the rich and powerful." And adds at Page
419, " This *Protection* of the inferior Claffes of his Subjects,
" produced, as a natural Confequence, a greater Freedom
" and Independency in the lower Houfe of Parliament. Sir
" THOMAS MORE oppofed a Subfidy with Succefs, in the
" laft Year of this King's Reign ; which is, perhaps, ☞ the
" firft Inftance of Oppofition to a Meafure of the Crown by
" a Member of the Houfe of Commons."

BUT though the Reprefentatives of the People began to acquire Confequence in Proportion as the People themfelves became lefs dependent on the Prince, or on his Barons;---yet
they hardly felt their full Strength till a much later Period.

In

Expences incurred. Hence therefore it was natural for them to confider the Diffolution of the Houfe at the End of every Seffions as a Matter of Grace and Favour; in order that they might have a Chance of not being elected a fecond Time. So that from this Circumftance we may trace the true Caufe, how it came to pafs, that at the End of every Seffions of Parliament, the Houfe of Commons was generally diffolved :—— I fay *generally:* For there were fome Exceptions: And moft affuredly the Prince was not then under the Obligation of any *pofitive Statute Law*

[as

In the fucceeding Reign a moft remarkable Inftance occurs of their Non-importance, even in their own Eyes. One RICHARD STRODE [fee Statutes at large, 4. H. VIII. C. 8.] a Tinner and Member for *Plimton* in *Devonfhire*, had very properly, as it feems, joined with other Members of the Houfe of Commons in promoting Bills for preventing his Brother-Tinners from monopolizing the Tin Trade. This was Crime enough in their Eyes. They therefore called a Parliament of the Stannaries to condemn the Culprit for what he had done in the Parliament at *Weftminfter.* And having fined him by Proceffes in their Law-Courts to the Amount of 160l. they " imprifoned him in a Dungeon, a deep Pit under Ground " in the Caftle of *Lidford*, the which Prifon is one of the moft " heinous, contagious, and deteftable Places within this " Realm, and put Irons upon him to his more greater Pain " and Jeopardy, and gave him but Bread and Water only." In which Situation he continued till he was releafed by a " Writ of Privilege out of the King's Exchequer" [N. B. A. Privilege, not as being a Member of Parliament; for that it feems, gave him then no protection; but] " as being one of " the [as he now is] for diffolving it at any particular given Time. It was wholely at his own Option, when to do it. The *Irifh* Houfe of Commons, copied from the *Englifh* Model, puts this Affair beyond Difpute. For in that Kingdom, when an Houfe of Reprefentatives was elected, at the Acceffion of a new King, it was to remain undiffolved ['till the late octennial Act altered the Cafe] during the Life of the reigning Prince, if he thought proper:—If not, he might diffolve it as often as he pleafed, and command new Elections to be made.—So much as to the boafted conftitutional Rights of annual Elections.

M m 2

How-

" the King's Collectors in the faid County for the firft of the
" two *Quindeims* granted at, and in this Parliament:---
" Wherefore the faid RICHARD humbly prayeth, that it may
" be ordained, eftablifhed, and enacted by the King our So-
" vereign Lord, and by the Lords Spiritual and Temporal,
" and the Commons in this prefent Parliament affembled, and
" by the Authority of the fame, that the faid Condemnations,
" and Condemnation of the faid 1601. &c. &c. be utterly
" void, and of none Effect."

The Legiflature having granted this moft reafonable Requeft, added a farther Security to Members of Parliament, viz.
" That all Suits, Accufements, Condemnations, Executions,
" Fines, Amerciaments, Punifhments, Collections, Grants,
" Charges or Impofitions put, or had, or hereafter to be put,
" or had unto, or upon the faid RICHARD, and to every
" other of the Perfon or Perfons afore fpecified, that now be
" of this prefent Parliament, or that of any Parliament here-
" after fhall be, for any Bill, Speaking, Reafoning, or de-
" claring

However, though our Modern-Patriots have failed moſt egregiouſly in this Point; yet, if they can make it appear, that annual or triennial Elections would be productive of more Good than Evil, every real Patriot will wiſh Succeſs to their Endeavours, whatever may have been their Motives.

And 1ſt. They aſſure us, " that annual Elec-" tions would put an End to all Bribery and Cor-" ruption." Good News indeed! But are you *really* ſure of that? " We are; for when Ge-" neral Elections were annual, there was no " Bribery."

" claring of any Matter or Matters concerning the Parlia-" ment to be communed and treated of, be utterly void, and " of none Effect."

To which Protection the Legiſlature added alſo a Penalty on ſuch Offenders, for this farther Security of the Liberty of Members of Parliament: Namely, that the Members might bring Actions on the Caſe, if moleſted for the future, and recover treble Damages and Coſts.----Such was the boaſted Privileges of the Repreſentatives of the People at this Period of Time! Reader, compare thoſe Times with theſe.

Again, during the long Reign of Queen Elizabeth, the Language of Parliament, I mean of the Houſe of Commons, was, That the Queen was abſolute, and her Prerogative unlimitted; ---conſequently, that no Act of the Legiſlature could curtail or abridge it. See Townshend's Collections of the many Debates for aboliſhing Monopolies; and D'Ew's Abridgement. On which Occaſion, the Speaker received a ſevere Reprimand

" Bribery."—Probable enough ; and if you intend to reduce the Power of the Houfe of Commons to the like *infignificant State* it was in during the Reigns of the *Plantagenets* and the
Tudors, that very Infignificance would effectually
remove all the Evils of which you now complain.
As a Proof of this, take the following Example
in modern Times.—The Clergy are no longer
taxed by their Reprefentatives in Convocation,
but by Laymen in the Houfe of Commons.—
And what is the Confequence ?—The Election
of Convocation-Men is now become one of the
moft peaceable Things in Nature. No Bribery,
no Corruption are even fufpected, not a Treat,
not an Intrigue is heard of, and Calumny herfelf

is

Reprimand from the Secretary of State, Sir ROBERT CECIL,
for fuffering the Heads of a Bill even to be read in that Houfe,
which feemed to limit or confine the regal Power. *You, Mr.
Speaker, ought to have known your Duty better:*---And in
another of his Speeches he faid, Hear what BRACTON faith,
Prærogativam meam nemo audeat difputare. Once more : The
fame Author, if my Memory doth not greatly fail me, mentions another curious Fact, namely, That one ARCHER,
who ftood and carried the Election for the Borough of *Read-
ing,* in Oppofition to a Candidate recommended by the
Queen's *Deputy Vice Chamberlain,* was imprifoned for this
atrocious Deed : Nor could he gain his Liberty, till the whole
Houfe of Commons had petitioned for his Releafe. Surely,
furely, the Reader will not difmifs thefe hiftorical Facts, without making his own Reflections upon them. The Influence
of the Crown ! The *encreafing* Influence of the Crown in thefe
degenerate Days ! O Liberty ! O my Country !

is dumb.　Now do you really wifh to have our
State-Difeafes cured, and our political Complaints removed after the fame Manner ? and is
this one of thofe *infallible Noftrums*, of which fuch
Boaftings have been lately made ?----However,
let us hear what you have further to propofe.

2*dly*.　You fay " Were Elections to become an-
" nual, Bribery would ceafe ; becaufe it would be
" worth no Man's while to bribe fo often, as
" every Year."　To this I anfwer, that there is
an Ambiguity in the Phrafe *worth no Man's*
while, which muft be firft explained : And then
the Merits of the Caufe will foon appear.
Among the many Motives which induce Men
to ftand Candidates for a Seat in Parliament,
fome good, and fome bad, two of the moft predominant are, AVARICE, and AMBITION.　Now,
as far as *mere Avarice* or the Thirft of Gain is
concerned, no Man in his fober Senfes would
think it worth his while to give 20,000l.—or
10,000l.—or 5000l.—or 2000l.—or even
1000l. annually, in Bribes, in order to procure
a Place, or a Penfion of 1000l.—2000l.—or at
the moft 3000l.—without any Security of holding it a Day :—I fay, no Man in his Senfes
would think it worth his while to rifque fuch a
certain Sum on fuch an Uncertainty.　And fo
far I agree moft cordially with you.　But remember that I have already proved [Page 247.]
that

that no Man doth act after this fenfelefs Manner, even at prefent.   But as to AMBITION, and Vain-Glory, and the Luft of Power, the Stings of Envy, Hopes of Revenge, Religious Bigotry, and Party-Rage, &c. &c. &c.—are thefe Evils to be cured by having Recourfe to annual Elections?   No, no: You cannot fuppofe any Thing fo foolifh and abfurd.   As foon might you undertake to quench Fire with Oil, as to cool and moderate the Paffions of Mankind, by keeping them in a perpetual State of Strife, Jealoufy, and Rancour.   It has ever been the Advice of medical People, to keep fore Places from being fretted ;—but it feems, our modern State-Doctors prefcribe the Ufe of continual fretting, as an infallible Means of Cure.

BESIDES, if Experience is to be our Guide, let the Experience of former Times decide the Queftion.   During the long Conteft between the Houfes of *Lancafter* and *York*, annual Elections were, according to this Hypothefis, the conftant Practice.   Whether that was the Cafe, or not, is immaterial.   If it was, what Good did thefe annual Elections then produce?   And how much of the Fury and Madnefs of the Combatants did they reftrain ?—If annual Elections were then fet afide, what was their Efficacy, if not ufed, when moft wanted ?—That Parliament upon Parliaments were held during thofe

troublefome

troublefome Times, is an undoubted Fact:—
And therefore if annual Elections are fuch a
fovereign Remedy, as here fuppofed, this was
the Time for them to have produced their falutary Effects.   Yet alas! the only Effect which
we can learn from Hiftory, was, That the victorious Side always reverfed what the vanquifhed
had enacted, and added new Confifcations, and
Attainders of their own.—Could any Thing
better have been expected from the annual Re-
vivals of civil Difcords?

But above all, if you will view the Matter in
a commercial Light, you muft acknowledge,
that annual, or even triennial Appeals to the
whole Mafs of the People, [each of whom, it
feems, hath an equal and an indefeafible Right
to be reprefented, and to be felf-governed, &c.]
would bring fwift Ruin and Deftruction on all
our Trade and Manufactures.   The Clubs and
Combinations of Tradefmen to raife the Price of
Goods, and of Journeymen to raife their Wages,
have a bad Effect on national Commerce even at
prefent:—judge therefore what would be the Confequences, were every Tradefman, and every
Journeyman, to be annually *authorifed* [as he
would be in effect] to make his own Terms with
the Candidate, before he would promife him his
Vote !   Moft undoubtedly *Birmingham* and *Manchefter*, *Leeds*, and *Halifax*, and many other po-
ulous

pulous Towns and manufacturing Places would
foon be reduced to mere Villages, when blessed
with equal Reprefentations, and frequent Elections: And the Trade and Manufactures, the
Shipping and Navigation of *England* would foon
migrate into *Scotland* : — Into *Scotland*, I fay,
where the common People have no Concern in
County Elections, and not much in moft of their
Cities and Boroughs ; and therefore they fuffer
but very little from the Drunkennefs and Intemperance, the Idlenefs and Diffipation, and
other Vices, which generally prevail in Confequence of contefted Elections.

But be that as it may, enough hath furely now
been faid to prove the Inefficacy of the Remedies hitherto propofed.   And if what I have to
offer in their Room fhould be found on Examination to be equally defective, I can only fay
that thefe Defects muft be charged either on the
Nature of the Difeafe, which will not admit of
a Cure,—or on the Incapacity of the Author,
who cannot difcover one.   [For as to Care and
Attention in confidering, and reconfidering the
Subject, nothing has been wanting in that Re-
fpect]   If therefore the Difeafe is really incurable, Patience and Refignation is the only Prefcription.   But if a great Part of the Evils now
complained of, might be rectified, and others fo
far redreffed as to be of fmall Importance,—it

is

is to be hoped that fome happy Genius may yet arife, who will propofe a Plan more efficacious in itfelf, and free from thofe Difficulties, which perhaps may be objected to what I have now to offer.

HAVING premifed thus much, I would now beg Leave to obferve, that the following Points appear to me of fuch Confequence, that every Man, who would propofe any Remedy either for removing, or palliating the prefent Evils, ought to have them conftantly in View, as the Scope and End of all his Endeavours.

1ft. TRUE Policy requires, that every Part of a compact [middle-fized] State, fuch as *Great-Britain*, ought to be well cultivated, and fully fettled ;—Therefore every Scheme, Plan, or Syftem, which has a contrary Tendency, ought to be difcouraged and oppofed, as much as poffible.

2dly. TRUE Policy requires, that in the well peopling of a Country, Abundance of fingle Farm-Houfes and Cottages, numerous Country Seats, Villages, and Towns, and not a few Cities of a moderate Size are much preferable to large, unwieldy Capitals in, or near the Centre, with Waftes and Deferts, or Diftricts thinly inhabited, at or near the Extremities :—Confequently every good

good and really patriotic Scheme fhould have an Eye towards promoting the former, and checking the Encreafe of the latter, as much as the Nature of the Cafe will permit.

3*dly*. THOUGH it would be highly abfurd, to admit indifcriminately every individual Moral-Agent to be a Voter, yet true Policy requires that the Voters fhould be fo numerous, and their Qualifications refpecting Property be fo circum- ftanced, that the actual Voters could not combine againft the Non-Voters, without combining a- gainft themfelves, againft their neareft Friends, Acquaintance, and Relations.

4*thly*. GOOD Policy alfo requires, that in the Matter of electing Reprefentatives, or fending Deputies to the great Council of the Nation, the general and particular, the national and perfonal Interefts both of the Electors, and of the Elected, fhould be made to harmonize as much as poffi- ble.

LASTLY, it alfo requires, that the propofed Alterations from the prefent Syftem, fhould de- viate as little as may be, from the prefent Forms of Government, and caufe no *remarkable* Changes in the external Police, and long eftablifhed Cuf- toms of the *Englifh* Nation.

ON

On these Positions, which I hope the candid, and judicious Reader will *readily* allow, I will venture to proceed in my intended Scheme of Amendment or Improvement.

The QUALIFICATIONS *of* VOTERS.

LET me therefore previously remark, that the Qualification for voting both as Freemen, and as Freeholders, ought to be raised a little. The public Good, as well as private Happiness, calls aloud for a Reformation in this Point; and none can reasonably object to such a Measure, but those who maintain the absurd, and often confuted Notion of the unalienable Rights of each Individual to be his own Legislator, and his own Director. But, I would beg Leave to observe, that this Qualification ought to be placed in such a Mediocrity of Condition, between the two Extremes of great Riches, and of wretched Poverty, that no sober, diligent, and frugal Man could well fail of raising himself by his Industry, in *a Course of* Years to the honourable Distinction of a Voter ;—and that almost every idle, vicious, and abandoned Spendthrift would be in Danger of sinking beneath, and of being degraded from the Privilege of voting. How different from this is the Case at present !

1*st.* THEN

1ſt. THEN, the Qualification for voting as a Freeholder for the County ſhould ſtill be no more *nominally* than that of Forty Shillings a Year above all Repriſals. But in order that this Qualification might not be ſubjeﬅ to any Fraud or Colluſion, it would be neceſſary to inſiﬅ that the Voter, or intended Voter ſhould be aſſeſſed to the Taxes both of King and Poor, for no leſs a Valuation of the Premiſes, than the whole Sum of forty Shillings ;—and that he himſelf ought to be in full Poſſeſſion of them, and to have paid the Tax or Taxes ariſing from ſuch Aſſeſſments, [Reference being had to the Books of the Collectors] a full Year before he could be entitled to give his Vote. This ſingle Regulation would cut off three-fourths of the bad Votes uſually obtruded on Sheriffs at conteﬅed Eleﬅions ; — nay, it would put an End to the whole Trade of ſplitting Freeholds on ſuch Occaſions.

2dly. THOUGH all Perſons ought to be free as to the Exerciſe of any handycraft Trade, or Calling, both in Town and Country [and all Laws, and Bye-Laws to the contrary ought to be repealed] yet none but *Reſidents* in Cities and Borough Towns ought to be allowed to vote at Elections as *Freemen.* And the legal Qualification of a *Reſident,* to entitle him to be conſidered as a *voting* Freeman, ought to be the having paid *Scot* and *Lot* in ſuch Town or City in his own Perſon,

and

and for his own Property, [Reference being had to the Collectors Book] for one clear Year, preceding the Time on which he tenders his Vote. Neverthelefs all Men, free or not free, refident, or Abfentees, who have *Freeholds* within the Precincts, Liberties, or Boundaries of fuch Cities, or Borough Towns, ought likewife to be entitled to the Privilege of voting for Reprefentatives in Parliament ;—provided that their Freeholds come within the Defcription of the full Sum of forty Shillings above-mentioned :—It being very evident that the Intereft of fuch Freeholder, generally fpeaking, is more permanent, and local, than that of a mere Freeman paying *Scot* and *Lot*. Now here again, the whole Syftem of electioneering Bribes, and of Borough-Brokage, would in a Manner be annihilated by this fingle Regulation ; and the remaining Evils be fo very few in Comparifon, as hardly to deferve our Notice.—So much as to the Qualification of Voters.

The QUALIFICATION of CANDIDATES.

RESPECTING the Gentlemen to be elected Reprefentatives. their Intereft, it is prefumed, would beft be connected with that of the Public in general, and of their Conftituents in particular, by the following Arrangement.

LET

1ſt. LET the Perſon offering himſelf a Candidate for a County, cauſe to be delivered to the Sheriff, or returning Officer, ten Days at leaſt before the Commencement of the Poll, a Liſt, or Schedule of his *landed* Qualification,—Shewing, that he has *not leſs* than 1,000 Acres of Land in ſuch a Pariſh, or Pariſhes, according as the Lands may lie contiguous, or diſperſed, within the ſaid County ; on which are erected ten Dwelling Houſes *at leaſt*, which are, and which have been for 12 Months laſt paſt inhabited by ten diſtinct Families; and that he himſelf hath enjoyed the ſaid Eſtate in his own full Right, and hath been the Landlord of the ſaid Tenants for at leaſt twelve Months preceding, having paid, either by himſelf, or by them, every Kind of Tax, which hath been legally charged upon the ſame. Moreover, he ſhould be obliged to cauſe a printed Copy of the ſaid Liſt or Schedule to be affixed on the Market-Houſe, Seſſions-Houſe, Town-Hall, Church Doors, and every other public Building of, and in every Market-Town within the ſaid County :—And ſhould alſo cauſe Duplicates of the ſame to be inſerted twice, or oftener, in the Journals or News-Papers of the ſaid County, if any ſuch ſhall be publiſhed ;—if not, of ſome neighbouring County or City, the moſt read by, and circulated among the Electors.

THE

2*dly*. The Candidates for Cities, or Boroughs, fhould be obliged to deliver fimilar Lifts, or Schedules, and to give equally long Notice to their refpective returning Officers, and indeed to all the Inhabitants of fuch Cities, or Boroughs, by caufing printed Copies to be affixed on the Market-Houfes, and on every public Building whatfoever, ten Days at leaft before the Poll begins: Nor fhould the Infertion of fuch Lift or Schedules in the public Papers (as related in the former Article) ever be omitted ; in order that Freeholders at a Diftance, as well as Freemen on the Spot, may be made perfectly well acquainted with the Pretenfions, and landed Qualifications of each intended Candidate :—Only refpecting the *Quantum* of the Qualification, it may be neceffary, [in order to approach nearer to the prefent Law] that no more Acres fhould be required than 500,—and five Dwelling Houfes, occupied or inhabited by five diftinct Families. But neverthelefs, that this Qualification may be a real one, and not pretended, or a borrowed, [which alas ! is too often the Cafe at prefent] it may be neceffary to infift, that *no Part* of this landed Eftate fhould be thirty Miles diftant from the City, or Borough, for which he offers himfelf a Candidate, fo that many of the Inhabitants might be able to detect the Cheats if any fhould be attempted :— The Miles to be meafured along the King's Highway, and public Roads, and not as the

Crow

Crow flies. But it is immaterial in what County or Counties the Eſtate itſelf ſhould happen to be ſituated, the Vicinity being the main Point to be regarded.

3*dly*. THE Penalties or Forfeitures for contravening, or not duly performing any of the above Rules and Conditions, ſhould be the following.

[1*ſt*.] THOUGH it would not be right to debar the accuſed, before his Guilt is legally proved, the Liberty of ſtanding a Candidate ;—yet as ſoon as the Election was ended, and for nine Months afterwards, it might be lawful for any Perſon whatever to proſecute him in the King's-Bench for the [ſuppoſed] Breach of this intended Law ;—provided, that the Plaintiff previouſly gave Security for paying 1000l. Damages in the Caſe of a County Election, and 500l. in that of a City or Borough, to the Defendant, if he did not, according to the Verdict of a Jury, make good his Charge :—But in Caſe he did, then the Defendant ſhould forfeit the Sum of 1000l. for a County, and 500l. for a City or Borough, with treble Coſts to the Plaintiff; and the *Onus probandi*, that he was actually and *bona Fide* poſſeſſed of ſuch an Eſtate, and that he had performed all the Conditions required by this intended Law,

fhould

should rest on the Defendant, because it would always be in his Power to prove his Innocence, if he was falsely accused.

[2*dly*.] In Case the Defendant should be cast, then, if he was returned Member, his Seat should be declared vacant, *ipso facto*, and a Writ be made out for a new Election :—But he himself should be rendered incapable of standing a Candidate for that, or for any other County, or Place, for at least three Years to come.

[3*dly*.] If any Thing else can be supposed yet to be wanting towards putting a total End to the numerous Frauds and Forgeries of *unqualified* Candidates, [now, alas ! so very common] and of their Adherents, Co-adjutors, or Abettors,—It may be thus supplied :—Let every Person who can be proved to have been an Accomplice, or Assistant in making up false Accounts, or publishing the same, (knowing them to be false) respecting the Property of, or Title to the Lands, —the Quantity of Acres which they contain,— the Number of Dwelling Houses erected on them, —the Families actually inhabiting them,—the Length of Time, in which the Candidate may have been in the Possession of them in his own Right ;—I say, let every such convicted Accomplice, Agent, or Assistant, be judged by this intended Law to have incurred the same Guilt as a Principal,

Principal, and be fubject to the like Penalties, and Difqualifications in every Refpect whatever.

HAVING laid down thefe feveral Regulations for afcertaining the Qualifications both of thofe, who are to *elect,* and of the Candidates to be *elected;* it is humbly conceived, that, were they duly executed, they would prove fuch a fufficient Guard to the Freedom of Elections, and fuch a preventive Remedy againft almoft every Kind of Fraud and Impofition, that more, or greater need not be required.   Indeed, it may be queftioned, whether in the prefent State of Things, more or greater would not embarrafs the main Defign, inftead of promoting it.   Let us therefore take a View of the whole Plan, as it lies before us.—Suppofing, that it was faiily fet in Motion, and when all the Parts are co-operating with each other.

BUT in order to do this, I muft premife, that fuch an important Bill ought not to be attempted to be introduced into Parliament, at or near the Diffolution of an old one, but about the beginning of a new one. Thofe, who know any Thing of the Spirit of Electioneering, which is ready to burft forth, as a Flood, when a Parliament is drawing near the Time of its Diffolution, and of the vile Arts and Stratagems ufually practifed on
fuch

fuch Occafions, to inflame the Populace with Names, and Noife, and Nonfenfe, can eafily comprehend my Meaning.

This being premifed, I am therefore to obferve,

FIRST of all, That when fuch a regulating Bill fhall have paffed into a Law,—even the loweft of the People, and thofe, who perhaps might be deprived thereby of their prefent Privilege of voting [a Privilege alas! which is now their greateft Misfortune] would foon find, that they would be Gainers by it in Reality, inftead of Lofers ;—*Gainers*, I fay, unlefs the Removal of the Power of doing Mifchief to others, and of ruining themfelves, can be called a *Lofs*. In fact, all the great Bleffings of Society, Life, Liberty, and Property, would be as much enfured to them under this Circumftance, as to any Set of Men whatever.

NAY 2*dly*, They would alfo foon find, that the Honor or Privilege of becoming a BRITIH VOTER [it would then indeed be a *real* Honour, and a great Privilege] lay within their own Reach to obtain ;—provided they were fo much their own Friends, as to live a Life of Induftry, Sobriety, and Frugality for a few Years ;—I fay, for a *few* Years; it being almoft demonftrable that any common Day-Labourer, or common Mechanic

chanic, acting uniformly on a Plan of Induftry, and
Œconomy, might raife himfelf [unlefs particularly unfortunate] to the Degree of a Voter, before he arrived at the middle Stage of Life ;—
Yes, he might raife himfelf to it by his own good
Conduct, without applying to any one for Intereft, or ufing any Sort of Solicitations.—Now,
when the Road to public Profperity, and to private Happinefs, to external Honours, and to internal Virtue, is thus made ftraight and eafy,
without any Turnings or Labyrinths whatfoever,
—What can any People upon Earth reafonably
defire more ?

3*dly*. THOSE, who fhould feel themfelves either elevated to, or confirmed in the Rank of
VOTERS, by Means of thefe new Regulations,
would prize this Privilege fo much the more,
and contend for it with the greater Zeal, in Proportion, as they found that it would be an *honourable Diftinction*, not conferred indifcriminately, as at prefent, on the very Dregs of the
People, or the moft worthlefs of Mankind; but
beftowed on the more deferving, both as a Reward for their own exemplary Conduct, and alfo as
an Incitement held forth to others to copy after.
Men in fuch a Situation will value that Conftitution, which diftinguifhes them from others, fo
much to their Credit and Reputation, for the
fame Reafon that they love and value themfelves.

And

And the Lockian Doctrine of *unalienable Rights* will neceffarily fall to the Ground.

4*thly.* WHEN the Time of electing Reprefentatives fhall draw near, the Electors for Cities and Towns, as well as for Counties, will be tolerably well fecured by thefe new Regulations from the Solicitations of thofe bribing Mufhroom Candidates, who always mean to *fell*, having no Chance to fucceed, unlefs they *buy*. Therefore, generally fpeaking, neither the Plunderers of the *Eaft*, nor the Slave-Drivers of the *Weft*, nor the Privateering, trading Buccaneers of the *American* Continent, nor our *Englifh Newmarket* Jockeys, nor *London* Gamblers, nor *Change-Alley* Bulls and Bears, &c. &c. will be able to fhew their Heads, when fuch *terra firma* Qualifications fhall be required, before they offer themfelves as Candidates. Yet thefe landed Qualifications are fo low and moderate in themfelves, and the Time required to be in Poffeffion of them fo very reafonable, that no Man in the Neighbourhood, who has any Title to the Character of a Gentleman, would be excluded from being a Candidate, if he pleafed.

HENCE therefore 5*thly*, it is very apparent that all Candidates for Boroughs, anfwering to this Defcription, would have a real Intereft in the Welfare of the Neighbourhood of the Place

they

they intended to reprefent. A Circumftance this, in which our prefent Syftem is too often very defe&ive: For when an Adventurer of the former Stamp, (as mentioned in the 3*d.* 'Article) whofe Wealth lies in far diftant Countries, or in the Funds (if indeed it is any where) happens to be ele&ed, he has no perfonal Motive to concern himfelf at all in the Profperity of the Borough, or in the Improvement of the Eftates, fituated in its Neighbourhood. Nay, indeed it may fo happen, that his own private Intereft as a Planter, a Monopolizer, a Jobber, or Contra&or, &c. &c. may be dire&ly oppofite to the true Intereft of that Place, or Diftri&, which he reprefents in Parliament: And therefore, if he can attach to his ele&ioneering Views two, or three leading Men of the Borough, either by pecuniary Bribes, or by the Promife of Places to them, their Relations, or Dependents,—his End is anfwered, and he looks no farther;—unlefs it be to affift thefe dirty Tools to opprefs and harrafs thofe, their fellow Burgeffes, who fhould dare to oppofe them.

5*thly*. When the general and particular Intereft both of the Ele&ors, and Ele&ed, of the Conftituents, and of their Reprefentatives, are thus made to con-center, Parliament-Men become in fa&, what they are always fuppofed to be in Theory, and Speculation, both *Guardians,*
and

and *Guarantees*: Guardians of the Rights of the People, and of their own Property againſt the Encroachments or Innovations either of the Crown, or of the Ariſtocracy—if any ſhould be attempted;—and *Guarantees* to both the Crown and the Nobility, that the People ſhall not abuſe the Liberty they enjoy, by aiming at too much, ſo as to overturn the Conſtitutional Balance; which indeed would ſooner or later prove their ·own Ruin:—For a turbulent, factious Democracy is quickly, and eaſily converted into the Tyranny of a ſingle Deſpot.

It has been often ſaid by certain Writers on Politics, that Wealth and Power naturally, and even neceſſarily infer each other. In a qualified Senſe this may prove true, but not univerſally. It would be true, were none but Perſons of ſome Property in Counties, Cities, and in Borough-Towns, [that is, were *ſubſtantial* Freeholders, and all Perſons paying *Scot* and *Lot*, and not the loweſt of Mankind, though frequently a Majority as to Numbers] were thoſe, I ſay, and *none but thoſe* to elect their own Repreſentatives, and to empower them to act in their Stead. In ſuch a Caſe the Wealth of Individuals thus confederated together under proper Heads to direct and govern the whole, would become its Strength;—And Strength ſo circumſtanced would be only another Name for Wealth.—Suppoſe, therefore, that in the Viciſſitudes of human Affairs,

our

our Body Politic fhould be threatened with fuch
a violent Shock as would greatly diforder it :—
As foon as the Danger was perceived, every
Voter or Eleftor, every Freeman, and Freeholder, would immediately unite with their refpeftive Reprefentatives to guard againft the approaching Evils, and repel the Blow.   All little
Divifions and Animofities would then be forgot :
The general Solicitude would fwallow up every inferior Confideration, and unite all Parties in the
common Caufe.   Suppofe again, that thro' Want
of Attention in fome, and from a much worfe
Caufe in others, the Blow was aftually given,
and that the Wound was almoft mortal ;—yet
even then, as long as Life remained, and any
Hopes were left, the whole Mafs of the [voting]
People, as well as their Reprefentatives, would
ftruggle hard to get the better of this dangerous
Convulfion, and to reftore the Body-Politic to
its antient Vigour.   Thefe Efforts they would
certainly make, becaufe they would then direftly
feel, that the Lofs of fuch a Conftitution as ours,
would be their own Lofs, and that they themfelves could never be of fo much Importance,
either in their private, or their public Capacity,
under any other Form of Government, as they
are under the prefent.

HERE therefore, it may be highly neceffary
to obferve, that the democratical Branch of our
Conftitution,

Conftitution has more to fear from its own internal Tendency, than from any external Caufe whatever.—I have, I hope, already proved, that neither the Crown nor the Peerage, according to the prefent State of Things, could either attack or undermine the Liberties of the People, with any Profpeft of Succefs. We may therefore confider ourfelves as fafe on that Side. But I own, I am not without Apprehenfions, that the People themfelves are ftrongly inclined to do thofe Things, which would in the Event prove a *Felo de fe.* Too many among them are always difpofed to think, that becaufe Liberty is a good Thing, *therefore they can never have too much of that good Thing.*—This fatal Miftake has been the Ruin of every free Government, both in antient, and modern Times; and will, if perfifted in, prove the Ruin of ours. The new Regulations here propofed, bid the faireft of any that I know of [confiftently I mean, with the Spirit of our Conftitution, and a due Regard to *real* Liberty] to check that ftrange Propenfity fo obfervable in our common People towards *Levelling,* and *Licentioufnefs,* and to give their Minds a better and more reafonable Turn. It is indeed a melancholy Refleftion, that in moft Cities, and Borough-Towns, and perhaps in Counties, the far greater Number of Voters are fuch, whofe Circumftances lead them to wifh for a new Divifion of Property, becaufe they have

little,

little, or nothing to lofe, but may have much to get in Times of Confufion, and by a general Scramble. Therefore every Rule of found Policy, not to fay Religion and Morality, fuggefts the Neceffity of raifing the Qualification of voting to fuch a Mediocrity of Condition, as would make it the Intereft of the Majority of Electors, to affift in the Support and Prefervation of Order and good Government, and not to wifh their Overthrow.

7*thly* and *laftly*. THE new Regulations here propofed, if carried into Execution, would caufe every Part of the Kingdom, the Extremities, and intermediate Places, [as well as the Centre, or Seat of Government] to be better reprefented than they are at prefent. The Complaint ufually brought againft *Cornwall* and *Wiltfhire*, is, that they return too many Members in Proportion to the reft of the Kingdom : Whereas thefe Counties might juftly retort the Accufation, by faying, that though they have *nominally* more Members than *London*, *Weftminfter*, and *Southwark*, yet in *Reality* they have fewer. For moft of the Members for the *Cornifh* and *Wiltfhire* Boroughs have their chief Refidence in the Metropolis, with Country-Seats perhaps in its Environs :—None of which Villas, generally fpeaking, are at a greater Diftance than 20 or 30 Miles from it :—And what is ftill worfe, moft of fuch Members have

not

not a Foot of Land *in*, or any where *near* the Places for which they were elected : So that having no perfonal Intereft in the Premifes, they might with much greater Propriety, be ftiled the Reprefentatives of *London*, *Weftminfter*, and *Southwark*, and of the feveral Diftricts in that Neighbourhood [where their Eftates and Fortunes are fuppofed to be] than the Reprefentatives of the Boroughs in *Wiltfhire* and *Cornwall*, where they have no Property at all.

When Men are determined to fupport a favourite Hypothefis, it is curious to obferve, what Pains they take, to make every Thing, however difcordant in its Nature, to bend and ply towards their beloved Syftem. The Boroughs of the two Counties juft mentioned return more Members to Parliament than any others : This is a Fact which cannot be denied. But how is it to be accounted for ? — The Difciples of Mr. LOCKE, who maintain, that all Perfons have an unalienable Right to choofe their own Legiflators, Governors, and Directors, gravely tell us, that thefe Boroughs, now fallen into Decay, were once very large, and extremely populous, and the Seats of various extenfive Manufactures :— And then the fhort Inference is, that as the Trade is gone, and the Inhabitants become very few, the Right of fending Members to Parliament ought to be transferred to more populous and flourifhing flourishing Towns. [*Birmingham, Manchester, Leeds, Halifax, Stroud, Bradford, Trowbridge,* and many such like Places, would not think themselves at all obliged to the Author of such a Proposal, and would certainly remonstrate strongly against it] But waving the Matter, let us, if we can, trace the real Origin of this Difference between the State of Representation of the Boroughs in the two Counties of *Wilts* and *Cornwall,* if compared with those of other Counties. * *Wiltshire* was long the Residence of the Kings of the *West-Saxons,* who in Process of Time conquered all the rest. Now where the Royal Residence was, there of Course would be the chief Domain: For the stated Revenue of our antient Princes, both *Saxon* and *Norman,* consisted chiefly in Landed Estates, that is, in

Castles,

---

* *Somersetshire* was originally much under the same Predicament with *Wiltshire,* being a Western County, where the Kings of the *West Saxons* had great Demesnes. WILLIAM the Conqueror gave large Possessions in this County to some of his Favourites, and Followers, and particularly to WILLIAM MALET, to whom he granted several Towns, which were called after the Name of MALET, such as *Shipton-Malet, Curry-Malet,* &c. The other Towns and Villages in Demesne, namely, *Axbridge, Charde, Dunster, Langport, Monterate, Stoke-Curry, Watchet,* and *Were,* sent their Deputies to Parliament in very early Times: But in Proportion, as these Estates were aliened from the Crown, or as the Inhabitants could get themselves excused from that heavy Burden and Expence, they do not no longer. The same Observation will extend to several

Towns

Caftles, with their Territories, Manors and Honours, and Towns and Villages, held by various Services, fome of them military or noble, and others bafe and fervile. *Cornwall* was in like Manner, and for the fame Ends and Purpofes the Domains of the Earls and Dukes of *Cornwall.* Hence therefore it naturally followed, that as the great Tenants of the Crown were obliged to attend *in Perfon* at the Courts of their Sovereign [thereby conftituting an Houfe of Peers] fo the fmaller Tenants, and inferior Vaffals, were to do the fame by Deputation; which Circumftance gave the firft Idea of an Houfe of Commons. Indeed there was a ftronger Reafon for the Attendance of the Deputies from thofe Towns and Villages, which belonged to the Crown, *if their Poverty did not prevent them;—*

Towns and Villages in *Devonfhire* [and to fome Places in other Counties] fuch as *Lidford, Bradnick, Crediton, Fremington, Modbury, South-Moulton,* and *Torrington;--* all which returned Members during the Reigns of one or more of the three firft EDWARDS;---but not afterwards. Dr. BRADY's Rule for diftinguifhing Towns of antient Demefne from thofe which were not, is here worth inferting, " That wherever the Mayor, " Bailiffs, or Burgeffes are chofen by a Jury in a Court-Baron, " or at the Leet; or what the Return of Parliament Members " have been, or are now made, by the Lord or Lady of the " Manor, or their Steward, fuch Towns are Towns in an- " tient Demefne."——For a further Confirmation of thefe Points, fee SQUIRE's *Enquiry into the Foundation of the* Englifh *Conftitution, &c.* Dedicated to the Duke of NEWCASTLE. London, 1753.

f

I fay, there was a ftronger Reafon for their Attendance in fome Refpeects, than for that of
others;—becaufethe Quantum of thofe Acknow-
ments, Services, and Quit-Rents, which they
were to pay to their great Landlord, the Crown,
as well as their Free-Gifts and Benevolences, if
they are difpofed to make any, were to be fixed
and apportioned at fuch Meeting. Moreover,
when the Duchy of *Cornwall* efcheated to the
King, the Tenants, and Borough-Towns, and
Villages of the Duke became a Part of the
Royal Patrimony ; in confequence of which,
they were obliged to do the fame Suits and Services at the King's Courts, which they had done
before to their ducal Mafters, or great feudal
Lords. I own indeed, that feveral of the
Cornifh Boroughs were not *chartered* to fend
Members to the General Parliament of the
Realm 'till the Reign of King JAMES I.—But
neverthelefs they were fuch Places as were fuppofed to have fent Deputies to the Courts of the
Earls, or Dukes of *Cornwall*, and therefore were
confidered as having a Kind of *equitable* Right to
fend Members to the General Council of the Nation, now that their own particular Courts were
fuppreffed, or rather fwallowed up. Therefore,
to return :——

SURELY there is nothing forced, or unnatural
in this Account of the Matter ;—nothing, but
wha .

what is perfectly analagous to the Cuſtoms and Manners of antient Times, and correſpondent to the Genius of the Gothic Syſtem. Why therefore ſhould we have Recourſe to an imaginary Hypotheſis of the great Commerce, great Population, and extenſive Manufactures of theſe two ſingle Counties of *Wilts* and *Cornwall*, to the Prejudice of all the reſt of *England*, without any Foundation in Hiſtory for ſuch a Suppoſition :—Why indeed, when it is farther conſidered, that ſuch an Hypotheſis can anſwer no other End, than to confirm, by forged Accounts, that falſe Notion of every Man having an unalienable Right to be ſelf-governed ;—a Notion which was not ſo much as dreamed of in thoſe Times?

THERE is but one Objection, as far as I can perceive, which can be made to the Account here given of the Reaſon, why a greater Number of Members are ſent by the *Wiltſhire* and *Corniſh* Boroughs, than by the Towns and Villages of other Counties :—And that is this ; " Were the " Caſe as here ſtated, it would be natural to ex- " pect from the Analogy of the Thing, that the " Dutchy of *Lancaſter*, now united to the Crown, " would have furniſhed Examples ſimilar to thoſe " of the Dutchy of *Cornwall* : -- But it doth not." —— This Objection, it muſt be owned, looks plauſible at firſt Sight :—But the whole Force of

it

it is built on a Miftake.—The Dutchy of *Lancafter* is, and ever was a fcattered Thing, compofed out of the forfeited Eftates of four great Barons, befides other Acceffions, which lay difperfed in almoft every County both of *England* and of *Wales*. It was therefore impoffible, that the fame Phœnomenon could have occurred in the one Cafe, as in the other. Had indeed thofe forfeited Eftates been fituated altogether in *Lancafhire*, or in any one fingle County, there is hardly a Doubt to be made, but that the fame, or nearly the fame Circumftance would have taken Place, on the Union of that Dutchy with the Crown.—And if it had, what ill Confequences would have enfued,—fuppofing, I mean, that the Regulations here propofed, had been adopted, as a Part of the Syftem?——For my Part, I can fee none:—Nay, I will not fcruple to declare, that it would be a much more rational Plan, that the Deputies from *Cornwall*, or *Weftmoreland*, *Cumberland*, or *Northumberland*,——or, if you pleafe, from *Sutherland* and *Caithnefs*, (now thefe Kingdoms are united) fhould out-number thofe of *London*, *Weftminfter*, *Southwark*, and the adjacent Parts, than that thefe latter fhould be more numerous than the former:——Becaufe the Centre and the Refidence of the Legifla-

tive,

tive, and executive Powers;——or in one Word, the Metropolis will never fail to take Care of itself:—Not fo, *vice verfa*.

PART

PART III.

Divers Collateral Circumstances

CORROBORATING

THE FOREGOING SYSTEM,

AND

CONFUTING THE LOCKIAN

C H A P. I.

The general Nature of the Gothic Conftitution defcri-
bed, which the barbarous Nations introduced and
fettled in every Part of Europe, and particularly
in England.—Various antiquated Cuftoms and
Laws explained relative thereto.—Thefe Laws
either not underftood, or wilfully mifreprefented
by our modern Lockians.

THOUGH I have in the preceding Work
endeavoured to illuftrate feveral antient
Laws and Cuftoms, the Knowledge of which are
totally unknown to the Generality of News-Paper
Politicians;—yet I find myfelf under a Kind of
Neceffity of giving a ftill more general Sketch
of the Out-lines, of our former *Gothic* Conftitution, in order to guard againft the Mifreprefen-
tations of certain late Publications, circulated and
difperfed with incredible Induftry;—whofe Authors muft have had an uncommon Share either of
Ignorance or of Difingenuity, intending only to
give the Out-lines of the *Gothic* Syftem, which

once

once univerſally prevailed. I will endeavour to be as brief, as the Nature of the Subjeƈt will permit.

SETTING aſide the Clergy, whoſe Office and Charaƈter created them a diſtinƈt Conſideration, there were but three *general* Claſſes of Men in this, and in every other Kingdom in Europe ;— The Villains,—the Tradeſmen,—and the Gentlemen.

1. The V I L L A I N S.

THE Villains were the loweſt Claſs, but they were by far the moſt numerous : For there was hardly any Kind of laborious, or ſervile Work in all Branches of Huſbandry performed by any other Claſs of Men. Neverthelefs, they too had their Gradation of Servitude. For ſome of them were Villains in groſs, other Villains regardant Manors [not to mention the Bordarii, Cottarii, &c. &c.] and the Reſt were Copy-holders ;—of which latter alſo there were various Kinds, and different Degrees.

THE Villains in groſs ſeem to have been on the ſame Footing with the Negro Slaves at preſent in the *Weſt-Indies*. And as one of the chief Articles of Export from *England* to other Countries,

tries, [even to *Ireland.*] during the Times of the
Anglo-Saxons, was this horrid Trade of felling
their Fellow-Creatures,—it is probable that fuch
Slaves were Villains in grofs.

The next Species were Villains regardant, or
appendant to Manors. Being attached to the
Soil [*Glebae afcriptitii.*] They could not *regularly*
be feparated from it, without their own Confent:
Confequently they paffed with the Manor from
Lord to Lord, as often as the Land changed its
Mafter or Proprietor by Purchafe, Donation,
Devife, or Defcent. However, Slaves they
were in every Senfe : For their Lords and Mafters might ufe their own Difcretion in impofing
upon them, what Burdens or Tafks they pleafed;
and might punifh them alfo very feverely, without being accountable to any one ;—provided
they did not maim or kill them. Moreover thefe
poor Wretches were not capable of acquiring any
Property for themfelves ; for all theirs were their
Mafters.

THE Severity of this Bondage became milder
in Procefs of Time, by the Inftitution of Copy-
hold Tenures. The Villains of this Denomination were comparatively happy; becaufe they had
certain Portions of Land affigned them, which
in fome Refpects they might call their own, provided they performed the Conditions annexed
thereto. Thefe Services were at firft fo much
manual

manual Labour, or fo many Days' Work, according as their Lord fhould appoint : Alfo the Copyholders were generally obliged to furnifh him with certain Quantities of Provifions of different Kind, of Corn, Cattle, Poultry, Meal for his Dogs, &c. &c. &c. Moreover there were often added to thefe Services, various other Stipulations, fome of them not amifs, and others very ridiculous and abfurd, to fay no worfe. But all, or moft of them, as they took their Rife from the mere Will and Pleafure, or *Caprice* of the firft Granter, became afterwards a Kind of Law to both Parties, that is, both to the Lord, and his Vaffal ; and were therefore called the Cuftoms of the Manor, and held to be facred for a long Seafon. However as the feudal Syftem was evidently more the Work of prefent Neceffity, than of cool and provident Deliberation, thefe Tenures were foftened by little, and little, into more liberal Holdings, according as the Times became more peaceable and fettled, The Services were often changed into annual Quit-Rents, and the Herriots, Efcheats, Forfeitures, Admittances, and Reliefs, were turned into Fines certain, and fixed Sums of Money. Moreover, feveral of thefe Holdings were made perpetual, according to the Cuftom of the Manor : And the Nature or Condition of moft of the Reft was fo changed, as to differ little from Lands held in Soccage. Indeed Soccage itfelf was a bafe, or fervile Tenure : For
whatever

whatever was not military, was bafe, according to the Ideas which then prevailed. The worft Part of this Inftitution, and what drew after it real Tyranny on the one Side, and Slavery on the other, was, that the Copy-holder feemed to be without a Remedy, in Cafe he was oppreffed by his Lord : For he had no other Jurifdiction, at leaft in the firft Inftance, and in Civil Caufes, to appeal to, but the Court Leet, or Court Baron of that very Man, his Steward, Bailiff, &c. who was his Oppreffor. Happily at prefent all thefe Evils are effectually removed : And indeed the Inftitution itfelf, as far as it carries an Idea of Slavery, is vanifhing away. For, as no new Copy-holds can now be erected, and as there are fo many Ways of turning the old ones into different Holdings [which are putting in Practice every Day] it is probable, that this Kind of Tenure will be extinct. [The whole Manor of *Taunton-Dean* in *Somerfetfhire*, containing fo many Thoufands of Inhabitants, is Copy-hold of Inheritance under the Bifhop of *Winchefter*, and might be turned into diftinct Freeholds for a trifling Confideration.] The feveral Tenures of bafe Condition [including Borderers, and Cotters, alfo Copy-hold and Soccage] were once fo numerous, as to fuftain a far greater Number of Inhabitants, than the noble, or military ;—and the Peafantry and Yeomanry of this Kingdom, and perhaps feveral other Orders

of

of Men, who now figure away in high Life, can trace their Pedigree from no other Origin, than that of Villainage, in one or other of its Branches.—Be it also remembered, that Villains of any Sort, were never confidered as CITIZENS at large, or as Members of the State,—but rather as Goods and Chattels of a fuperior Kind. belonging to their refpective Owners or Proprietors. Nay, Magna Charta itfelf confidered thefe human Beings in no better Light than as fo many Head of Cattle, or other live Stock, upon an Eftate; ordaining [fee Article the 5*th*.] That, whilft the Eftate of a Minor was in Wardfhip, the Guardian fhould make *no Deftruction or Wafte of the Men, or Things* belonging to it. Such were the Ideas of Humanity, and its Rights, which then prevailed. In fhort, Slaves of any Sort were never allowed to vote. They were not reprefented in Parliament, and they had no Share in the Legiflature. Therefore,—Whether Parliaments were to be held annually, or not,—and what was to be the Qualification either of a Freeholder, or of a Freeman, in order to entitle him to vote; was a Queftion in which they were not concerned; nor was it of any Confequence to them how thefe Matters were to be determined.—In one Word, the Majority of the Nation, as to Numbers, were not *Electori ab Initio.* This is FACT.

UNDER

UNDER the prefent Head the following Obfervations may be ranged, as they tend to throw a general Light on the Subject;—namely, That formerly almoft every Lord of a Manor had three Sorts of Lands within the Boundaries of his Lordfhip. The firft Sort was for his own peculiar Ufe, that is, for the Support of himfelf and Family, and for the keeping of what was then called great Hofpitality. This Lot of Land was generally large and extenfive, lying compact, and convenient round his Caftle, or Court-Houfe, and not interfected by, or intermixed with the Property of others. The fecond Sort was for his military Tenants, or Freeholders, who were to pay him annually fome fmall Acknowledgment in Money, or perhaps none at all, the Eftate being only fubject to Reliefs, Wardfhips, Heriots, the furnifhing of fo many Pieces of Armour, warlike Stores, and the like. But all thefe Tenants were to do Suit and Service at the Court of his Manor-Houfe, according to their refpective Holdings; which Attendance was then equivalent, or nearly equivalent to what the calling over the Mufter-Roll of Soldiers is at prefent.— But it is remarkable, that the Eftates granted to thefe Warriors, or fecond rate Gentlemen, were not only of lefs Extent than the former (which is natural enough to fuppofe) but alfo greatly interfperfed and intermixed with the Eftates of other Tenants; fo that (excepting the mere

Homefteads,

Homesteads, or Lands surrounding the Mansion-
Houses) the chief Part lay confusedly disperfed
in Common Fields, and Common Meadows.
—However these were not scattered in any Degree fo much as the last Clafs to be mentioned and
the moft numerous, viz: The Estates of Copy-
holders; for these Men had hardly five Acres
lying together; on the contrary an Holding of
40, or 50 Acres might be found to be divided
into Bits and Scraps, called Langlets, Head-
lands, Gores, Rudges, Lands, &c. &c. perhaps
to the Number of Fourscore, or an Hundred
Pieces.—It is difficult to discover what could
have been the Policy of fuch a Contrivance:
—For that a *Contrivance* it was, [and not what
happened by mere Chance or Accident] is evident beyond Difpute: The very Univerfality of
it, were there no other Proof, being fufficient to
shew, that fome End or other was intended to be
answered by it.—I acknowledge myfelf at
a Lofs to guefs what that End could be;
—unlefs it was to keep both Sorts of Tenants the
more dependant on their original Lords, by
Means of thofe frequent Appeals, which muft
be made to his Courts, in order to fettle the Difputes, which fuch an Intermixture of Property,
and mutual Encroachments, (fome perhaps voluntary, and others involuntary) would necessa-
rily create.—Such a Motive as this for the Inftitution was certainly a very bad one;—and yet
bad

bad as it was, it is hard to affign a better.—[If it was to increafe the Fees and Profits of the Court for the Benefit of the Steward, or Court-Keeper, that was certainly a worfe.] Be that as it may, Fact it is, that it has coft this Nation already many Scores of Acts of Parliament, and almoft as many Thoufands of Pounds to undo thofe Mifchiefs which have fprung from this Intermixture of Property, the Confufion of Interefts, and the Difcord of Inclinations of different Landholders.

ARTIFICERS and TRADESMEN,

The Second Class.

As no Trade was honourable among barbarous Nations but the Trade of War, it is therefore highly improbable, that a Gentleman-Soldier fhould fo far degrade himfelf, as to take to any other Employment, than that of the Sword. Neverthelefs there was a Neceffity that other Trades, befides that of deftroying Mankind, fhould fubfift even in Times of the greateft Simplicity. Villains of different Kinds were to furnifh the Warrior with Victuals :—But how was he to be fupplied with *Raiment*, and *Dwelling*? and who was to ferve him with all the Articles whatever of Profit, or of Pleafure, of Ufe, or of Oftentation

belonging

belonging to Cloathing and Habitation? Things thefe, which require many Hands, and infinitely more Skill and Judgment, and much larger Capitals, than are neceffary for the bare Preparation of coarfe Food.—To get over thefe Difficulties, both the Prince and his great Lords condefcended to invite as many Tradefmen and Artizans as they could colleĉt, or as they thought neceffary, to fettle in fome commodious Spot on their principal Domains, near their Caftles and Places of Refidence, under their own immediate Patronage and Proteĉtion.—And for their greater Security and Encouragement, they granted them Charters, which were originally defigned to anfwer much the fame Ends to Artificers in Towns as Copies of Court Rolls were to thofe poor Dependants, who were called Villains in the Country.—For as the leffer-Lords of Manors did not chufe that any fhould tyrannize over their own Vaffals but themfelves; fo likewife the Magnates, the *Proceres Regni*, and the Sovereign, took efpecial Care to guard their Traders and Mechanics from any Infults but their own. At firft thefe Charters of Proteĉtion were very fparingly granted, and contained little more than general Promifes of Favor and Good Will.—During this Period, thefe Colleĉtions, or little Nefts of Pedlars and Artificers, were not confidered as Members of the State; for they had no Reprefentatives in the natiohal Councils; and of courfe had no Share in the Legiflature. On the contrary, they were regarded as the private Property of their refpective Patrons and Protectors, the King, and the great Barons, who were to anfwer to the Public for their good Conduct and Behaviour. But a Circumftance arofe, which gave them much greater Weight and Importance in the Community, than otherwife they would have acquired, perhaps for Ages.—This remarkable Revolution in their Favour came to pafs in the following Manner: When there were no more Countries in Europe for the Northern Barbarians and Freebooters to fubdue, thefe Heroes by Profeffion would have been greatly at a Lofs, how to have employed their Time, had not a certain enthufiaftic Monk, whofe Name I think, was PETER, hit on an Expedient to employ vaft Numbers of them, in the military Line, and affuring them at the fame Time, that the more Throats they cut, the greater would be their Reward in Heaven. The Scheme propofed was to undertake Pilgrimages to *Jerufalem*, and to fight for the Recovery of the *Holy Land*, out of the Hands of the Infidels. Joyful News indeed! For no fooner had this Fanatic announced his Commiffion, and got the Pope and fome Councils to ratify the Promifes of eternal Happinefs, than the whole Hoft of *idle Warriors* throughout moft Parts of *Europe* were feized with an epidemical Madnefs to engage

in

in this Holy War [The Cause of God, as it was called]; and to purchafe Heaven on fuch foldier-like Terms. So great was their Phrenfy, that they never reflected that in paffing from *Europe* to *Palestine* they would be under a Neceffity of laying in great Quantities of Provivifions, Hay, Straw, &c. in order to form Magazines, and of ftoring up Medicines for the Ufe of Hofpitals, to accommodate not only the Troops of *God, but alfo the prodigious Numbers of other Pilgrims [among whom were Swarms of Females of Quality] during fo long a March, or fo long a Voyage. But furious and frantic, they rufhed headlong on the Expedition, expecting to be fed and cured by Miracles. The firft Hoft of thefe pious Mad-Men and Women miferably perifhed, fome few excepted, who brought home with them that loathfome Difeafe called the *Leprofy*, and likewife the Knowledge and Experience, that long Marches and long Voyages require many other Things befides enthufiaftic Zeal, and brutal Courage.

Therefore whilft the blood-thirfty Zealots, the Monks, were preaching up a Revival of the Crufade, with Croffes in their Hands, the

---

* Gestae Dei apud Francos was the Title of a famous Treatife recording the Exploits of thofe holy Murderers, the *Croifes.*

fecond

fecond, and third, and fourth Swarms were col-
lecting together, various Ways and Means were
fuggefted towards raifing Money for defraying
the enormous Expence of thefe frantic Expeditions. Among other Expedients, it was conceived, that the emancipating thofe little Societies of Tradefmen, who were fettled in different
Parts of the Kingdom, and empowering them to
elect their own Magiftrates, and to make Bye-
Laws for their own internal Government; alfo
exempting them from all arbitrary Impofitions,
Tolls, or Taxes, would bring good Sums of
Money to the King, and to the great Lords,
on whofe Eftates they were fettled,—at the fame
Time, that the Meafure itfelf would be highly
acceptable to the Purchafers of fuch Charters.
Therefore it is not improbable, but that WIL-
LIAM II. HENRY I. STEPHEN, and HENRY II.
availed themfelves, as did likewife fome of the
greater Barons, of this Mode, this very *popular*
Mode of raifing Money. But above all, our
glorious RICHARD I. [that Lion-hearted Man,
Cœur de Lion, who went in Perfon to the Holy
War, and who had great Need of this Kind of
Merit, to atone for the Want of almoft every
moral Virtue.] I fay, it is not to be doubted,
but that RICHARD I. fold as many Charters as
he could find Purchafers. Which Example was
moft probably followed by JOHN, by HENRY III.
and the three firft EDWARDS. [Indeed Charters
of

of Exemption were to be had in fuch Plenty on
all Occafions, in thofe Times, that even private
Perfons ufed to purchafe them to be freed from
being *impannelled in Affizes' Juries, and Inquefts:*
[See 52d of HENRY III. Chap. 14.] Nay, I
believe, it would be found on Examination, that
almoft all the old Charters to Cities, or Towns-
Corporate, were granted during the Phrenfy of
the feveral Crufades, which lafted from the Time
of WILLIAM II. to EDWARD III. or thereabouts, that is, during the Space of upwards of
200 Years! Aftonifhing Infatuation! and utterly incredible—had we not Inftances of as great,
or even greater national Infanity in our own
Times, in fighting for Countries ftill farther off,
and of much lefs intrinfic Value than *Palefline* or
Syria,—yet who knows, but that Providence may
in this, as in the former Cafe, bring much Good
out of Evil?—But to return.   Certain it is,
that in the Reign of EDWARD I. not a few of
thefe trading Places were grown up into fo much
Confequence, as to be thought worthy to be fummoned to fend Reprefentatives to Parliament:
Which Summons, as far as appears, was the *firft*
they ever had; for there are no * Records extant

---

* The Authority I make Ufe of, on this Occafion, is the
Appendix, No. 2, to the Enquiry into the Foundation of the
Conftitution above mentioned.   The Title of the Appendix is,
An Accounts of all the Cities, Towns, and Boroughs in
England

tant of their fending Reprefentatives before the 23d of EDWARD I.—or even of their being required to fend them.

HOWEVER thefe newly-erected Corporations were fo far from efteeming the being obliged to fend Deputies to Parliament as an Honour conferred upon them, that the Generality confidered it as a fore Burden, from which they wifhed moft heartily to be releafed. So little had the Idea of *unalienable Rights* prevailed in thofe Days! Nay, feveral Boroughs, after having once obeyed the Sheriff's Precept, defifted from making Returns for a long Time afterwards, till they were *compelled* to do it by the 5th of RICHARD II. Stat. 2d. C. 4. [The Claufe refpecting the Returns made, or to be made by the Sheriffs, is fo much in Point to the Cafe here before us, that it would be almoft unpardonable to omit it, viz. " And if any Sheriff of " the Realm be from henceforth negligent in " making his Returns of Writs of the Parlia- " ment; or that he *leave out of the faid Returns* " *any Cities or Boroughs, which be bound,* and

---

England and *Wales*, which have been ever fummoned to fend Members to Parliament, with the Date of their firft Returns : Extracted chiefly from the three Vols. of Dr. BROWN WILLIS's *Notitia Parliamentaria.*---Many Vouchers from BRADY and MADOX are likewife produced in the Notes annexed.

" of

" of old Time were wont to come to the Par-
" liament, he fhall be amerced, &c." Be it likewife remembered, that there are Inftances of
fome Boroughs being fummoned, and of ap-
pearing at firft, which neverthelefs got themfelves releafed afterwards; which Releafes or
Exemptions remain valid to this Day; by what
Authority, or on what Ground this was done
after paffing the above Act of Compulfion, is not
my Bufinefs to enquire. Nay more, when the
two famous Acts were made in the Reign of
EDWARD III. for requiring that Parliaments
fhould be held once a Year, or more often, if
need be, they [the Boroughs] fhewed plainly
by their Actions, what were their Sentiments
concerning this Privilege; for, according to
the Account given in the Appendix juft mentioned, not one of thofe, which had omitted or
neglected to make Returns during the two former Reigns, embraced the Opportunity of re-
covering their unalienable Rights, by complying
with the Laws lately made for annual Parliaments;—On the contrary, and —(what is ftill
more extraordinary) fome other Boroughs, which
had not omitted to make Returns before, chofe
to be refractory or negligent on the Occafion, till
they were compelled.—So that, it is evident,
that the Laws, which required even *annual*
Meetings of Parliaments [without faying a Word
about annual Elections of Citizens or Burgeffes

to

to be prefent at fuch parliamentary Meetings]
were unpopular at the Time to one Part of the
Community, tho' perhaps very popular to
another. They were generally unpopular to
Tradefmen, Shopkeepers, and Artificers, becaufe fuch frequent Meetings put their Corporations to an Expence which many of them
could ill bear, and becaufe alfo they detained
fome of the principal Inhabitants, chofen to reprefent the reft, from their proper Trades and
Bufinefs,—by obliging them to attend on Affemblies, where they had but fmall Influence, and
lefs Refpect. For not only the great Barons be-
held them with Difdain, and treated them with
Contempt, but alfo the *Reprefentatives of the
leffer

* The Stile of Parliament as low down as the Reign of ED-
WARD III. plainly proves, that there was a Diftinction then
exifting in Point of Dignity and Honour, between the Knights
of Shires and the mere Citizens and Burgeffes chofen to reprefent their refpective trading Societies. Statutes made at Weftminfter Anno 10. EDWARD III. Stat. 1. Anno Dom. 1336.
Becaufe our Lord the King, EDWARD III. after the Conqueft
(which fovereignly defireth the Maintenance of his Peace, and
Safeguard of his People) hath perceived as the *Complaint* of the
Prelates, Earls, Lords, Barons,—and alfo as the *fhewing* of
the Knights of the Shires,—and his Commons, &c.—hath ordained and eftablifhed by the *Affent* of the faid Prelates, Earls,
Barons, and other Nobles of his Realm,---and at the Requeft
of the faid Knights and Commons, &c. &c----By the Words
of this Preamble, it is evident to a Demonftration, that the
Reprefentatives of the leffer Barons [the Freeholders of Coun-
ties] were of a fuperior Rank, and not to be confounded, as
they

leffer Barons, (the Knights of Shires) looked on them as an Order of Men much inferior to themfelves. Hence it came to pafs, that the Deputies from Towns and Boroughs were very often in great Hafte to depart, and to retire to their refpective Homes, whilft the Barons and Knights of Shires wifhed to ftay longer, and complete the Schemes they had in Contemplation. The Fact was, to fpeak the Truth at once, the *landed* Intereft, as it was *then erroneoufly* underftood, was fuppofed to be directly oppofite to the *trading* Intereft of the Kingdom. For the perfonal and immediate Intereft of the Barons, great and fmall, was to preferve their own Importance in the State, and their Authority and Jurifdiction over their Vaffals and Dependents, in Contradiftinction to the regal Power. Whereas Shopkeepers, Traders, and Mechanics, could have had no fuch Views. Therefore the former were always defirous of having frequent Meetings of Parliament, in order to confult and affociate together againft the Crown, whom they

---

they are now, in the fame Clafs with the Reprefentatives of Cities and Boroughs. Before the Admiffion of Citizens and Burgeffes, the greater Barons, and the Deputies from the leffer, fat in the fame Room.----But the Deputies from the trading Places never did. In fhort, the one were Knights Milites, Soldiers, or Gentlemen,---the others more Commoners, that is, common People, Tradefmen, or Mechanics; who were only one Step above the Villains or Slaves.

regarded

regarded as their common Enemy: [Magna
Charta itfelf was owing to this very Principle.]
Whereas the latter, the Corporate-Towns and
Boroughs, which had Reafon to efteem the
Crown more their Protector than their Oppreffor, had no fuch Motives, either offenfive or
defenfive, for affociating together. In one
Word, the Crown, and the Law-Courts of the
Crown, were then the only Security and Defence
which trading Corporations could have had a-
gainft the Power and Infults of the feudal
Baronage.—The great Barons having attempted
feveral Times to bring almoft all Caufes into
their own Courts, to be judged by themfelves,
or by Deputies, Stewards, Bailiffs, &c. &c.

To confirm what I have here advanced, I will
relate two very curious Facts. The firft is, that
though the Towns and Boroughs had gained their
Liberty, and were no longer in a State of Slavery
either to King or Barons,—yet they ftill retained
fuch a Jealoufy of the encroaching Nature of the
feudal Syftem, and fuch a Dread of being
brought again into Bondage, that many of them
caufed every new Member of their Body, when
he took up his Freedom, to promife upon Oath,
that he would not take one who was *bound in
Blood*, to be is Apprentice. This Claufe is continued in the Oath of a Freeman of *Briftol* to
this Day, and I think was formerly in that of
London,

London, and of feveral other Places: Though moft undoubtedly not one in a Thoufand know its antient Meaning, or to what it referred. The Cafe, of which they are at prefent fo happily ignorant, I will endeavour to explain, becaufe it throws great Light on the Subject now before us.   When the trading Towns, and efpecially the Metropolis, were grown into fuch Importance as to afford fome Sort of Shelter to thofe miferable and diftreffed Objects, who were in a State of Slavery, many of them [Male and Female, Villains and Neifs] fled to thefe Places, as to an Afylum, to be protected from the Tyranny of their cruel Mafters.   When there, they entered into the Service of fuch Perfons as would employ them, in order to get a Livelihood.   And it is very probable that they offered to work or ferve on lower Terms than others.   In fhort, the Towns found their Account in this Affair; and therefore efpoufed the Caufe of fuch Refugees, as far as they dared,—by granting them the Privileges of defending themfelves in the Law Courts of thefe local Jurifdictions.—In thefe Courts they alledged, when claimed by their Lords, that they were the Servants or Apprentices of fuch, or fuch Citizens, or Burgeffes, and therefore owed no Submiffion or Subjection to any others.   This Plea, it muft be owned, was not ftrictly juftifiable, being little better than a pre-

varicatory

varicatory Subterfuge. However, as the Tradefmen were willing that thefe Fugitives fhould urge
it againft their former Mafters, – the Barons and
great Men got two remarkable Laws to pafs,
which enabled them to purfue their Slaves, and
to feize and take them, as well within the Liberties of Cities and Towns, as without. The firft
was made the 25th of EDWARD III. Stat. 4.
Chap. 18. and the other, which is ftill more exprefs, the 9th of RICHARD II. Chap. 2. The
Words of this latter Act are the following,

    " Whereas divers Villains and Neiffs, as
" well of great Lords, as of other People, as
" well fpiritual as temporal, do fly within Cities,
" Towns, and Places *enfranchifed*, as the City of
" *London*, and other like, and feign divers Suits
" againft their Lords, to the Intent to make them
" free by the Anfwer of their Lords : It is ac-
" corded and affented, that the Lords, nor other,
" fhall not be forebarred of their Villains, be-
" caufe of their Anfwer in the Law." Had the
Cities and Towns perfifted in their Defigns of
protecting the Fugitives, it is eafy to conceive,
that this Affair would have embroiled them with
every great Lord, and with the whole landed
Intereft of the Kingdom : For which Conflict
they were, by no Means, a Match at that Time
of Day. Therefore they gave up the Caufe with
a good Grace ; for they paffed a Bye-Law,
obliging all the Members of their refpective Fra-
ternities,

ternities, not to harbour or employ any of thefe
poor Runaways for the future ;—at leaſt not to
employ them in ſuch a Manner, as would give
them any Colour or Pretence to demand the
Franchiſe of the Place: For every Man at the
Admiſſion to his Freedom, was to ſwear, that he
would take no Perſon as an Apprentice, who was
bound in Blood. By this Regulation. they not
only avoided numberleſs Quarrels with the Lords
of Manors, but alſo preſerved the Credit of
their own Body, by refuſing to mix or incorporate
with Perſons of a baſe Condition, or Slaves by
Birth.

2dly. THE other Anecdote is, that the corporate Towns required every Member at his Admiſſion, to bind himſelf by an Oath, that he
would wear no Man's Livery, except Mr. May-
or's, or the Maſter of his Craft. This is another
Regulation, which, if underſtood according to
the modern Practice of wearing Liveries, muſt
appear a moſt ridiculous Thing, and a very improper Covenant. Neverthelefs, at the Time it
was made, I will be bold to ſay, it was a wife, and
even a neceſſary Caution.—But as the right Explanation of this Prohibition will fall more properly under the next Head, I ſhall defer it for
the preſent, 'till we ſhall come to an Opportunity of aſcertaining its true and original Signification.

BEFORE

BEFORE I conclude this Article, perhaps it may not be amifs to mention a Circumftance or two, which, though not immediately connected with the Subject now before us, yet will give us fuch a Picture of the Manners and Modes of thinking and acting in antient Times, as may ferve to correct many Miftakes, which modern Politicians are too apt to commit, either through Inattention, or through Ignorance,—if not from Motives of a much worfe Nature.

IT has been obferved already, That the Baronage, or Landed Intereft, during the feudal Syftem looked down on the Trading with fovereign Contempt, hardly allowing them the Rank of Fellow Subjects,—and very unwilling to fuppofe, that they were entitled to equal Law and Liberty with themfelves. Now, would not any one have inferred from this Treatment that the feveral Cities and Boroughs of the Kingdom would on their Parts endeavour to form themfelves into fome Kind of League or Union, like the Hanfeatic Cities of *Germany*, in order to repel the Infults, and defend themfelves againft the Oppreffions of fo formidable a Body? Certainly this is a natural Suppofition:—Yet the Fact was far otherwife. For the *Londoners* were continually attempting to engrofs all the little Trade of the Kingdom to themfelves; treating the other trading Corporations with as

little

little Ceremony as if they had been their Slaves
and Vaffals : And thefe latter, inftead of being
the more firmly united, carried on a Kind of
Hoftility againft each other. It was thought
lawful at that Time for the Inhabitants of one
Town to make Reprifals on thofe of another,
like the Subjects of different States, when at
open War. Thus, for Example, if a Tradefman of *Glocefter* was a Debtor *to,* or had committed an Offence *againft* a Tradefman of *Briftol,* the *Briftolian* thought himfelf warranted to
feize on any other Burgefs of *Glocefter* by Way
of Reprifal, and to oblige, him to make Re-
paration for the Offence or Debt of his Brother-
Burgefs. [See COKE's Inftitute, Page 204,
and Statutes at large, 27th EDWARD III. Stat.
2, C. 17.] Now, can any Thing be more repugnant to Order and Government, not to mention Honefty, Induftry, and commercial Intercourfe than fuch Proceedings ? Yet this was the
Cafe : For, as the Barons were continually
plaguing one another with their Robberies and Inroads, their Quarrels, and private Wars ; [as
I fhall fully fhew under the next Head] fo
thefe *tiny* Heroes chofe to mimic their Betters,
by being as mifchievous as they could. — In fhort,
the Spirit of Envy and Jealoufy was fo predominant in thefe trading Bodies, that they could
hardly agree about any Thing, except in their
mortal Averfion to Foreigners : In that they were
unanimous;

unanimous; as moſt of their Succeſſors continue to be to this Day. Indeed they alſo conſidered their Fellow-Subjects in the Light of Strangers, ſtiling them ſuch in all their public Acts;—becauſe forſooth they were not of the ſame Guild, Fraternity, or Corporation with themſelves: And the above Quotation ſhews in what Manner they treated them. But though they uſed their Fellow-Subjects ill, yet their Conduct was mild and gracious, in Compariſon to the Fury with which they perſecuted *outlandiſh* Strangers: For in reſpect to them, their Antipathy knew no Bounds. EDWARD III. was a ſagacious Prince, as well as a great Warrior. His Laws for the Extention of Commerce, and Increaſe of Manufactures, indicate a liberal Mind, much more enlightened than could be expected in thoſe Times of general Darkneſs. In the 11th Year of his Reign [Anno. 1337] he cauſed four Statutes to be made for the Encouragement of the Woollen Manufacture, then in its Infancy among the *Engliſh*. In one of which Laws, Foreigners are invited to come in by the Offer of large Privileges. " It is accorded, that all the Cloth-
" Workers of ſtrange Lands, of whatſoever
" Country they be, which will come into *Eng-*
" *land, Ireland, Wales,* and *Scotland, within the*
" *King's Power,* ſhall come ſafely and ſurely, and
" ſhall be in the King's Protection and ſafe Con-
" duct, to dwell in the ſame Lands, chuſing
where

" where they will. And to the Intent the said
" Cloth-Workers shall have the greater Will to
" come, and dwell here, our Sovereign Lord
" the King will grant them Franchises as many,
" and such as may suffice them." Yet, notwith-
standing this Protection of an express Law, Complaint was made against the Mayor and Bailiffs of
Bristol, that they greatly obstructed the Execution
of it, by extorting Money from the Undertakers
under various Pretences, and by molesting them
in different Ways ;—the King therefore required
them by a special MANDAMUS, under heavy Penalties, to desist from such Practices for the future. This was about two Years after passing the
above excellent Law [See RYMER's FÆD.
Vol. v. Page 137.] And this, one would have
thought, would have been Warning sufficient to
the rest of the trading Corporations to desist from
such scandalous Practices ; but it was not.—
For about five Years afterwards, and seven
Years from the first passing of the Law, the Freemen of *London* were so far from being intimi-
dated by the Reprimand sent to *Bristol,* that
they became so much the more outrageous,
threatning, that they would *knock these Foreigners
on the Head, and break their Bones,* [*de vita, &
membris minitantur*] if they should dare to exercise their Trades of Cloth-making within the Liberties of the City of *London.* On which Account

count the royal Authority was obliged to interpofe, by iffuing another MANDAMUS more ftrict,
and penal than the former. [RYMER's FÆD.
Vol. v. Page 429.]

Now from the Behaviour of Tradefmen on
this, and fimilar Occafions. and particularly from
the Conduct of the City of *London*, which always
takes the Lead, and which generally obftructs
the moft public national Good, through narrow
monopolizing Views,—let the Reader judge,
whether the modern Doctrines of unalienable
Rights,—of Self Government, Self Legiflation, &c. &c. &c. are fit Doctrines to be
inculcated into large Mobs, and the Mafs
of Mankind?—-And whether the Bulk of
ignorant, fhort-fighted People, Men, Women,
and Children, would not do, both themfelves and others, much greater Harm than
Good, were they to be left at Liberty to put fuch
Plans into Execution according to their Wifhes
and Caprices?—But alas! thofe who know better, and yet inculcate thefe pernicious Doctrines,
have the more to anfwer for.

GENTLEMEN. *The Third, or higheft Clafs.*

It has been obferved already, that amongft all
barbarous Nations, and before Civilization has
been fufficiently introduced. there are never
found more than three Claffes of Men in Civil
Life,

Life, the *Slaves,*—*Mechanics,*—and *Warriors.*
Thefe latter are of Courfe the Men of Confequence, or the *Gentlemen* of that Country. For
they hold the others under great Subjection, and
therefore efteem themfelves, and are efteemed,
as Perfons of a fuperior Rank.

Now, whether our *Saxon* Anceftors were utter
Strangers to the feudal Syftem, or whether they
were in Poffeffion of the *Subftance.* without the
Terms of Art belonging to it (which is the more
probable Opinion) is a Matter of no Confequence in the prefent Cafe. For it is an undoubted Fact, that the Chieftains of the feveral
Tribes of *Angles, Jutes, Saxons,* &c. &c. feized
on vaft Tracts of Country, according as they
drove the antient Inhabitants before them ; and
that they afterwards divided thefe Diftricts into
fmaller Shares among their numerous Relations,
Followers, and Dependents. It is alfo equally
certain, that *Lands,* and *Jurifdiction* originally
went together. So that the fame Perfon, who
was the *Landlord,* or the *Lord* of the *Land,*—was
alfo the *Judge* over the Inhabitants of that Land
in Times of Peace,—and their *Leader* in Times
of War. For thefe three Offices, now fo feparate, were in Times of great Simplicity, and before the Refinement of Government, hardly fuppofed to be capable of a Separation. The only
Diftinction neceffary to be obferved in thofe
Times,

Times, was the different Nature of the Tenure, whether it was bafe, or noble,—fervile or military,—by the Soc, or by the Sword. If the Lands in Queftion were held by *antient* Soccage, that is, by a fervile or ignoble Tenure, the Occupiers were *Slaves*, and bound to *work* for their *Mafters*:—But, if by the Service of the Sword, that is, by a military, a frank, or noble Tenure, the Occupiers were the *Frankmen* of the Realm. *Liberi Homines Regni*, were Freeholders, Warriors, GENTLEMEN; whofe Duty it was to *fight* for their *Chief*. And thefe Diftinctions were thought to be fo important, as not only to influence all the Rules of Conduct and Decorum, and to fettle the Claims of Rank and Precedency in the Departments of Civil Life;—but alfo to deferve a Place in the fundamental Conftitutions of the Realm. For even in Magna Charta it is enacted, in the 7th Claufe, that *Heirs fhall be married without Difparagement;* which Words were underftood then to mean, that all *Minors*, Male or Female, who were the Wards of the Crown, or the Wards of any great Baron, fhould not be married to Perfons below their Rank. Money was not then the greateft Object: For the greateft Wealth or Fortune with *ignoble Birth*, was a *Degradation*; and therefore a Breach of Magna-Charta.—Whereas, to have married the Ward to a Beggar of high Blood, was no *legal* Objection. In a fubfequent Statute, made

made the 20th of HENRY III. C. 6. the Word
Diſparagement is more particularly explained ·
It is there made to ſignify. the cauſing of a Ward
to be married either to a *Villain*, or to a *Burgeſs*:
For either of thoſe would be a Diſparagement. The
ſame Rules prevail throughout almoſt every Part
of Europe to this Day. In *Germany* in particular (from whence our Anceſtors originally came)
if a poor *Count of the Empire*, not worth a
Shilling, ſhould marry a rich Burgher's Daughter of *Amſterdam*, worth Half a Million ſterling,
the Children cannot inherit the Family-Titles,
but muſt be reputed as no other than the *Baſtards*
of the Empire, though born in lawful Wedlock.
And if a Lady of this high *German* Quality, tho
without a Penny of Fortune, ſhould condeſcend
to give her Hand in Marriage to a rich Merchant or Mechanic, the Friends and Relations of
this *illuſtrious* Spouſe, may proſecute the low-
born, preſumptuous Huſband, even to Death, if
they pleaſe, for a *Rape*,—not indeed of Violence,
but of *Seduction*.—[And this latter Law likewiſe
takes Place in *France*, with very little Alteration.]
However, we find that here in *England*, the
Caſe was ſomewhat different even in the moſt an-
nient Times. For long before the Inſtitution of
a Lord Mayor, the *principal* Citizens of *London*
were ſtiled *Barons*, by Way of Eminence and
Diſtinction; ſo that they were plainly diſtinguiſhed from common Burgeſſes; and therefore

we

we may naturally conclude, that an Inter-
marriage with any of thefe *London* Barons was no
legal Difparagement.   But, be that as it may,
one Thing is certain, that the Exception here
mentioned is fo far from invalidating the Obfervation refpecting Mechanics and Tradefmen, that
it ftrongly confirms it.

WE have now feen what it was to be a
GENTLEMAN, and what was his original Occupation, let him be rich, or poor, a Prince, or
a Beggar, in regard to outward Circumftances.
His Trade was *Fighting* : And it would have
been a Blot in his Efchutcheon to have taken to
any other Employment.   But the Misfortune
was, That Fighting was not a conftant Trade :
For there are fo many Intervals in it, that a
Man who has nothing elfe to do, and is fit for
nothing elfe, is at a Lofs how to employ his
Time.   Befides, the Number of thefe Heroes
greatly encreafed during the Continuance of a
long Peace, at the fame Time that the Means
of fubfifting them on their own frank Eftates were
as much leffened by their Multiplication.—Not
to mention, that the younger Brothers of pro-
lific Families, and the Decay of others, through
private bad Management, public Misfortunes,
and various other Caufes, added to the Diftreffes
of this Order of Men, without pointing out any
effectual Means for their Relief.   In fho.t, till
the

the Pride of Family, and the Notions of Birth and Blood can be, in fome Degree, got over, perhaps a more miferable Being cannot exift, than a POOR GENTLEMAN,—without any vifible honeft Means of mending his Condition.

I mentioned under a former Article, [Page 311] that PETER the Hermit found out Employment for great Numbers of thofe idle free People, by fending them to the Holy Land, to be knocked on the Head. But ftill, thofe who ftayed at home, on various Accounts,—and thofe who were born between one Crufade and the other, alfo the rifing Generation, after the Crufades were out of Fafhion :—All thefe had nothing to do, unlefs they would employ themfelves in doing Mifchief. And a very little Infight into human Nature may enable us to judge, that Mifchief of fome Sort or other would become their principal Imployment.—The only Queftion therefore is, What Sort or Kind it would probably be ?—

ALL the fuperior Barons, and many of the fmaller, had great Royalties, and extenfive Jurifdictions. befides Poffeffions intermixed with each other, and rival Claims. Thefe Things naturally occafioned inteftine Quarrels and Difputes; fo that when the Grandees of the Realm were not leagued together againft their Sovereigns,

reigns, they were hardly ever free from Broils
and Contentions with each other, which were
fure to *end in Blood*. Here then was created a
Sort of Neceffity of imploying many of thefe
Gentlemen Bravos;—and that too in their own
Way. For if any one of the great Barons
fhould entertain a Band of fuch Defperadoes in
his Caftles, or about his Perfon,—his Neighbours, or his Rivals were obliged to do the like,
merely from a Principle of Self-Defence or Self-
Prefervation. So that every Caftle, of which
there were then fuch Multitudes, and every
great Houfe, efpecially if trenched or moated
round, became of Courfe little better than a
Den of Thieves and Robbers. A modern *Englifh* Reader may poffibly be furprifed to hear,
that in Times of profound *public* Peace, fuch
ftrange Proceedings fhould be permitted; but
ftrange as they were, they were not only
permitted, but countenanced in every Part of
Europe, in fpite of the fovereign Power, according to the Ideas of thofe Times. Nay, they
were dignified by the Name of *Private Wars.*
Thofe who wifh to fee a true and faithful, and
at the fame Time an elegant, Account of thefe
barbarous Tranfactions, may confult the preliminary Difcourfes of Dr. ROBERTSON's inftructive Hiftory of CHARLES V.—But as my Bufinefs is confined to *England*, I fhall chufe to
borrow my Account from the very Words of
Englifh

English Acts of Parliament, rather than in-
dulge myself in the Pleasure of tranfcribing
Paffages from an Author, whom I will dare to
pronounce excellent, though a *Scotchman.*

In the Reigns of HENRY III. EDWARD I.
II. III. and IV. RICHARD II. and HENRY
IV. V. VI. and VII. many Laws were exprefsly made either to prevent or fupprefs fuch
Outrages,—the Opprobrium of Common Senfe,
as well as the Deftruction of all Order and good
Government. [And befides thefe, many other
Statutes were enacted, which occafionally referred to the fame Affair,] One of the moft
antient, tho' not the oldeft of all, exhibits fuch
a curious Picture of thofe bleffed Times of *Old
England,* which fome of our modern Patriots wifh
us to prefer to our own, that I fhall produce it at
full length, and then quote fome Paffages out
of other Statutes, as Comments upon it.

" *A Definition of Conspirators made Anno* 23.
 " EDWARD I. *Stat.* 2. *Anno Dom.* 1304.
 " [PICKERING's *Edition.*]

Who be CONSPIRATORS, *and who be* CHAM-
PERTORS.

 " *Conspirators* be they that do confeder or bind
 " themfelves by Oath, Covenant, or other Alli-
 " ance,

" ance, that every of them fhall aid and bear the
" other falfly and malicioufly to indite, or falfly
" to move, or maintain Pleas: And alfo fuch as
" caufe Children within Age to appeal [accufe]
" Men of Felony, whereby they are imprifoned
" and fore grieved ; and fuch as retain Men in
" the Country [in the Country is not in the ori-
" ginal *Norman-French*] with Liveries or Fees
" for to maintain their malicious Enterprifes; and
" this extendeth as well to the Takers, as the
" Givers. And Stewards and Bailiffs of great
" Lords, who, by their Seignory, Office, or
" Power, undertake to bear or maintain
" Quarrels, Pleas, or Debates that concern other
" Parties, than fuch as touch the Eftate of their
" Lords, or themfelves. This Ordinance and
" final Definition of Confpirators was made and
" accorded by the King and his Council in his
" Parliament, the 33d Year of his Reign. And
" it was further ordained, that Juftices affigned
" to the hearing and determining of Felonies
" and Trefpaffes, fhould have the Tranfcript
" hereof.

" *Champertors* be they that move Pleas and
" Suits, or caufe to be moved either by their own
" Procurement, or by others, and fue them at
" their own proper Cofts, for to have Part of the
" Land in Variance, or Part of the Gains."

I x

It is a Pity, that the very learned and ingenious Commentator on the more ancient Statutes,
had not made his Obfervations upon this, which
fo much wanted the Affiftance of his able Hand ;
being wrote, (fhort as it is) in three different
Languages, the Beginning in old Norman
French, the middle Parts in Law-Latin, and the
Conclufion in *Englifh* ; and not without fome
Difficulties in each. To fupply this Defect to the
beft of my Power, and to make Ufe of his Authority as far as I can, I would obferve in the firft
Place, that though the *poor Gentleman* of every
Country looked upon Trade with Horror and
Difdain ; — yet it was *no* Difparagement to him to
ferve a rich Brother-Gentleman in the meaneft
Capacity, efpecially if he was a great Baron.
In that Cafe it was no Difgrace to wear a Livery,
and to ferve at Table,—and even to make Beds
in the Caftles, or great Men's Houfes, and to
fweep the Rooms, if *they were to be fwept at all.*
The fame Cuftoms ftill prevail in *Poland* ; which
is a Country that exhibits a true Picture of what
Old England was.—N. B. The Croifade never
got much Footing in *Poland* ; therefore the *Polifh* Nobles ftill remain in *Statu quo.*

Respecting the giving, taking, and wearing
of Liveries and Hats [*Chaperons*, Kind of Caps
or Bonnets ; Hats being not then in Ufe] alfo
Badges, and of ufing Watch-Words, Signs, or
Signals;

Signals ;—thefe Practices were grown to fuch an
enormous Height, that Multitudes of Statutes
were made to prevent, or punifh them. For
there was hardly a Seffion of Parliament from
the Time of HENRY III. to HENRY VIII. but
Laws were enacted for reftraining the Feuds,
Robberies, and Oppreffions, of the Barons and
their Dependants, on the one Side,—and to
moderate and check the Exceffes and Extortions
of the royal Purveyors on the other : — Thefe being the two capital Evils then felt. Refpecting
the Tyranny of the antient Baronage (the only
Evil I am now confidering) even Squires as well
as others were not afhamed to wear the Liveries
of fuch Leaders, and to glory in every Badge of
Diftinction, whereby they might be known to be
retained as the Bullies of fuch or fuch great Men,
and to engage in their Quarrels, juft or unjuft,
right or wrong. In fact, the *Old Englifh* Hofpitality fo much boafted of, and fo little underftood, was for the moft Part dedicated to the
very Purpofes of retaining and feeding, in the
great Halls, Numbers of thefe unhappy People,
to be the general Pefts of Society, and a Tor-
ment to each other. The Hiftories of thofe
Times, together with the Statutes of the Realm
inform us, That they *affociated*, (or, as they
called it, *confederated* together) in great Bodies,
parading on Horfe-back in Fairs and Markets,
and clad in Armour, with Lances or Javelins in
their Hands, to the great Terror of all peaceable
Subjects;

Subjects;—Nay, that they attended their Lords
to Parliament, equipped in the same Military
Dress;—and even dared sometimes to present
themselves before the Judges of Affize, and to enter the Courts of Justice in a hostile Manner, whilst
their Principals sat with the Judges on the Bench,
intimidating the Witnesses, and influencing the
Juries by Looks and Nods, Signs and Signals.
And as one Species of Iniquity generally begets
another, it was no unusual Thing with the weaker
Party [weaker I mean, in *these Kinds of Arguments*] to apply to the King in Council for a
Commission of Inquiry, Whether the Profecutor
commenced the Suit out of a sincere Desire of
obtaining Justice? or from Motives of Revenge,
Avarice, or Oppreffion?* And as the Ap-
pellant was allowed to name his own Com-
miffioners, it is no difficult Matter to guess, on
which Side these impartial Commissioners would
determine. This Method of proceeding was
therefore considered as a Kind of previous Queftion; so that the Logic of the Times was,

——— Nec lex est justior ulla,
Quam necis artifices arte perire sua.

But amongst the strangest of these Doings,
perhaps nothing would more surprise a modern

---

* Many Examples of this Nature occur in RYMER's FÆD.

Reader,

Reader, than to be told, That Gentlemen of the long Robe made a Part of the Retinue of the great Men of thofe Days ; that they lived in their Houfes or Caftles, and wore their Liveries. Yet this was the Fact. Their Employment, befides that of being Stewards of the Courts, and keeping the Records, and Title Deeds of the Baron, [who, generally fpeaking, could himfelf neither write, nor read] was to find out Flaws in the Titles and Conveyances of fome rival Baron,—or (what anfwered the fame End) in the Titles or Claims of fome of his Adherents, Partizans, or Dependents. The next Step was to fuborn Witneffes, of which, it feems, there was a very great Plenty to be had on all Occafions, and then to undertake the Caufe by fharing in the legal Plunder, if they fucceeded;—or elfe by making an abfolute Purchafe thereof, and taking the Chance of the Suit to themfelves.

THIS accounts for the many fevere Prohibitions in the old Statutes againft fuch horrid Abufes of the Law, efpecially by the * Profeffors of it. One of the moft remarkable of thefe Pro-

---

* Perhaps there never exifted a greater Contraft between the Proceedings in the Courts of Law in antient Times, and in thofe of the prefent. It is really a Matter of Aftonifhment (and furely ought to be of Thankfgiving) that fuch *pure* Streams fhould flow from fo *very impure* a Fountain.

hibitions

hibitions has never been tranflated from the *Nor-man-French*. It is the 13th of RICHARD II. Stat. 3. I will endeavour to give the general Senfe of one Paffage in it, without attempting to explain all the Law-Terms, or making myfelf anfwerable for the Juftnefs of the Tranflation in every *technical* Part.

" THE King to the Sheriff of *Kent*, Health." [The like Writ was directed to all the Sheriffs in *England*.]

" WHEREAS by the Laws and Cuftoms of our Realm, which we are bound to obferve, by our Coronation Oath, all our Liege Subjects within the faid Realm, as well poor as rich, ought freely to fue, defend, receive, and obtain Juftice and Right, and the Accomplifhment and Execution of the fame, in all our Courts, and elfewhere, without being difturbed, or oppreffed by *Main-tenance*, [fee JACOB's Law-Dictionary for the Explanation of all thefe Terms] *Menace*, or by any other Manner ;—and whereas alfo in many of our Parliaments held in Times paft, and par-ticularly in the Parliaments lately held at *Canter-bury* and *Weftminfter*, grievous Complaints, and great Lamentations have been made, as well by the Lords Spiritual and Temporal, as alfo by our Commons of our faid Realm, of the great and outrageous Oppreffions and Maintenance com-

mitted,

mitted, to the Damage of us, and our People, in different Parts of the faid Realm, by divers Maintainers, Menors, Baratters, Procurers, and Embracers of Quarrels and Enquefts, in the perpetrating of which, many are the more emboldened and hardened ;—☞ becaufe they are of the Retinue of Lords, and others of our faid Realm, by [Means of] Fees, Robes, and other Liveries, ftiled the Liveries of Company [Affociation.] THEREFORE We ordain and enjoin by the Advice of our great Council (the Parliament) that no Prelate, nor any other of Holy Church, nor Batchelor, nor Squire, nor any other of inferior Rank fhall give the Livery, called the Livery of Affociation : And that no Duke, Earl, Baron, or Banneret fhall give fuch Livery of Affociation to a Knight or 'Squire,— unlefs he be *retained for Life*, as well in *Peace* as *War*, by Indenture, without Fraud, or evil Engine :—Or that he be an Officer in his Family, and that he refides in his Houfe : -- Neither fhall any Duke, Earl, Baron, &c. grant any Livery (whatever) to a Valet, or Yeoman, an Archer, or to any Perfon of a Degree lower than a Squire, unlefs he be his menial Servant, or Domeftic, making a Part of his * Houfhold.

THUS

---

* As this Tranflation is not warranted to be *technically*, but only *fubftantially* juft, I would here obferve once for all, after

the

THUS ftood the Cafe with the higher Ranks
in Society: And as Vice and Wickednefs are
generally contagious, in Procefs of Time, the
very Cities and Boroughs began to ape their
Betters in doing Mifchief. They too had their
Affociations, their Liveries, and Retainers.
Therefore a Law was made to reftrain them,—
at leaft fo far as to prevent them from hiring
themfelves out to be the Bullies and Retainers
of the Great Barons. They might indeed affociate, and parade in Armour and Military
Array among themfelves, as the proper Garri-
fons of their own Franchifes, but were to proceed no farther (fee particularly 7th of HENRY

IV.

---

the judicious Mr. BARRINGTON, that the common Tranflation, printed in a Column oppofite to the Original in the Sta-
tute-Books, is miferably defective and incorrect. In a very fhort
Paragraph from a Statute, which I am going to quote, there
are two very capital Miftakes in almoft as many Lines. The
Words of the firft are thefe, *Notables Chevilers, et Notables Ef-
quiers,* which are rendered notable Knights, and notable Efquires : Whereas the Senfe itfelf, as well as the original Language, requires, that they fhould be tranflated, *refpectable*
Knights, and *refpectable* Efquires, that is, Men of Eminence
and Property in their Country. In this Senfe, the Duke de
Sully fays in his Memoirs, that when he was the Baron de
Rhoni he affifted at an Affembly of the *Notables* of *Britanny.*
The other Senfe is perfectly ludicrous. FALSTAFF was a
very notable Knight in that Senfe : But furely he was not a *refpectable* one. Apropos ; the Humours of FALSTAFF, *extra-
vagant* as they may now appear, were the Humours of thofe
Times. He was not the firft Knight by a great many, whofe
Profeffion

IV. C. 14.] Moreover Care was taken by the Magiſtrates of ſeveral of theſe incorporated Places, and particularly by thoſe of *Briſtol*, that every Perſon, when he came to take up his Freedom, ſhould engage by an Oath, that he would wear no Man's Livery (the Livery of Aſſociation, Maintenance, or Retaining) except Mr. Mayor's, or the Maſter's of his Company.

But perhaps ſome may ſay, " During all " this while, there is not a Word about the " Complaint and Grievance of the preſent Day, " BRIBERY AND CORRUPTION." To this I an- ſwer, that reſpecting the Prevalence of Corrup- tion, there ſurely has been a great deal ſaid,— and alſo *proved*: Reſpecting Bribery there has not. And the Reaſon is obvious. The moſt corrupt could not bribe, unleſs they had the Means;

Profeſſion it was, to enroll a Band of poor ragged Gentlemen Adventurers, and to rob on the Highways. The other Miſtake is a capital Omiſſion, *Gentil-hommes del Nativitée*, that is, *Gen- tlemen by Birth, or Gentlemen born*; whereas the Words *del Na- tivitée* is totally left out in the Tranſlation, as if of no Conſe- quence, though the Senſe of the Paſſage, and the Contraſt of what follows, lay a particular Streſs upon it. Here I will alſo note a remarkable Change in the Signification of ſome Words in our Language. We now ſay, *I ſigned my Name,* meaning thereby, *I wrote my Name:* Whereas it originally ſignified, when very few People, even of the Grandees, could write a Letter, I made a *Mark* or *Sign* [generally the Sign of the Croſs] for my Name. Thoſe that were ſuch Scholars, as to be able to write, frequently added, *Ego A. B. propria manu ſubſcripſi.*

Means;—and even then, they would not, unlefs there was fome End to anfwer. But, generally fpeaking, neither of thefe was the Cafe in
thofe Times. Indeed, if any Bribery was at
all introduced, it is moft natural to fuppofe, that
it was among the Cities and Boroughs:—Among
them, I fay, not to obtain the Election, as at
prefent,—but to avoid being elected. For when
none but *refident* Citizens and Burgeffes were
eligible by Law,—alfo when almoft every one
of thefe Tradefmen or Mechanics deemed the
Office of a Deputy to Parliament a *fore Burden*, not attended with a proportionable Degree
of Honour or Profit to counterbalance it, the
likelieft Thing to have happened in fuch a Cafe,
was for the Perfons in Danger of being elected,
to make private Applications to the Electors, to
be fet afide; or if elected, to the Sheriffs, or
Returning Officers to be excufed, or omitted,
and others to be fent in their Room. Moreover Application was made fometimes to the
Crown, for Letters Patent to be exempted
[See 29th HENRY VI. C. 3.] Abufes of this
Nature, we find, did frequently happen: For
there are many fevere Penalties in the old Statutes againft the Partiality of Sheriffs, and Returning Officers for *excufing*, as well as againft
the Patents of Exemption granted by the Crown.

THE Knights of Shires, the Reprefentatives of
Freeholders, or of the leffer Barons, were on a
much

much more honourable Footing. Their very Inftitution required them to be of the Order of Knighthood, and confequently to be *girt with Swords* as *Milites*, or military Men ;—by which Circumftance, as well as by their Rank, they were greatly elevated above the Reprefentatives of Tradefmen and Mechanics. Not to mention that their Pay or Wages in fome Counties was a *confiderable Object*. Moreover, as they were to be of the honourable Order of Knighthood,—this required a certain Qualification in Land, to be held, not by a bafe, but by a noble Tenure [See particularly the Statute for Knights, made 1ft EDWARD II. Stat. 1.] which muft have a-mounted, as far as I perceive by comparing diffe-rent Accounts together, to an Income of about 400l. a Year of modern Rent.—Whereas no fuch Qualification was ever required from the Repre-fentatives of Citizens, and Burgeffes. They were eligible, though not worth a Groat. Nay, in Procefs of Time, when the Requifition of *actual* Knighthood was a good deal difpenfed with, as appears by the 23d of HENRY VI. C. 15.—yet ftill it was thought neceffary, that Candidates for Counties fhould be, if not re-fpectable Knights, at leaft refpectable Squires, and Gentlemen by their *Nativity*, who were *able* to take upon them the Order of Knighthood, whenever required fo to do: And it was added,

that

that no *Perfon of the Degree of a *Vadlet*, [a Varlet, or Serving-Man] much lefs a Plebeian, or Mechanic, fhould be permitted to be the Knight of a Shire, or to reprefent the leffer Barons.

Now taking all thefe Circumftances together, the Elections of the Reprefentatives of the leffer Barons muft have become a moft turbulent and bloody Affair, in which, *Might* would be fure to overcome *Right*; and the ftrongeft Sword, as in *Poland*, be the *Returning Officer*;—or elfe fuch a Number of the pooreft, and moft dependent of thefe *Gentleman-born* Electors muft be excluded,

as

---

* The *Vadlet*, Varlet, Valet, or Serving-Man mentioned in this Statute of HENRY VI. feems to explain the whole Drift and Intention of the Law. Evidently there was fome fhameful Abufe about that Time committed in the Choice of a Knight of a Shire, which this Statute was intended to correct. And the moft probable Account is the following: When fome great Baron, fuch as an Earl of WARWICK, of LANCASTER, GLOCESTER, NORTHUMBERLAND, NORFOLK, &c. &c. had perhaps more than Half a County his own Property, and when the Freeholders of moft Part of the reft were in Dependance on him, wearing his Livery on all public Occafions; he might nominate whom he pleafed to reprefent the County. For none dared to oppofe him openly, or conteft the Election. If therefore the Great Baron had a favourite Valet to recommend, he muft be obeyed, and the Favourite be elected. But moft undoubtedly the Knights of the other Counties could not be pleafed with being claffed in fuch Company. ·Therefore, they caufed a general Law to be made, requiring

that

as would render Elections a reasonable and practicable System.   Therefore, as the Evils of Affociations, Liveries, and Maintenance were rifen to fuch an alarming Height, as to become more and more intolerable, the Legiflature chofe the latter ; that is, they wifely refolved to ftrike at the Root at once, by excluding all thofe diminutive Gentlemen-Barons from voting, who had little or nothing to lofe in any Conteft, but might have fomething to get by ftirring up Riots and Batteries in every public Meeting, and breaking the Peace of Society.   See the 8th of H. VI. C. 7.

But let the Preamble of the Statute fpeak for itfelf.

Item " Whereas the Elections of Knights of " Shires to come to the Parliament of our Lord

" the

---

that for the future the Candidate fhould be not only a Gentleman born, which it was no uncommon Thing for a Valet to be at that time of Day, but alfo a *refpeftable* Gentleman, a Man of Character and Fortune, even fuch an one as was *able* to fupport the Expence of Knighthood, if required.   This effectually difqualified all Vadlets, Varlets, or Valets from being Candidates for Knights of Shires.   Some Anecdotes concerning the infolent Behaviour of the great Nobility towards the inferior Gentry in former Times render this Conjecture very probable.   And hence alfo a much better Reafon may be affigned for the Anxiety which the Houfe of Commons, have expreffed of old, as well as in modern Times againft any Peer of the Realm interfering in the Election of their Members, I fay a much better Reafon than that which is ufually given.

" the King in many Counties [moſt Countries]
" of the Realm of *England*, have now of late
" been made by a very great and exceſſive Num-
" ber of People dwelling within the ſaid Coun-
" ties, of the which moſt Part was of People of
" ſmall Subſtance, and of *no Value*, [no Pro-
" perty] whereof every of them pretended to
" have a Voice equivalent, as to ſuch Elections
" to be made, with the moſt worthy Knights and
" Squires (that is, Knights and Squires of the
" greateſt Property, *les plus Valants*) dwelling
" within the ſame Counties, whereby Man-
" ſlaughters, (Murders) Riots, Batteries, and
" Diviſions among the *Gentlemen*, and other Peo-
" ple of the ſame Counties, ſhall very probably
" riſe, and be, unleſs convenient and due Re-
" medy be provided in this Behalf:— Our Lord
" the King, conſidering the Premiſes, hath pro-
" vided and ordained by the Authority of this
" Parliament, that the Knights of Shires to be
" choſen within the Realm of *England* to come
" to the Parliaments hereafter to be holden, ſhall
" be elected in each County by People abiding
" and reſiding therein, of whom each ſhall
" have a *Frank Tenement* of the Value of 40s. a
" Year at leaſt, (or over and above) Repriſals,
" or Out-goings."

THESE are the Words of the Statute, rendered
as literally, as perhaps they well can be, from
                                                        -one

one Language to another. The Things which deferve our more attentive Regard, are principally thefe:

1*ft.* THE Nature of the Tenure itfelf: It was to be a *frank Tenement;* that is, fuch as was fit for a *Frank,* a *Liber Homo,* a Freeman of the Realm, a Gentleman, or a leffer Baron to hold, *without Difparagement.*—So that the *Suit* and *Service* belonging to it (Words which imply, *to follow,* and *to ferve)* were to be of the *noble* Kind, and not *bafe* or *fervile;* therefore would not have degraded him into the State and Condition of a Villain, or a Slave, by performing them.

2*dly.* THE Value of fuch a *Frank Tenement,* is another Confideration.—It was to be 40s. at leaft, above all Out-goings. Here therefore be it remembered, that originally, eleven Ounces of Silver of Troy-Weight (with a Fraction) together with a certain Quantity of Copper fufficient to harden it, were cut into 20s. now into 62s. —So that a Pound Sterling, and a Pound Troy were then of equal Weight. But in Procefs of Time, fuch very difhoneft Arts were practifed at the Mints, that the juft Proportion between *Weight* and *Currency,* could not eafily be afcertained. When this Law was made (Anno 1429) I

think

think the Weight of One Shilling was equal, or nearly equal to the Weight of 2s. 6d. of modern Coin: So that 40. sat that Juncture muft have been nearly as heavy as 5l. in Silver is now : And if to this you take into Confideration the Difference between paft and prefent Times, refpecting both the Rents of Lands, and the Prices of Provifions, furely, it muft be allowed, That a Mafs of Silver of that Weight was equal to at at leaft 40l. Value of prefent Income.—Befides, the Framers of this Law feem to have had in their Eye a certain Proportion proper to be obferved between the Gentlemen *Electors*, and the Knights to be *elected.* The Qualifications for a Candidate to be elected, (that is, for a refpectable Knight girt with a fword, to reprefent the leffer Barons) was, that he was to be in Poffeffion of a *Freehold* Eftate of at leaft 20l. a Year in *Tale* (See the Statute for Knights, 1ft of EDWARD II. Stat. 1.) And probably about 50l. in Weight of prefent Silver ; which we may well fuppofe was then equal to 400l. a Year of modern Rent. So that the Proportion between the refpective Qualifications of the *Electors* and the *Elected,* was intended to be as one to ten, or nearly thereabouts : That is, as 40l. to 400l. a Year.

3*dly.* THE Evils propofed to be prevented by thefe Regulations, are a farther Proof of the Ufe

Ufe and Advantage of this Law. The Preamble affures us, that it was made to prevent Murders, Riots, Batteries, and Divifions among Gentlemen, &c. affembled to elect the Knights of Counties, or the Reprefentatives of the leffer Barons refiding in fuch Counties. Motives good, and very commendable! But how could thefe Evils have been reftrained at *that Juncture* by any other Method, than by that which this Act prefcribes? Liveries and Affociations every where prevailed; Maintainers and Retainers were the Appellations, by which all the Barons might have been known and defcribed from the higheft to the loweft, either as *Givers*, or *Takers*. And the whole Clafs of them had a Right to affemble themfelves together, and to give their Votes for Knights of Shires, 'till this Law thinned their Numbers: For none were excluded but Villains, Copy-holders, Burgeffes, and Mechanics. In fhort, the Number of Pauper-Gentlemen-Barons was become fo public a Nuifance, continually encreafing, that it called aloud for fpeedy Reformation. Nay, the very Laws, which both preceded, and followed the prefent Act in the fame Statute [for it is a capitular Statute, compofed of various Articles] I fay the very Laws both preceding, and fubfequent thereto, plainly point out thofe Evils then intended to be redreffed.

I 4

In the 4th Chapter we read, That notwithstand-
ing the many Laws which had been made (I
might fay *Multitudes* of Laws, during the Space
of upwards of 300 Years) to prevent the giving
of Liveries, forming Confpiracies, or Affociations, maintaining of Quarrels, riding in Armour, and the like ;—the Evils ftill remained
uncorrected, and were likely to encreafe;—
therefore it is ordained, " that if any Perfon
" after the Feaft of Chriftmas (1429) fhall buy
" or wear for his Clothing any Cloths, or Hats
" called *Liveries*, of the Sort, or Suit of any
" Lord, Lady, Knight, Efq; or other Perfon,
" for to have *Supportation, Succours,* or *Main-*
" *tenance,* in any *Quarrel,* or in any *other Man-*
" *ner,* if he be thereof duly convict by Exami-
" nation, or otherwife, before by the Statutes
" declared, he fhall incur the Pain before li-
" mitted of them that take Liveries of Lords,
" or other Perfons aforefaid, and moreover fhall
" have a whole Years' Imprifonment without be-
" ing let to Bail or Mainprife, for their Falfity,
" and fubtil Imagination in this Part."

THIS was a preceding Law ;—a fubfequent
one (Chap. 9.) in the fame Statute was to this
Effect, That whereas the " Statutes and Or-
" dinances made, and not repealed, of them
" that make Entries with *ftrong Hand* into
" Lands, Tenements, or other Poffeffions what-
" ever,

" foever, and them hold with *Force ;* · likewife
" of them that make Infurrections, Riots, Routs,
" Ridings [Chivaches] or Affemblies in Dif-
" turbance of the Peace of the Common-Law,
" or in Affray of the People, fhould be holden
" and fully executed ;"—And, after having re-
cited divers others grievous Complaints, it adds
alfo, Whereas it was a common Practice with
thofe who had forced themfelves into the Poffeffion of other Men's Eftates, without juft Title of
Law, to make over fuch ufurped Poffeffions by
Deeds, or Feoffments, ☞ *to Lords, and other
puiffant Perfons ;*—or even to Perfons utterly unknown, whereby the legal Recovery of fuch
Eftates or Poffeffions was rendered the more difficult, tedious, and expenfive :—Therefore it
enacts, That all the former Laws fhould be re-
inforced with new Penalties, and new Provifions.
One of the new Provifions was, that for the Recovery of the ufurped Poffeffions, the Juftices of
Affize, or Juftices of the Peace, might direct the
Sheriff to impannel a Jury of the Vicinage to enquire into the Truth of the Premifes : And every
Juror thus to be impannelled was to have Lands
or Tenements of the *clear* yearly Value of at leaft
40s. or about 40l. of modern Rents, the better
to fupport the Character of a creditable Man.
But, N. B. the Act is filent as to the Nature of
this Tenure, whether it was to be military, or
fervile : So that a Villain, a Copy-holder, or a
Yeoman,

Yeoman, if poffeffed of an Income of 40s.
might have been impannelled on fuch a Jury, yet
he could not have voted as one of the leffer Barons at a County Election, becaufe he held by a
bafe, or *fervile* Tenure.   But what Need of mul-
tiplying Proofs ?—Every Inftance ferves to fhew
that the Legiflature meant at this Juncture to co-
operate with,   and   render effectual, thofe good
Laws, which had been made from Time to Time
againft Liveries, Badges, Signs, Signals, Confpiracies, Riots, Ridings, Maintenance. &c.
&c. &c. ;—Evils, which it was impoffible to
have prevented by any other Means, than by
difcarding the numerous beggarly Gentlemen-
Barons from having any Thing to do with electioneering Contefts, and by vefting the Right of
voting in Men of Weight and Property.   N. B.
The modern Doctrine of *unalienable* and *indefeafible* Rights had not then been difcovered.—This
was referved for the Honour of the prefent Age !
And great Bleffings are likely to attend it ! fome
of which we very lately felt.—One Thing more
is neceffary to be obferved, namely, That during
all the Times under our prefent Confideration,
that is, about the Space of 400 Years, and upwards, no Mention is made of any Difturbances at Elections in Cities and Boroughs,—the
very Places where the greateft Diforders are now
committed :—And the Reafon is plain : A Candidate even in our Days for a burdenfome, difagreeable

greeable Office, attended with no Honour, and lefs Profit, would be fure to have a peaceable Election.

THIS was beyond Difpute the Cafe with almoft all Cities and Boroughs in antient Times. Nay, what is ftill more extraordinary, we learn from PRYNNE, as quoted by Mr. CARTWRIGHT [Page 71 of the People's Barrier, Note at the Bottom] " That the *elected* Perfon was com- " pellable to find Manucaptors, or Sureties, " fometimes four, five, or fix, for his executing " the Office of Reprefentative; and, if he " failed, his Goods were diftrained." Can a better Proof be ever given of the Truth of the Facts here infifted on, than what may be drawn from this Quotation? Would any Man wifh or defire a ftronger?

From a View and Retrofpect of all thefe Things, it is natural for every honeft Man to think, that had he lived in thofe corrupt Days, he would have acted a better, a more confiftent, and a more honourable Part. A Thought which ought to be cherifhed in every virtuous Breaft. But at the fame Time, let the *real* Patriot reflect, that we have Abufes in our Days, which approach too nearly to thofe of our Fore-fathers; and therefore cannot be viewed by an honeft Man, but with Horror and Indignation,—

Ind'gnation.— Tis true, our modern Champions do not wear Liveries, or ftalk about in Caps of Maintenance : Tis true, we have none at prefent, who parade in Armour, and ride in Harnefs at Fairs and Markets, tilting againft each other, Badge againft Badge, and Colour againft Colour. But alas! What we have left off in the Field, we have too much adopted in the Senate. For there we have fomething, which is too much a Kin to the former Badges, Signs, and Signals :—There we find too much of an *Eaft-India* Livery :—too much of a *Weft-India,* of an *American,*—of an Oppofition,— of a Minifterial Livery :—And alas! a great deal too little of that, which ought to be the only Badge of a *Britifh* Senator, THE CONSTITU-TIONAL LIVERY OF HIS COUNTRY.

CHAP.

C H A P. II.

Certain Objections and Cavils answered and confuted.

THE Man who embarks in the Cause of Truth, without any Party Views, must be an entire Stranger to the Ways of the World, if he expects to be better treated on that Account.— It is well, if his Treatment will not be worse: For, as his Conduct is a Reproach to both Sides, he will not find any Favour from either: So that his very Impartiality will be considered as his most unpardonable Crime. I was not ignonorant of these Things when I undertook the present Work; nevertheless I wished to persevere in the Pursuit of Truth, in Spite of all Discouragements. Two Antagonists have appeared already; and others have threatened to commence Hostilities, as soon as the Publication of my Work shall enable them to erect their Batteries. I therefore here dedicate one Chapter for the Purpose of replying to the Objections which have been already made, in order that the Reader may have some Sample of what he is to expect from the Productions of such Kind of Adversaries.

The

The 1st of these is JOHN CARTWRIGHT, *Esq.*

An Author, whose indefatigable Zeal and Industry would deserve great Commendation, were they employed to more rational Purposes, and were he less attached to a System which cannot be defended. To do him Justice, his *Integrity and Fair-dealing are more conspicuous than what is discoverable in many of his Brother-Patriots. For in general he misrepresents but little through Wilfulness and Design: What he doth through Ignorance or Inattention, ought to be ascribed to the Errors of the Head, and not to the Corruptions of the Heart. Respecting Lockianism, he is a very just and consistent Writer, advancing nothing but what is fairly deducible from his Master's Principles. If in doing this he falls into palpable Contradictions,

---

* Mr. CARTWRIGHT's Quotations from the Dean of *Glocester*, are from Works already printed, and *published*. This was fair and honourable. He did not have Recourse to a Manuscript, or, what was the same Thing, to a Copy printed for the Use of a few select Friends, and their Acquaintance, in order to obtain the Benefit of such Correction;—to which an Advertisement was prefixt, that the Press was no other than an expeditious Amanuensis.---Mr. CARTWRIGHT, I dare believe, would have acted a Part very different, on such an Occasion, from what Mr. Professor DUNBAR, of *Aberdeen*, has thought proper to do in his late Publication: *The History of Mankind.*

he

he doth no more, than what his Mafter did before him. Thus, for Example, he is fo inconfiftent with himfelf, that he will not allow that
Right to Females of the Human Kind, which
he exprefsly declares in many Places, to be a
Right *infeparable* from Human Nature. "I
" have DEMONSTRATED [fays he, Page 127
" of the People's Barrier] that Reprefentation,—
[he means the Right of chufing Reprefentatives,]—" depends on *Perfonality* alone : And
" that all Regulations for making it depend on
" Property, muft be capricious, arbitrary, and
" unconftitutional." In other Places, he allows, that Women are *Perfons*, and Moral
Agents, as well as Men ; and that they have
Souls to be faved. Yet in fpite of all thefe Conceffions, he maintains, that it is abfurd to fuppofe, that Women have thofe Rights of voting
at parliamentary Eleftions, which belong to,
and are, according to him, unalienable from
human Perfonality. But why, good Mr. CART-
WRIGHT, is this abfurd,—I mean, on your
Principle ?—He is fure it is abfurd : And he
refers the Dean of *Glocefter* (fee Page 46 of
Legiflative Rights) " to the Scriptures,—to the
" Laws of Nature, and the common Law of
" *England*,—and to the fair Sex themfelves, in
" order to fettle this Point." Authorities fully
fufficient, I allow, were they as decifive in this
Gentleman's Favour as he imagines them to be.
But that is the Queftion. 1/2.

1*st.* My kind Inftructor refers me to the Scriptures :—So far I am obliged to him. —— In them
he fays [Page 27. of the People's Barrier] it
will be found, " that God, as an Example to
" all other Kings, infifts upon the People's exer-
" cifing their RIGHT of *choofing* their firft Ma-
" giftrate (GOD) and of *affenting* to the Laws,
" under which they were to live." [For it feems,]
" God would not take upon him the Civil Go-
" vernment of their State, until the People had
" ELECTED him, and by their *voluntary* Affent
" had JOINED in enacting the Laws of the Com-
" munity, &c. &c." This he affures us is the
Doctrine of Scripture.—I do moft willingly acknowledge it to be the Lockian Doctrine,—and
a neceffary Confequence of that rafh, inconfide-
ate, Pofition, ' That all Governments whatever,
' antient or modern, good as well as bad, are
' fo many Ufurpations, 'till the People fhall have
' given their actual, explicit, and pofitive Con-
' fent, both to the Formation and to the Conti-
' nuance of them.' But even to hint at Ufurpations of any Sort, when we are fpeaking of the
Formation or Continuance of the Government
of the greateft and beft of Beings, WHO FIL-
LETH ALL IN ALL :—I fay, even to furmife that
his Authority over us depends, in any Senfe, on
our own good Will and Pleafure, or that his
Laws are not *binding,* till we fhall have *ratified*
and *confirmed* them, is a Liberty which I dare

not

not take. Mr. CARTWRIGHT muſt therefore excuſe me, if I decline the Diſcuſſion of ſuch a Topic.

2*dly.* HE directs me alſo to learn from the Scriptures, that the Rights of voting, chuſing, or electing Delegates to Parliament, though un-alienable in themſelves, are all alienated from *married* Women, and transferred to their Huſ-bands by a *poſitive* and *expreſs* Law. The Wife is commanded to ſubmit herſelf to her Huſband in *every Thing* ; Ergo ;—Huſband and Wife are in Scripture called one Fleſh ; Ergo,—(that is, from thence we muſt infer, elſe what would be-come of Mr. CARTWRIGHT's Argument ?) that the Huſband is appointed in Scripture to vote for his Wife in all public Relations whatever, and to be her Lord and Maſter in Politics, as well as in domeſtic Concerns. [See Page 46, of Le-giſlative Rights.]

WERE it neceſſary to ſhew, that the Gentle-man grosly miſapplies theſe Texts of Holy Writ, and that he aſcribes to them a Meaning, they were not intended to convey ;—it would be a very eaſy Matter ſo to do. But I chuſe rather to let him confute himſelf, as the beſt Way of an-ſwering ſuch an Adverſary. In this very Page, in which he condeſcends to correct the Dean of *Gloceſter*, for his Ignorance of the Scriptures, he
ſays,

fays, that the " Sexes are *equal* in Dignity with
" Regard to God, and his Salvation." By which
he plainly means, that Women have an equal
Right with the Men to judge for themfelves in
the Concerns of Religion.   For the Rights of be-
lieving, of thinking and praying, and of performing all religious Duties, are *unalienable*
Rights, which cannot be transferred from the
Wife to the Hufband, or executed by any Kind
of Deputation.—Confequently in regard to thefe
Points, the Hufband cannot be authorifed to reprefent the Wife,—nor is he her Lord and
Mafter in this Senfe.—About what then is my
fhrewd Antagonift now difputing ?—If he intends
to fay, that civil, and religious Rights are Things
of a very different Nature, becaufe the former
are *transferrable*, whereas the latter are not :—
He would indeed affert a very capital Truth;
but it is fuch a Truth, as deftroys the whole
Lockian Syftem at once.   On the other Hand,
were he to maintain, [which he, and Dr. PRICE
really do] that thefe two Rights are fuch exact
Parallels to each other, " that the Perfons who
" are to judge for themfelves with refpect to *re-*
" *ligious* Salvation, EQUALLY ought to be the
" *Judges* of their *political* Salvation" (which are
his own Words, at Page 134, of The People's
Barrier, in order to prove, that the very loweft
of Mankind, fuch as Footmen, Draymen, and
Scavengers, whom he there particularifes, as having

ing an *unalienable* Right of voting) he then muſt allow, whether he will or not, that the Wives of theſe Footmen, Draymen, and Scavengers have in civil, as well as religious Concerns, the ſame *unalienable* Right with their Huſbands.—Either therefore the Caſes are parallel, or they are not:—Let him take his Choice.

3*dly.* IN reſpect to Law, and more particularly the Law of the Realm ;—if he means to ſay, that Women (whether married or ſingle) have no *legal* Right to vote for Members, I ſay ſo too: And will add this as a plain Proof, that, in the Eye of the Legiſlature, the civil, and religious Rights of Mankind are very different Things; and therefore ought not to be confounded together: Which is the capital Error of Mr. LOCKE, and his Followers.

But 4*thly.* My greateſt Misfortune is yet to come. For the fair Sex are to be appealed to in this Diſpute. And they will—my generous Adverſary doth not ſay, *What they will do,* But at Page 46 above-mentioned, he ſays, " Were the " Rev. Dean to receive no greater Thanks from " the Miniſtry than he is likely to obtain from " the fair Sex for ſuch Attempts, poor indeed " would be his Reward! Women knew too well " what God and Nature require of them, to put " in ſo *abſurd a Claim* for a Share in the Rights of " Election."

" Election."—What Reward the Miniftry intend the Dean of *Glocefter* is to me a Secret. But how great foever they may be, [as I hope they will not be of an *unalienable* Nature] I do hereby freely and voluntarily make a *Transfer* of them all to Mr. CARTWRIGHT, with my grateful Acknowledgments for his kind Inftruñions :—I have not the Honour of his perfonal Acquaintance ; but if he fhould be like the Majority of his Brother Patriots, he may ftand in greater Need of minifterial Favours than the Dean of *Glocefter* :—The Dean is a Man, who, with a very moderate Income, [which many People would think rather fcanty] can truly fay, that he has all he wifhes to have, and more than fufficient to fupply his Wants. Would to God, that the Majority both of the *Inns*, and of the *Outs* could lay their Hands on their Hearts, and fay the fame Things.

As to the Judgment which the fair Sex is to pafs upon us, when the Caufe is to be brought before their Tribunal,—I own I am rather anxious for the Safety of us both, at fuch a Juncture. Becaufe, if Mr. CARTWRIGHT, after the Example of his Brother-Patriot, Lord G. GORDON, fhould fummon the Wives of Footmen, Draymen, and Scavengers, and *all the Ladies of their Acquaintance* to meet in *St. George's Fields*, then and there to debate the folemn Queftion,
Whether

Whether they fhould furrender up their unalienable indefeafible Rights, or infift on the FREE
EXERCISE of them, I will not be anfwerable for
the Confequences of fuch an Affembly of 20,000
patriotic Ladies, warmed with — Zeal for
their Rights and Liberties.

ONE Thing more I have to add on this Subject, and I have done.—During an Experience
of upwards of Fifty Years, I have obferved,
that in every contefted Election, the Females of
all Ranks, Ages, and Conditions, both in high
and in low Life, married or unmarried, thofe of
rigid, and thofe of *eafy* Virtue,—fo far from not
concerning themfelves at all in fuch Matters,—
have entered into the Spirit of Electioneering
with much greater Zeal, and keener Appetites
than the Males.—And let Mr. CARTWRIGHT
himfelf be the Judge, if he pleafes, whether he
thinks they would chufe LOVELACES, or HICK-
MANS to be their favourite Reprefentatives, had
they the Privilege of voting. [See RICHARD-
SON's *Clariffa* for the Explanation of thefe oppo-
pofite Characters.]

The Cavils of Mr. Professor D U N B A R, of Aberdeen.

WHEN I first undertook the Task of an-
swering Mr. LOCKE, I thought it ne-
cessary to proceed with the greater Caution, as
I had so many popular Prejudices to encounter
with. Mr. LOCKE's Writings on Government
had obtained a Reputation and Character little
short of political Infallibility ; therefore any
Man who dared to depart from this Standard of
Orthodoxy, was deemed a State-Heretic, and
condemned of Course, as an Enemy to the just and
unalienable Rights of Mankind. Finding myself oppressed by this Weight of undeserved
Censure, I caused the Press to strike off about
50 or 60 Copies of the principal Parts of the
present Treatise. My View therein was to con-
sult the Learned and Judicious both far and near,
concerning the Plan of the Work, and the Nature of the Undertaking ;—likewise to entreat
the Benefit of their Corrections and Amendments, in Case they should judge so favourably
of this Specimen, as to encourage me to proceed.

AMONG other respectable Personages to whom
I applied on that Occasion, I mention with sin-
gular

gular Pleafure and Efteem, the Reverend Dr. CAMPBELL, Principal of Marifchal College at *Aberdeen*; a Gentleman to whom the whole Republic of Letters is greatly indebted; and from whom the Dean of *Glocefter* has received more Affiftance, than from all others. I glory in the Declaration; and am much afraid, that the critical Reader will too foon difcern thofe Portions of the Work which received the Benefit of his judicious Correftions and Amendments, from thofe, which were never fent, becaufe I ceafed to take off Copies of the remaining Parts.

WHEN thefe Papers were at *Aberdeen*, it is probable, that a Mr. *Profeffor* DUNBAR got a Sight of them. A Gentleman, who appears from his late Publication, *The Hiftory of Mankind*, to be capable of making an ufeful Writer, could he add a little more found Senfe, and logical Confiftency to his *florid Periods, and high dreffed Stile*. Be that as it may, the Impatience of this Gentleman, and his patriotic Zeal, were fo ungovernable, that he could not ftay 'till the Book was publifhed, but hurried his Confutation of the poor Dean of *Glocefter* into Print, before the Dean's *confuted* Book was itfelf publifhed. This is rather a *new* Cafe. But, that the Reader may not be deprived of the Benefit fo kindly intended by Mr. *Profeffor*, I will here beg Leave to quote, firft my own Words, and then his Cenfures

Cenfures upon them, in the Order in which he himfelf was pleafed to place them, that the Reader may make his own Reflections ; and if Mr. *Profeffor* fhould be diffatisfied with this Mode of Proceeding,—I muft fubmit to his Difpleafure.

The Dean of Glocefter [*fee Page* 171 *of the prefent Treatife.*]

I.

ALL that we know of *America*, relative to the prefent Subject, feems to be this, That the *far greater* Part of the Native Indians [Indians I mean, as they were *formerly*, before their Subjection,—or thofe at prefent, who are *not* in Subjection to any *Europeun* Power] may be divided into three different Ranks, or Claffes, *mere Savages,—Half Savages*, and *almoft civilized.* ☞ I do not mention thefe Diftinctions, or Claffes, as accurate Definitions, according to logical Rules, but as Defcriptions of Men and Manners fufficiently exact for our prefent Purpofe.

Mr. Profeffor DUNBAR's *Cenfure on the Preceding* [*fee his Note to his Hiftory of Mankind, Page* 204.]

" A well known Writer in Politics affects to " have Ideas of the State of Mankind fo *mathematically.*

" *matically* precife, that he divides the Indians
" of *America* into three Claffes, *mere Savages,*—
" *Half Savages,*—and *almoft civilized.*"

II.

The Dean of Glocefter [*fee Page* 190 *of the
prefent Treatife.*]

With refpect to the firft Clafs of thefe bad
Qualities *(their Want of Tendernefs, Sympathy,
and Affection)* all Hiftorians agree, *without one
Exception,* that the Savages in *general* are very
cruel and vindictive, full of Spite and Malice ;
and that they have little or no Fellow-feeling
for the Diftreffes even of a Brother of the fame
Tribe,—and none at all, no not a Spark of
Benevolence towards the diftreffed Members of
an hoftile Tribe. But the Miffionaries (of
Paraguay) to their eternal Praife be it fpoken,
have converted thefe blood-thirfty, unfeeling
Animals into a very different Sort of Beings :
So that if the Accounts given of them (by Muratori, and others) are *true,* or even *near the
Truth,* there can hardly be a more humane and
benevolent People upon Earth, than the Indian
Converts of *Paraguay.*

Mr. Profeffor Dunbar's *Cenfure on the Preceding.*

" The Savages he (the Dean of *Glocefter*) de-
fcribes, in *all* refpects, as a blood-thirfty, unfeeling

" ing Race, deftitute of *every* human Virtue.
" But Miracles have not yet ceafed. The Mif-
" fionaries of *Paraguay*, we are told, can tranf-
" form thefe *infernal* Savages into the moft bene-
" volent Race under Heaven. A Metamorphofis
" which, though celebrated by a Dignitary of the
" Church, will hardly command Belief in this
" fceptical Age : Yet it ferves to fupport a new
" Theory of Government, which is founded on
" a *total Debafement of Human Nature*, and is
" now oppofed to a Theory that afferts its
" Honour, and derives from an happier Origin
" the Image of a free People."

III.

The Dean of Glocefter *[fee the Preface to the 2d Part of the prefent Work.]*

THE Author imagines, that he has confuted the Lockian Syftem in the foregoing Part of this Work. And he is fupported in this Opinion by the Judgment of many Perfons, not only diftin-guifhed for their Learning and good Senfe, but alfo for their zealous Attachment to the civil and religious Liberties of this Country. If this be the Cafe, that is, if he has really confuted Mr. LOCKE, he may now, he hopes, with fome Pro-priety, venture to fubmit to public Confideration, a Syftem of his own ; which he is *inclined to think*,
may

may ferve as a Bafis for every Species of Government to ftand upon.—At the fame Time he is
well aware, that it doth not follow, that his
muft be true. becaufe Mr. Locke's may have
been proved to be falfe : He is alfo very fenfible, that it is much eafier to pull down than it is
to build up ; and that many a Man can demolifh
the Syftem of another, who cannot defend his
own.   For thefe Reafons he is the more defirous
of proceeding with due Referve and Caution ;—
not expecting that his Plan fhould be adopted, as
foon as propofed, - nor yet fuppofing. that it
will be totally rejected, ☞ before it fhall have
undergone fome Kind of Examination.

*Mr. Profeffor's Cenfure on the preceding, is as
        follows :*—

" See a Work by Dean Tucker,   Part II.
" containing, as the Writer *modeftly* declares, the
" *true Bafis* of Civil Government, [*True Bafis*
was the running Title at the Top of the Leaf,
which gave Offence] in Oppofition to the Syftem
" of Mr. Locke and his Followers."

This third Blow of Mr. Profeffor is fo well
aimed, and fent with fo much Good-Will, that
it may be confidered as the *Executioner's Coup de
Grace*, to put the *condemned* Anti-Lockian out
of his Mifery.   However, as the Malefactor,
                                    though

though executed in his *Manuscript-State*, might come to Life again under the Shape of an Author in public Print, and by that Means do the more Mischief to the Lockian Cause; Mr. Professor seems to have been desirous of preparing some further Punishment for such a Criminal, as soon as he should revive, and appear in his former Character. With this View it is probable, that he added the following Clause.

" WHEN the Benevolence of this Writer [the
" Dean of *Glocester*] is exalted into Charity,
" when the Spirit of his Religion corrects the
" Rancour of his Philosophy, he will learn a
" little more Reverence for the System to which
" he belongs, and acknowledge in the most un-
" tutored Tribes some Glimmerings of Humanity,
" and some decisive Indications of a moral Na-
" ture."

THE Words *Benevolence, Charity, Religion,* are undoubtedly very good Words. And (as I do not set up for a Judge of fine Writing) perhaps I might likewise allow, that the Period which contains them, is well turned. Nevertheless, what Reference all this can have to the Conduct of the Dean of *Glocester* in the present Dispute, is a Thing which surpasses my Comprehension. And I do freely acknowledge, that I am myself so far one of the untutored Tribes, not-
withstanding

withftanding the Profeffor's great Pains to *tutor* me, that I have not the leaft Idea of having, tranfgreffed the Bounds of Benevolence, Charity, or Religion, in what I have faid concerning the Savages of *America*. The Relation, it feems, has incurred the high Difpleafure of the Profeffor of Philofophy at *Aberdeen*.—Be it fo.—But did the DEAN forge this Relation? No. Did he falfify the Accounts he had received from others? No. Did he mifquote, or mifreprefent any of his Authors? No. What then was his Offence? And what Provocation has he given to this Lockian Champion?—HE HAS DARED TO CON-FUTE THE LOCKIAN SYSTEM.—A moft unpardonable Crime indeed! For the Punifhment of which, the Rules of Decorum are to be violated, and the Modes of dark Attack to be practiced. Surely, if the Lockian Caufe is no otherwife to be defended, it is high Time that fuch a Syftem fhould be banifhed from the Society of Men.

HAD this Gentleman cited but one Author of Note, who had given an Account different from thofe of Dr. ROBERTSON, MURATORI, and others, to whom I referred, fomething like the Shadow of an Excufe might have been framed for the Rancour of his Invective. But as he has not, I will help him to a Writer as full of Romance, and as paradoxical as himfelf. The *Jefuit* LAFITAU in his *Mœurs des Sauvages*, has faid more to apologize for the Conduct of the Savages, than any

Writer

Writer that I have feen.   Neverthelefs, the general Chara&er which he gives of them, tallies fo exa&ly with the Relation of other Hif-torians, that plain Men of common Senfe, like myfelf, cannot fee the Difference.   The *Je-fuit's* Words are thefe, ' Leur bonnes Qualités (which he had been enumerating in the preced-ing Paragraph) ' font mélées fans doute de plufieurs ' defautes: Car ils font legers et volages, faineans ' au dela de toute expreffion, ingrats avec excefs, ' foupçonneux, traitres, vindicatifs, et d'autant ' plus dangereux qu 'ils fcavent mieux couvrir, et ' ils couvrent plus long temps leur refentiments: ' ils font cruel a leur ennemis, brutaux dans leur ' plaifirs, vitieux par ignorance, et par malice.' (Tom 1, P. 106.)

Such is the Portrait, which their own Apo-logift has drawn of this unhappy People.   But neverthelefs, though it is much to be feared, that this is too truly their general Chara&er, yet we will charitably fuppofe, and do moft will-ingly hope, that many Exceptions are to be found among them.   St. PAUL in his firft Chap-ter to the *Romans*, prefents us with a Pi&ure of the degenerate Heathens not much unlike this of the benighted Indians.   But no Man ever underftood the Apoftle in that rigid Senfe, as if he intended to fay, that there was not one fingle Exception to the Defcription he had given of Men and Morals, to be found in all *Rome*.

FOR

For my Part, I think it reasonable and right, that Exceptions should be made to all general Characters. Sometimes indeed I am obliged to make them with Regret: This is my present Case.—I have admired and respected the Literati of *Scotland* for upwards of 30 Years: The present is certainly their shining Period, their Augustan Age. They are now become not only a Credit to themselves, but an Honour to enlightened *Europe*. And were some of them to attend more to *Facts* than to *Theories*, and to pay a greater Regard to the Strength of an Argument, than to the Arrangement of Periods, or the Choice of Words, their Excellence and Usefulness would still be greater.—Unconnected as I am with them, and unbiassed in my Judgment, I pay this free-will Offering to their distinguished Merit.—Nor shall the unprovoked, and unjustifiable Behaviour of one of their Members lessen my Esteem for so illustrious a Body.

CHAP.

C H A P. III.

An Enquiry how far the Authorities of Great Names, and particularly how far the Opinions of ARISTOTLE, CICERO, GROTIUS, *and* HOOKER *can be serviceable to the* LOCKIAN *Cause.*

HAVING proceeded moſtly in the argumentative, or controverſial Way in the preceding Parts of this Treatiſe, it may not be amiſs here to alledge the Authority of reſpeƈtable Writers in Confirmation of what has been already advanced. I know, indeed, that the Gentlemen, with whom I have the Misfortune to differ, diſdain the very Thought of paying a Deference to any human Opinion whatever. But I know likewiſe, that there are not a Set of Men under Heaven, who make more Parade with the Honour of a great Name, than they do, if they are able to quote any Paſſage from his Writings, only *ſeeming* to be favourable to their Cauſe : ‒ A ſtriking Proof of which will be given in the Courſe of this Chapter, reſpeƈting the great and judicious Mr. HOOKER.

MEER Authority, it muſt be confeſſed, is not ſufficient in many Caſes to determine our Aſſent: But Authority, added to other Arguments, in thoſe *peculiar Circumſtances*, where the Mind is equipoiſed between oppoſite Reaſonings, ought certainly to turn the Scale. And indeed it generally will; for many of the moſt capital Affairs in human Life, are often conducted on no other Principle. [Thoſe, who wiſh to ſee this important Subject handled more at large, and properly exemplified, may conſult my two Letters to the Rev. Dr. KIPPIS, printed for RIVINGTON.]

THE Diſciples of Mr. LOCKE differ from the reſt of Mankind, antient and modern, in two eſſential Points.

I.

THEY often maintain in expreſs Terms, and the Tenor of their Argument always doth, that Mankind have no natural Biaſs, no innate Inſtinct or Propenſity towards Civil Society, as an *End*, or *Object*. Nay, many of them have not ſcrupled to declare, That were Men left to follow their own ſpontaneous Inclination, they would never have incorporated at all; but would have led a Life of abſolute Freedom and Independance. Mr. LOCKE's own Expreſſion is, That Men are DRIVEN into Society.—But
why

why driven ? And who drives them ? Their own
Wants and *Fears*, he tells us. For, it feems,
that after having deliberated on the Matter, *pro*
and *con*, Men at laft refolved to abandon the
Charms of native Liberty, in order to guard
againft thofe Dangers and Inconveniencies,
which they found to be unavoidable in their natural and folitary State. Hence therefore it
neceffarily follows, according to the Lockian
Idea, that Government itfelf, even in its beft
Eftate, and when beft adminiftered, is no other
than a *neceffary Evil*, which muft be endured,
for the Sake of efcaping from fuch other Evils
as are ftill more intolerable.

II.

In Conformity to this leading Principle, they
infer very logically, and indeed very juftly, [rea-
foning right from wrong Principles] that no Man,
tho' born within the Confines of fome certain
State, and all along protected by it, ought to be
deemed a Member thereof, 'till he himfelf hath
made an *actual Choice*; that is, 'till he has voluntarily entered into a *folemn Contract* with that, or
with fome other State, by an *exprefs, pofitive,*
and *perfonal* Engagement.—For 'till that is done,
he is in fact an independent, unconnected Being,
the Subject of no State whatever.

Now,

Now, to combat thefe two erroneous Opinions, which would in Practice be attended with
the moft fatal Confequences, I might obferve,
firft of all, that all the Notices, which we have
from profane Hiftory relative to Government,
are about the *Improvements*, or *Alterations* of thofe
Societies, which were already formed, and not
about the original, or *impulfive* Caufe, which firft
gave them an Exiftence, and brought them into
Being. *Minos*, *Solon*, *Lycurgus*, *Numa*, and
many others, who were juftly honoured with the
Title of Legiflators, were only fo in this fecondary Senfe of the Word: That is, they either
improved, or reformed, or new modelled fome
of thofe Societies, which already exifted in a
rude, and imperfect State. But they did not
erect new ones among a Set of human Creatures, who were before totally independent of
each other;—that is, who were *utter Strangers*
to any Kind of Subordination whatfoever. This
is a weighty Matter, and deferves to be well confidered. But as it would carry us too far from
the Points now *immediately* before us, if purfued
to its full Extent, I fhall wave it for the prefent;—
and content myfelf with producing only four Authorities in Oppofition to the Lockian Syftem:—
But thefe four are fuch, as are worth Thoufands
of others, the Lockians themfelves being Judges,
were their Teftimonies to be weighed, and not
numbered. The four I mean are no lefs than
ARISTOTLE,

ARISTOTLE, CICERO, GROTIUS, and HOOKER;
—the three firſt of whom were born, and educated under Republican Governments; and the
fourth is the very Perſon to whom Mr. LOCKE
and his Followers always appeal in diſputed
Caſes.

A R I S T O T L E.

THIS firſt of Men in the Pagan World delivers himſelf in the ſecond Chapter of his firſt
Book of Politics to the following Effect,—That
Man is by Nature a *political* Animal, much more
ſo than Bees, or any other Animals of the *gregarious* Tribes;—becauſe he is endowed with the
Uſe both of *Speech* and *Reaſon*:—Of Speech, to
make known his Wants, his Feelings, and Intentions;—and of Reaſon to judge, what is
right, and what is wrong, and to diſcern Good
from Evil.   Therefore *as Nature makes nothing
in vain*, any Man, who, through Choice, and not
from Neceſſity, is not a Member of ſome Civil
Society, muſt be ſuppoſed to be either much
better, or much worſe than the common Lot of
Human Nature.   Conſequently, if any Being in
a human Shape either has no Propenſity for the
politico-ſocial Life, or has ſuch a Sufficiency of all
Things within himſelf, as not to want it, that
Being is either a *God*, or a Beaſt of Prey.   For
Nature hath implanted in all Men a ſtrong Inſtinct [*Ormé*] for this Kind of ſocial Life.

SUCH

Such is the Substance of Aristotle's Argument, in a free Translation, when the different Parts of it are brought together, and cleared from some metaphysical Niceties, foreign to the present Subject. On which I must beg the Reader's Indulgence to make a few Remarks.

In the first Place, it is evident, that this first of Philosophers [as Mr. Hooker, by using a Greek Term (Arch Philosopher) justly calls him] was not here delivering an Opinion, which he thought would ever have been called in Question, or so much as doubted of. He took it for granted, that no Man would be so very absurd as to suppose, that Mankind had not a natural Instinct, Impulse, or Inclination towards forming political Unions or Connections of some Sort or other. Had he suspected that this Point would ever have been controverted, he would certainly have done more ample Justice to his Subject.

For 2dly. Whereas he barely affirms, that Men are Animals *much more* political in their Nature than Bees, or any of the gregarious Tribes, he might have corroborated his Assertions with such Reasons, as would have been unanswerable. Meer gregarious Animals are not political simply on that Account;—as I have shewn before in the Instances of Sheep, Horses

Horfes, Cattle, &c. [See Pages 131 and 132.]
But gregarious Animals then become political,
when they divide their common Labour into feparate Shares or Portions, each Individual having a diftinct Occupation, and acting within his
own Sphere. For fuch a Police evidently infers
a certain Subordination and Government, wherein fome are to act in Obedience or Subferviency
to others :—Or, to fpeak ftill plainer, fome are
to direct, and others to be directed. Hence it
follows, that not only Swarms of Bees, whom
ARISTOTLE mentions, but alfo Ants and Beavers, and every other Tribe of Animals in like
Circumftances [if any fuch there are] muft have
a Plan or Regulation, or a fixt Mode for the
Diftribution of Labour ;—that is, they muft have
a general Law, and Conftitution of Government
fettled amongft them.

Now, if this be the Cafe among the inferior
Animals, ARISTOTLE might have obferved with
great Juftice, that the Reafons or Motives for im-
planting fuch Inftincts in human Animals, as
would caufe them, not only occafionally to *herd*
together, but to form *lafting Connections*, are fo
much the ftronger in Proportion to the greater
Exigencies of their Condition : For even the
natural Wants of Men, *Food*, *Raiment*, and
Dwelling, are a thoufand Times more numerous,
and diverfified than the natural Wants of either

of

of the Tribes of Animals above-mentioned :—
And if to thefe we fhould add the *artificial,* which
comprehend all the Elegancies, Comforts, and
Conveniences of Life,—(not to mention the infinite Number of fantaftic, and imaginary
Wants) it muft appear next to a Demonftration,
that Mankind were formed with much ftronger
Propenfities for Society, than any Tribe of Animals whatever.   And ARISTOTLE's favourite
Maxim, that *Nature doth nothing in vain,* thus
returns with more than redoubled Force.

NAY, 3*dly.* Whereas ARISTOTLE obferves,
that Mankind are endowed with *Language,* and
Reafon,—(Gifts, which he apprehends are appro-
priated to the human Species, in order to enable
them to form political Affociations) he might
have added another Circumftance, which is ftill
more peculiar to the Human Race :—The Circumftance I mean is the Power of captivating the
Paffions by Means of public Declamations, or
folemn Harangues ; for this is a Thing quite
diftinct from the mere Ufe of Speech, or of
Reafon.   And it is obfervable, That when thofe
Geniuffes, whom Nature has formed to be great
Orators, harangue the liffening Crowds, they
are frequently able to enchant their Audience in
fuch a Manner, as to caufe them to move and
act, to refolve, or to refcind former Refolutions,
juft as they would have them.   Marvellous Talents

lents thefe! And happily for Mankind, they are not common: For, as in a free State, fuch as ours, they are more frequently employed in doing Mifchief, than in doing Good, we do not fo often experience their falutary Effects, as we do their fatal Confequences.—But however that may be, thefe Talents are fo much the Pre-rogative of Man, that we are not able to dif-cover the leaft Traces of them either in Herds of Cattle, or Flocks of Sheep, or in any other Animals whatever.

Upon the whole, though ARISTOTLE gave his Opinion after a tranfient or curfory Manner, and without any previous Study to inveftigate the Nature of the Subject;—yet it is fuch an Opinion, as leaves not the leaft Doubt in any Man's Mind, how fully he was perfuaded, that Mankind were formed by Nature to be *political Animals*, and that civil Government, of fome Form or other, was the State or Condition which was moft natural to Man. The next great Man is

C I C E R O.

This eminent Statefman and Philofopher was much in the fame Situation with his Predeceffor. For he too was a total Stranger to the Paradoxes of modern Days refpecting Government. Therefore

fore his Obfervations can be but fhort, being, as it were, occafionally uttered. In his *Firft Book of Offices*, §. 44, he had been comparing different Duties or Offices together ; and he gave the Preference, very juftly, to that Duty, or to that Imployment of a Man's Time, which was dedicated to the Service of his Country,—and not to mere fcientific Speculations, or abftract Theories. He placed the Contraft between *Communitas*, or the Duty owing to the Community, and *Cognitio*, or the Manner of entertaining one's felf in private with literary Amufements Which perhaps was intended as a gentle Reproof to his Friend ATTICUS.] And then obferves, " *That as Bees do not form them-" felves into Communities for the Sake of " making their Honey-Combs ; but being na-" turally united into Communities, called " *Swarms*, they therefore fet about this Work : " So Men, who are formed with much ftronger " Inftincts [than Bees] for a political Life, ufe, " that is, ought to ufe, their Powers both of " Action, and of Thought [for the public " Good."]

---

* Ut apum examina non fingendorum favorum causâ congregantur, fed, cum congregabilia naturâ fint, fingunt favos ; fic homines, ac multo etiam magis *naturâ congregati,* adhibent agendi, cogitandique folertiam.

THE

THE Conſtruction of the latter Part of this Sentence ſeems to be a good deal embarraſſed; probably becauſe a Word or two are miſſing. But be that as it may, there is no Manner of Obſcurity in the Words, *ſic homines, ac multo etiam magis Naturâ congregati.* For they are as clear as the Day : And it was for their Sakes alone, that the Paſſage was quoted.

AGAIN, in his Treatiſe concerning the Boundaries between Good and Evil, towards the Cloſe of the third Book, where he is ſumming up the principal Dogmata of the *Stoics* concerning Morals, Politics, Religion, &c. &c. which he highly (and in general very juſtly) extolls, he expreſſes himſelf after this Manner, * " As " we alſo uſe our Limbs [in Childhood] before " we have been able to learn for what Uſe, or " with what Intent they were given us; ſo we " are mutually connected, or joined together " by Nature herſelf into a Civil Community, or " Body Politic."

ONCE more, In his *Firſt Book concerning Laws*, §. 9, where he is enumerating the ſuperior Gifts and Advantages, which Nature or

---

* Quemadmodum etiam membris utimur, priuſquam didimus cujus ea utilitatis causâ habeamus ; ſic inter nos naturâ ad civilem communitatem conjuncti, et conſociati ſumus.

Providence

Providence has beftowed on Man, he mentions, among others, the Power of Speech, as particularly ferviceable in the Formation, and Confervation of human Society. [Orationis vis, quæ conciliatrix eft humanæ maxime focietatis.]

INDEED in his Oration for P. Sextius he has a Paffage, which feems (and perhaps only feems) to contradiＢ thefe two Quotations. The Paffage is to the following Purport :—

* WHICH of you, my Lords Judges, needs be told, that, according to the natural Progreffion of Things, there was a Period, not charaＢerifed by an Obedience either to the Law of Nature, or to Civil JurifdiＢion, when Men ran wild in the Woods, fubfifting by Rapine and Plunder, and having nothing which they could call their own, but what the ftrongeft could either fnatch from, or keep from the weakeft ? Therefore thofe who excelled in Wifdom and

Virtue,

---

* Quis veftrûm, judices, ignorat, ita naturam rerum tuliffe, ut quodam tempore homines nondum neque naturali, neque civili jure defcripto, fufi per agros, ac difperfi vagarentur, tantumque haberent, quantum manu, ac viribus per cædem ac vulnera aut eripere, aut retinere potuiffent ? qui igitur primi virtute et confilio præftanti extiterunt, ii perfpeＢo genere humano docilitatis, atque ingenii diffipatos unum in locum congregarunt, eofque ex feritate illa ad juftitiam, atque manfuetudinem tranfduxerunt. Tum res ad communem utilitatem,

Virtue, having obſerved a certain Docility, and innate Diſpoſition in human Nature, gathered theſe wandering Savages together, and brought them out of their former Ferocity, to have a Regard for Juſtice, and the Duties of a ſocial Life. Hence a Concern for the public Good may date its Origin; hence thoſe little Congregations, which afterwards grew up into civil Communities, or Bodies politic; and hence alſo Men were not afraid to build their Huts nearer to each other, which afterwards became Towns and Cities, and were ſurrounded with Walls, under the Sanction both of divine, and human Law.

Now, though it muſt be acknowledged, that this Paſſage ſeems to claſh with the three preceding, yet the following Conſiderations may perhaps reconcile the ſeeming Contradiction.

---

tem, quas publicas appellamus, tum conventicula hominum, quæ poſtea civitates nominatæ ſunt, tum domicilia conjuncta, quas urbes dicimus, invento diviɴo et humano jure mœnibus ſepſerunt.

In the above Paſſage, whether the Adjective *deſcripto* ſhould be joined with the Subſtantive *tempore*, or with the Subſtantive *jure*, is perhaps a doubtful Point. But the Senſe, in the ſubſequent paſſage, ſeems to require, that *perſpecto genere humano docilitatis, atque ingenii*, ſhould be altered into *perſpectâ generis humani, docilitate, atque ingenio*. However, either of theſe Senſes or Conſtructions will ſerve in the preſent Caſe.

FIRST then, it may be obferved, that no great Strefs ought to be laid on what is here advanced; becaufe it is the Orator, and not the Philofopher, the meer Pleader at the Bar, and not the moral Inftruĉlor, or faithful Hiftorian, who is here fpeaking. And CICERO's avowed Principles, as an Academic, (indeed perhaps they are the Principles of all Pleaders, and in all Courts whatever) led him to ftudy *Plaufibili-ties,* [*Verifimilia*] more than Truths, in order to make the belt of his Client's Caufe.

2dly. THE latter Part of this Paragraph weakens the Authority of the former. For if there ever was fuch a Time as above defcribed, when every Savage was independent of, or unconneĉted with, the reft, fubfifting like a Beaft of Prey on Rapine and Plunder; it is inconceivable, how fo much *Docility* and *good Difpofition* as CICERO mentions, fhould be difcoverable in an Animal fo very unfocial, fierce, and cruel;—efpecially, if the pretended Difcoverer was himfelf (according to the Hypothefis) no other than a Brother-Savage of the very fame Sort.—The Truth therefore feems to have been this: On the Difperfion of Mankind, which, according to the Scripture-Account, came to pafs after the Attempt to build the Tower of *Babel,* it is very probable, that the Multitude were fcattered abroad *far* and *wide,* by breaking themfelves

themfelves into very fmall Societies, if not fingle Families. For not only the facred Hiftorian, who is likewife the moft antient of Writers, favours this Conjecture, but alfo the local Traditions of almoft every Country feem to corroborate it. Thefe little Nefts of Men, or fingle Families, afterwards fo encreafed and multiplied, as to become large Clans, Tribes, or Hordes; each of whom had an *internal* Form of Government of fome Sort or other, probably of the *patriarchal* Kind, diftinct from the reft, and peculiar to itfelf:—A Government, which anfwered all the general Ends of being a Terror to evil Doers, and for the Praife of them that did well. And if ever there was fuch a Time, as the *Golden Age*, this was the Period for it,— I mean, as far as their own internal Modes of Living were concerned. HORACE is alfo of the fame Opinion;

> Beatus ille, qui procul negotiis,
> Ut PRISCA GENS mortalium.

But neverthelefs, as the People of thefe feveral Clans, Tribes, or Hordes raifed alfo the Neceffaries of Life within their own Diftricts, and had no Intercourfe or Communication with other Countries, unlefs by Accident, or in order to carry on fome bad Defign,—they very foon mutually conceived both a Contempt for, a Jealoufy of, and an Averfion to each other

(The

(The fame is but too prevalent among the common People of moft Countries to this very Hour) So that *Stranger* and *Enemy* became convertible Terms. It was therefore deemed lawful, and not only lawful but *honourable* for one People to make Incurfions into the Territories of their Neighbours, and to commit thofe Violences and Depredations, which CICERO mentions;—only with this Difference, that the Pillages, which he complains of, as the Outrages of Individuals againft Individuals, were (at leaft for the moft Part) the Hoftilities of one Tribe againft another. For, like the Pirates or Banditti, or the roving Arabs both of antient and of modern Times, they obferved the Rules of Juftice, Equity, and Humanity among themfelves at the fame Time that they robbed, and plundered, and perhaps maffacred thofe unhappy Strangers, who became the Victims of their Power.

Now this State of the Cafe reconciles CICERO with himfelf; and, what is ftill better, with the Truth of Hiftory, and with Matter of Fact. Therefore the Orator's Obfervation feems to be a very juft one, that fuch Men as excelled in Wifdom and Sagacity, and were eminent alfo for Goodnefs of Heart, endeavoured to reconcile thefe jarring Tribes, by explaining to them the Folly and Abfurdity of their Conduct, and by expofing the horrid Nature of their Crimes,

in

in thus violating that natural Senfe of Juftice, and thofe very Inftincts of Humanity, which they themfelves mutually recognized, and revered in each other.   And one would hope, for the Honour of our common Humanity, that fuch good Men, and *real Patriots*, did frequently fo far fucceed, as to perfuade many of the *Heads* and *Leaders* of thefe hoftile Bands to lay afide their ill-grounded Antipathies, to look on each other as Friends and Brothers, and to acknow-ledge the Ties of Nature in a wider Extent. Hence therefore it was poffible, indeed it was very probable, that the original narrow Circles of Civil Polity became fo widened and extended, as to comprehend many leffer ones within their Bounds.   For by thefe Means, every Tribe, Clan, or Hord, might fo far join, or coalefce with others, as to have one common Intereft, one common Head, or Government, in the greater Concerns of State, and yet retain its own Peculiarities, its own Cuftoms, and Tradi-tions in other leffer Matters.   Now this will ac-count (which perhaps no other Syftem can do) for the vaft Variety of different Laws and Cuftoms that prevail in different Parts of the fame Com-mon-wealth, the fame Kingdom, or Empire throughout the World.

Upon the whole, take Cicero in what Light you pleafe, and it muft follow from his Principles, than an Inclination for Government is *na-tural to Men*. For in the three Inftances, where he is inftructing us in the true Principles of Morality and Philofophy, he directly afferts it: And in the fourth, where, in the Exuberance of his Eloquence, he deviates a little from the right Path, he affords us fuch a Clue, as might eafily ferve to bring him back, and to make the latter Part of his Affertion harmonife with the former. So much as to the firft Head, in Oppofition to the Lockians.——We come now to the fecond grand Point, Whether Children are the *natural-born* Subjects of that State, to which their Parents were fubject at the Time of their Birth ? Or whether they are fuch perfectly independent, unconnected Beings, as to belong to no State whatever, 'till their own *free* and *unconftrained* Choice hath·fixt their political Relation ? This is a Point, which cannot admit of a long Difcuffion.——For not only Aristotle and Cicero, but the Antients to a Man, *Greeks* and *Romans*, were fo far from favouring the Lockian Notion, that they carried the contrary Doctrine of an implicit Veneration for the Inftitutes, Rites, and Cuftoms of their Anceftors to very great Exceffes. They bred up their Children from their Infancy, with fuch enthufiaftic Conceits concerning the Goodnefs, the Superiority, and even Sacrednefs of what their Fore-fathers had ordained, and eftablifhed, both in civil and religious

gious Concerns, that it was deemed a Kind of Impiety or Sacrilege, to fet up any Thing elfe in Oppofition to them. Happy therefore was that Youth, who fhould expofe his Life in their Defence: And *Dulce et decorum eft pro patriâ mori*, or Expreffions of the fame Import, whether in *Greek* or *Latin*, were Maxims to be inculcated on all Occafions. Hence that contracted Love for their own Country, its Cuftoms, and Conftitutions, which caufed them not only to defpife, but even to *deteft* almoft all others; and confequently to perfecute them when in their Power.—And hence alfo, that falfe and fpurious Patriotifm, which in many Inftances, blotted out the very Ideas of Juftice and Humanity, towards the reft of the Human Species. But as this is a Subject of a moft important Nature, opening the Way to many others, both in religious, as well as civil Concerns, and highly deferving a more thorough Difcuffion, than can here be given it, I muft refer it to fome others, who have more Leifure, and greater Abilities, than I can pretend to, to do Juftice to it.

Pass we on therefore at prefent to another great Authority, namely

GROTIUS.

This learned Writer, and experienced Statefman is my third *Republican* Voucher. In the

Pro-

Prolegomena, to his celebrated Work, *De Jure Belli ac Pacis* [A Work which cannot be too much admired, notwithſtanding a few Slips and Imperfeĉtions.] He tells us, that he was entering upon an important Taſk, wherein he was to explain and vindicate the Rights of War and Peace ;—Rights, which derive their Obligation [not from aĉtual Compaĉt, but] partly from the Voice of Nature,—partly from the Commands of God,—partly from the Nature of moral Duties,—and partly from the tacit or implied Conſent of Mankind : - He then delivers himſelf after the following Manner :—" Not a few there are who doubt, whether any ſuch Law of Nature [prior to ſome Compaĉt, Regulation, or Agreement] can poſſibly exiſt, eſpecially in Time of War ; and others, who poſitively deny the Exiſtence of it :" Some of theſe he particularly mentions, and then refers us to many others, as aĉting according to the ſame miſtaken Principles.

* " Seeing therefore, ſays he, it would be in " vaintocompoſe a Treatiſe about *Natural Right*, " or the *Law of Nature*, if no ſuch Right, or Law " exiſts,

---

* Cum vero fruſtra de Jure fuſcipiatur diſputatio ; ſi ipſum jus nullum, et ad commendaɩdum, et ad præmuniendum opus noſtrum pertinebit, hunc graviſſimum errorem breviter refelli. Cæterum ne cum turba nobis res ſit, demus ei advocatum. Et quem

" exifts, it will be incumbent on us in the firft
" Place, and in order to protect and defend the
" enfuing Work, briefly to confute this moft
" pernicious Error. And that we may not con-
" tend with a Multitude of anonymous Adverfa-
" ries, let us affign fome Perfon, or other, as
" the Advocate for, or the Patron of fuch an
" Opinion. And who fo proper, as CARNEA-
" DES, the Academic, or rather the Sceptic?
" for he carried the Maxims of his difputatious
" Sect fo far, as to maintain that the Powers of
" Eloquence ought to be employed as much in

---

quem potius quam CARNEADEM, qui ad id pervenerat,
quod academiæ fuæ fummum erat, ut pro falfo, non minus
quam pro vero vires eloquentiæ poffit intendere ? Is ergo cum
fufcipiffet juftitiæ, hujus precipuæ de qua nunc agimus
oppugnationem, nullum invenit argumentum validius ifto :
Jura fibi homines utilitate fanxiffe varia pro moribus, et apud
eofdem pro temporibus fæpe mutata : Jus autem naturale effe
nullum : Omnes enim et homines, et alios animantes ad uti-
litates fuas natura ducente ferri : Proinde aut nullam effe juftitiam, aut fi aliqua, fummam effe ftultitiam, quoniam fibi no-
ceat alienis commodis confulens.

Verum quod hic dicit Philofophus, [CARNEADES] admitti
non debet. Nam homo animans quidam eft, fed EXIMIUM
ANIMANS multoq; longius diftans a cæteris omnibus, quam
cæterorum genera inter fe diftant : Cui rei teftimonium perhi-
bent multæ actiones humani generis propriæ. Inter hæc autem, quæ homini funt propria eft APPETITUS SOCIETATIS,
id eft COMMUNITATIS non qualifcumq fed *tranquillæ*, et pro
fui intellectus modo ordinatæ, cum his qui fui funt generis,
&c. &c.

the

" the Defence of Falſhood, as of Truth. There-
" fore when he undertook to oppoſe the general
" Idea of Juſtice, eſpecially of that Branch of
" of it now before us, he found no Argument
" more plauſible than the following : That Men
" had from Time to Time made various Laws
" relating to Morals, meerly from a Principle of
" Self-Intereſt, or Convenience ; — and had
" changed ſuch Laws as often as theſe Circum-
" ſtances had varied. Cònſequently there was
" no ſuch Thing as an invariable Rule, or Stan-
" dard for Morals, becauſe Men, like all other
" Animals, are guided by Nature to gratify their
" own Appetites :—If ſo, there can be no Juſ-
" tice in oppoſing Nature ;—or if there be, it
" muſt be the Height of Folly, to promote the
" Happineſs of another, at the Expence of our
" own.

" But this philoſophic Deluſion is by no Means
" to be admitted. For though Man is indeed
" an Animal as well as others :—Yet he is an
" Animal of a ſuperior Claſs in the Scale of Be-
" ing ;—and placed at a much greater Diſtance
" from other Tribes of Animals, than they are
" from each other. In Proof of this, many
" Actions or Qualities might be mentioned, as
" the diſtinguiſhing Prerogatives of the Human
" Race : Among others, that APPETITE for So-
" ciety, or for a political State, which is ſo peculiarly

" arly human.   For this Inclination is of a par-
" ticular Sort [not like the Inftinêts of other
",Animals, barely to herd or flock together, but]
" to live in a *regular and peaceable Community* with
" thofe of his own Species, according to the Na-
" ture of a rational Creature, &c. &c."

THE firft Head of this Enquiry being thus
eftablifhed beyond the Poffibility of Doubt,
namely, that, according to the Teftimony of
GROTIUS, Mankind are *naturally* inclined [not
to live unconnefted with, or independent of each
other, but] to join in a focial State, and to par-
take of the Bleffings of a Body Politic :—Let us
now proceed to the fecond Point of Inquiry,
Whether it was his Opinion, that Men are under
any Obligation to obey thofe *civil* Laws, to which
they never gave, and in moft Cafes never could
have given, their perfonal Confent, or pofitive
Approbation ?—Now this is in faft to afk the
Queftion, Whether GROTIUS wrote fuch a Book,
or not ?—For every Page, and every Line of
his Treatife, concerning the *Rights of War and
Peace*, tend either mediately, or immediately to
eftablifh this momentous Truth.   And he de-
monftrates in various Parts of his Book, that
private Subjefts, *young* as well as old, are bound
in Duty to pay a prompt and willing Obedience
to all the Laws of that State, under which they
live, and by which they are protefted, ex-

cept in thofe unhappy Cafes (if any fuch fhould
happen) where the Laws of the State are mani-
feftly and direftly repugnant to the Laws of Nature, and of God.

THUS therefore it appears, that the Authority
of the three moft eminent Writers, that perhaps
ever lived, all born and bred in Republics,
ARISTOTLE, CICERO, and GROTIUS;—[of
whom the Poet who wrote the Epitaph upon
upon MILTON, might likewife have juftly faid,

> Three Writers in three diftant Ages born,
> *Greece*, *Italy*, and *Holland* did adorn.]

Thus, I fay, it appears, that their Authority is
as oppofite to the Lockian Syftem of Government, as the Sentiments of any Writer whatfoever.

H O O K E R.

IT remains now, that we attend to what Mr.
HOOKER has faid on the fame Subjefts. This
excellent Man has obtained the Epithet of
JUDICIOUS by a Kind of univerfal Confent;—
a Confent, by the by, tacitly given, never voted,
or ballotted for in any Refpeft whatever. But
waving that Point, he certainly deferved thofe
Honours in every Senfe, which the grateful
Public have beftowed upon him. For his fuperior

perior Judgment appeared not only in what he
profeffedly treated of and largely expatiated
upon, but alfo in what he more briefly hinted
at, and did not fo amply exprefs: Would to
God, that one of his Cautions contained in his
fecond Book, had been better attended to!—
That Caution, I mean, which was levelled at a
very weak Notion entertained by too many Proteftants at the Beginning of the Reformation, concerning the Ufe of the Bible.   For they conceived it to be a Book, which was intended to
furnifh them with every Plan, every Syftem,
every Mode, and Species of Reformation, which
their diftempered Fancies wifhed to introduce
both into Church and State.   Full of this abfurd
and dangerous Perfuafion, they found, or
thought they found, all their own crude and vifionary Reveries authorized by the Word of
God.   Confequently having *Divine Right* on
their Side, what could they do lefs than contend
for it even unto Death, by appealing to the God
of Battle for the Juftice of their Caufe? They
did appeal; and in the Conteft they deluged
their Country with Seas of Blood, by fighting
and fighting fo long, 'till at laft they reared up a
bloody Tyrant, to ferve them in the fame Manner as they had ferved others.—It is well, if the
modern Doctrine of *unalienable* Rights, which
feems to be a Kind of a Succeffor to the former,
be not attended with the like fatal Confequences.
   But to return.—

THE

THE firſt Lockian Error mentioned at the Beginning of this Chapter, is, that Mankind are *driven* into Society, as having no *natural* Inclination of their own to become the Members of a civil State. Now, what ſays the judicious HOOKER concerning the natural Diſpoſition of Mankind in this Reſpect? He ſays, [Book I. Sect. 10, Page 17,] that they *have* a natural Diſpoſition; and a ſtrong one too; ſo very ſtrong, as to become one of the great Foundations on which Civil Society was originally built, and is now ſupported. " Two Foundations there " are which *bear up* public Societies ; the one a " NATURAL INCLINATION, WHEREBY ALL " MEN DESIRE SOCIABLE LIFE AND FEL- " LOWSHIP ; the other an Order *expreſsly*, or " *ſecretly* agreed upon, touching the *Manner* of " their Union in living together."

CAN any Words expreſs my own Sentiment more clearly and emphatically than thoſe ? Or can any Teſtimony more ſtrongly corroborate the whole Syſtem of my Book ? I own, when I firſt entered upon this Work, relying on the Teſtimony of Mr. LOCKE, and others, I took for granted that Mr. HOOKER was not favourable to my Opinion: This I ſignified in a ſhort Note at the Bottom of the Page of that *printed* Specimen, which I diſperſed among my Friends —*Aliquando bonus dormitat Homerus.* But, having

having found Caufe to diftruft the Truth of certain Affertions, though uttered with amazing
Confidence, I began to fufpeḋ, that too much
Art and Colouring had been ufed in the prefent
Cafe; and I was confirmed in the Sufpicion, by
the Confideration, that as the whole Scope and
Tenor of Mr HOOKER's Writings were to con-
fure the Republican Rant, and to chaftife the
faḋious Behaviour of CARTWRIGHT and TRA-
VERS, it was not credible that fuch a Man as he,
one of the beft Reafoners in the World, fhould
be fo far overfeen as to favour the very Schemes
he was confuting and condemning. For thefe
Reafons I determined for the future to fee with
my own Eyes, and to truft no longer to fuch
Guides; and my earneft Requeft to every Reader
is to do the fame by me.

2dly. ANOTHER grand Principle of the Loc-
kian Syftem, and a neceffary Confequence of
the former, is—That no Man ought to be re-
puted the Subjeḋ of any State (tho' born and
proteḋed by it) 'till he has acknowledged his
Subjeḋion by fome particular, pofitive, and ex-
prefs Engagement. Now this comes to the fame
Thing with that other Lockian Declaration,—
That Laws cannot bind us without our own
Confent, either given in Perfon, or by fome
Reprefentative, or Proxy, *chofen* by us for that
Purpofe.

IN

In Contradiction to thefe Pofitions, hear Mr. HOOKER. He has already faid in the former Quotation, that one of the Foundations which bear up public Societies, is an Order [or Rule, a Plan, or Conftitution] either exprefsly, or *fecretly agreed* upon, touching the *Manner* of Man's Union in living together. Now here I afk, What is this *exprefs* Agreement but the fame with my *actual Contract?* And what is Mr. HOOKER's *fecret Agreement* but my *Quafi-Contract* in other Words? Find out a Difference if you can.—But further: In the fame 10th Section (Page 19 of Fol. Edit. 1723) is this remarkable Paragraph;

"APPROBATION not only they give, who
" *perfonally* declare their Affent, by Voice, Sign,
" or Act, but alfo when others do it in their
" Names by Right, *originally at leaft*, derived
" from them as in Parliaments, Councils, and
" the like Affemblies, although we be not per-
" fonally ourfelves prefent, notwithftanding our
" Affent is [prefent] by Reafon of other Agents
" there in our Behalf. And what we do by
" others no Reafon [can be affigned] but that
" it fhould ftand as our Deed no lefs effectually
" to bind us than if ourfelves had done it in
" Perfon. ☞ In many Things Affent is given,
" they that give it not imagining they do fo, be-
" caufe the Manner of their affenting is not ap-
" parent.

" parent. As for Example, when an abfolute
" Monarch commandeth his Subjects that which
" feemeth good in his own Difcretion, hath not
" his Edict the Force of a Law, whether they
" approve, or diflike it ? Again, that which
" hath been received long fince, and is by
" *Cuftom* now eftablifhed, we keep as a Law,
" which we may *not tranfgrefs* ; yet what Confent
" was ever thereunto fought, or required at our
" Hands ? Of this Point therefore we are to note,
" that fithence [feeing] Men naturally have no
" full and perfect Power to command whole po-
" litical Multitudes of Men; therefore *utterly*
" [altogether] without our Confent, [expreffed
" or implied] we could in fuch Sort be at *no*
" Man's Commandment living. And to be com-
" manded we do confent [that is, we confent to
" be commanded] when that Society whereof we
" are Part, hath *at any Time before confented,*
" without revoking the fame after by the like uni-
" verfal Agreement. Wherefore as any Man's
" Deed paft is good as long as he himfelf con-
" tinueth it ; ☞ fo the Act of a public Society
" of Men done 500 Years fince, ftandeth theirs
" who prefently are [who are at prefent] of the
" fame Society, becaufe Corporations are im-
" mortal : We were then alive in our Prede-
" ceffors, and they their Succeffors do live ftill.
" Laws therefore human of what Kind foever are
" available by Confent, [either expreffed or im-
" plied."]

I

I have ventured to add a few Words within Crotchets [ ] by Way of Explanation. Let the Reader judge whether the Senfe doth not require *fome* of thefe Additions, in order to acommodate the Author's Stile to modern Ears; —and whether the leaft Injury has been done to his true Senfe and Meaning in any of the reft. In fhort, this whole Paragraph is fo full an Il- luftration of, and doth fo effectually corroborate, all that I have faid concerning the Nature of an actual Contract and of a Quafi Contract, and of the peculiar Ufes and Advantages attending each of them,—That I am in no Pain on that Ac- count.—Nay, I repeat it again, let the keeneft of my Adverfaries difcover, if he can, wherein Mr. HOOKER's Opinion, *in thefe Refpects,* dif- fers from mine.

BUT further, I had faid throughout my Work, That Civil Government was fo *natural* to Man, that *hardly* an Inftance could be given of a Peo- ple, Hord, Tribe, or Clan living together for any Length of Time, without a Civil Inftitution of fome Sort or other. Mr. LOCKE and his Fol- lowers do not controvert this Affertion, as far as relates to all the Regions of *Europe, Afia,* and *Africa:* At leaft, I never found that they did. But they fay, that there are a few Exceptions to this general Rule among fome of the Savages in the more interior Parts of *America:* Savages who live, efpecially in Times of Peace, without any
Degree

Degree of Civil Rule, or Power, or Subordination. Whether this be the Cafe or not, is very immaterial to determine; becaufe I have affigned Reafons at large from Page 181, to Page 200 of the prefent Treatife, why fuch Exceptions (if indeed any fuch there be) are no Prejudice to the general Rule. But as drowning Perfons will catch at a Straw, fo it has happened with our Difputants in the prefent Cafe. Mr. HOOKER, they tell us, befriends their Caufe; and helps them in Time of Need. For he fays in the fame Section of the 1ft Book,—" That " there is *no Impoffibility in Nature*, confidered " in itfelf, but that Man might have lived with- " out any public Regimen."—Therefore they infer, that what is not *naturally* impoffible is perhaps *probable* :—And what is *perhaps* probable, is *very* probable :—And what is *very* proba-ble, muft be a Matter of Fact. Moft curious Reafoning this! And worthy of fuch a Caufe!

But the Misfortune is, that this very Matter of Fact, on which fo much is built, is not only controverted, but abfolutely denied. For LA-FITAU, who fays he was five Years a Miffionary among the Savages of *North America*, and had had a perfonal Acquaintance with many, and even a Friendfhip with fome of them, pofitively denies the Charge, and is very angry with thofe, who fur-mife any thing fo much to the Difadvantage of

the

the native Indians. His Words are thefe:—
" On n'a pas fait une moindre *Injuftice* aux Sauvages de l'*Amerique*, en les faifant paffer pour des
Barbares fans *Loix et fans Police*, qu'en difant,
qu'ils n'avoient aucun Sentiment de Religion,
et qu'on n'en trouvoit chez eux aucun Veftige,"
&c.—See the whole Chapter *Du Gouvernment
Politique* Tom I. p. 456.

Now, whether Father Lafitau is right, or
wrong in thefe Affertions, is of no Confequence
to the prefent Argument. If he is right, then the
whole Lockian Objeftion to the Univerfality of
Civil Government falls at once to the Ground.
But if he is wrong, furely one fingle Exception
to the Praftice of all the Nations, and in all the
Ages of the World, (and for which very probable Reafons have been affigned) ought to be
confidered in no other Light, than as fome *mon-
ftrous Produftion ;* which in every other Cafe is
never efteemed to be an Objeftion of Weight a-
gainft the regular, ftanding, permanent Courfe
of Nature. Either Way therefore the Conclufion is much the fame : And Mr. Profeffor Dunbar, Mr. Cartwright, &c. &c. &c. may
take their Choice.

In the mean Time it is of much more Importance, to the Friends of Truth, to find that the judicious Hooker has been refcued out of the
Hands

Hands of our modern Republicans, and reftored
to his own proper Province, the Defence both
of Church and State. He certainly was no
Favourer of the debafing Doctrine of *abfolute* and
unlimitted paffive Obedience, and Non-refiftance.
And if that is fufficient to denominate a Man, a
Lockian, I too muft humbly requeft to be enrolled among their Number. For I maintain the
Right of refifting in certain Cafes of *extreme Neceffity,* as warmly as any modern Patriot whatever.
But be it ever remembered, that when Mr.
HOOKER avoided one Extreme, he did not run
into the other. On the contrary, he rightly
diftinguifhed between Liberty and Licentioufnefs, keeping at an equal Diftance from the Machinations of factious Demagogues, and the fervile Submiffion of cringing Slaves. In fhort,
though the Terms Whigg and Tory were not
then in Ufe, yet his Principles and Writings were
of fuch a Nature, that he might have been cha-
racterifed (as foon as the Meaning of thofe
Terms was known) as a true Friend to a limitted
Monarchy, and a Conftitutional, (though not a
Republican) *Whigg.*

CHAP.

C H A P. IV.

*The Doctrine of Scripture relative to the Obedience
due from Subjects to their Sovereigns; together
with the Grounds of, and Reasons for the Duty.*

IT is evident, that all thofe Circumftances, on
which relative Duties are founded, muft be
prior, in the Order of Things, to the Duties refulting from them. It is no lefs evident, that fuch
Relations or Conneftions ought to be Matters of
public Notoriety, before their refpeftive Duties
can be enjoined, and enforced. The Relations
between Parent and Child, between Hufband and
Wife, Mafter and Servant, Sovereign and Sub-
jeft, muft not only exift,—but the Exiftence of
them ought to be publickly known, before the
feveral Duties of Honour, Fidelity, and Obedience on the one Hand,—and of Proteftion,
affeftionate Regard, and providential Care on
the other, can be preffed on the Confciences of
Mankind with due Force. For the Holy Scriptures do not inform us, who are Parents, and
who are Children,—who are Hufbands, Mafters,
or Sovereigns,—nor yet, who are Wives, Servants,

vants, or Subjects :—No ; this is not their Province, and it would be abfurd to expect fuch Information from them :—But, after thefe feveral Relations are become fufficiently known from other Sources of Intelligence, then the Holy Scriptures proceed to inculcate the Duties refpectively belonging to each Relation, with proper Motives.

THERE is, indeed, one Exception, and but one, as far as I can perceive, to this general Obfervation. It became an excepted Cafe, becaufe it was plainly a Deviation from the common Courfe of Things.—The Circumftance I refer to, was that *peculiar* Relation, which fubfifted between the Children of *Ifrael* and their Prince, JEHOVAH. For after the LORD GOD of *Ifrael* had brought his People out of *Egypt,* by a mighty Hand, and a ftretched out Arm, it pleafed him to bind them to himfelf by a peculiar Covenant, condefcending to be their temporal King and Governor, and exalting them to the Honour of being his immediate and political Subjects. Now as this was a fupernatural Connection, it could have been made known to them only by Means of a fupernatural Revelation.

HOWEVER, thus it came to pafs, that the political Conftitution of the Sons of JACOB differed from the Polity of all other States upon the Face of the Earth. Confequently, as their
State,

State, or Kingdom, under their King JEHOVAH, was very literally of *Divine Appointment*, the *Ifraelites* firſt, and the *Jews* afterwards could ſay, with ſtrict Juſtice, as well as with great Propriety, that they had received a political Conſtitution, and a temporal Kingdom, *ordained of God:* Which no other Nation could ſay, beſides themſelves, in the ſame Senſe.

BUT alas! whilſt this Theocracy, or Divine Government laſted, we do not find, that the Subjects of it were more loyal, dutiful, and ſubmiſſive than thoſe, who lived under other Forms.—On the contrary, the Scriptures are every where filled with Relations of the Perverſeneſs, Ingratitude, Rebellions, and Apoſtacies of this very People.—Yet, when this Theocracy had ceaſed, and when they were reduced to a Level with the reſt of Mankind, reſpecting the Nature of their Government, then they became ſenſible of their Error,—though indeed not from the beſt of Motives; and then they moſt earneſtly wiſhed (certainly not with the pureſt Intentions) for a Return or Reſtoration of that very Government, which they had ſo frequently deſpiſed, and offended.—Hence therefore they became ſo very impatient in their Subjection to any other Power, and were continually longing, and attempting to free themſelves from every foreign Yoke.

THIS

This appears, as from the general Expectation, which every where prevailed among them,
that their MESSIAH was fhortly to appear (to
whofe triumphant Standard the whole *Jewifh*
Nation intended to refort);—as alfo from the
particular Emulations, and mutual Jealoufies of
the Apoftles themfelves,—ever contending, *which
of them fhould be the greateft*, that is, which fhould
be the moft in Favour with their victorious
Prince. Nay, it was this very Perfuafion of a
temporal MESSIAH, which induced the *Pharifees*
to join with the *Herodians* (whom they mortally
hated) to put certain enfnaring Queftions to our
Lord. *Matt.* Chap. xxii. 15, 22. " Then
" went the *Pharifees*, and took Counfel,
" how they might *entangle* him in his Talk.
" And they fent out unto him their Difciples
" with the Herodians, faying, Mafter, We know
" that thou art true, and teacheft the Way
" of God in Truth, neither careft thou
" for any Man; for thou regardeft not the
" Perfon of Men. Tell us therefore, What
" thinkeft *thou*, Is it lawful to give Tribute
" unto Cæfar, or not, [fhall we give or fhall we
" not give? fays another Evangelift] but Jefus
" perceived their Wickednefs and faid, Shew me
" the Tribute-Money, and they brought unto him
" a Penny" [A Piece of Money fomewhat larger
than our Sixpence] " And he faith unto them,
" whofe is this Image and Superfcription? They
" fay

" fay unto him, Cæfar's. Then faith he unto
" them, render therefore unto Cæfar, the
" Things which are Cæfar's; and unto God,
" the Things that are God's. When they had
" heard thefe Words, they marvelled, and left
" him and went their Way." St. LUKE alfo farther informs us, " That they could not take hold
" of his Words before the People, and that they
" marvelled at his Anfwer and *held their Peace*."

Indeed to hold their Peace, in their Situation,
was the wifeft Thing the Pharifees could do:
For had they proceeded to have raifed Objections
to the Sentence which our Lord had pronounced,
concerning the Payment of Taxes, they would
have fallen into the very Pit they had dug for
him. Had they acknowledged the Lawfulnefs
of paying Tribute unto Cæfar, they would have
loft their Popularity and Credit with the Multitude, who expected the Appearance of a temporal Prince to conquer Cæfar; and had they
maintained the Unlawfulnefs of fuch a Compli-
ance, the Herodians themfelves would have been
the firft to have impeached their Loyalty, and to
have informed the *Roman* Governor of their
feditious Conduct: Therefore they marvelled
and held their Peace.

AGAIN, when our LORD was brought to his
Trial before PILATE, the *Roman* Governor, the
fame Queftion was revived, only under fomewhat of a different Form. ST. JOHN informs us,
that

that Pilate afked him, whether he was a King ?
and particularly whether he was the King of
the *Jews* ?—Meaning thereby, whether he was
that great Perfonage, whom the whole Nation of
the *Jews* had fo eagerly expefted, and for whofe
Caufe they were all ready to revolt. To which
Queftion our Lord replied, " My Kingdom is
" not of this World: If my Kingdom were of
" this World, then would my Servants fight, that
" I fhould not be delivered to the *Jews:* But
" now is my Kingdom not from hence." [See
John xviii. 36.] This Anfwer was fufficient to
convince the Governor, that he had nothing to
apprehend from Jesus, as a dangerous Enemy
to the State : And moft certain he was, that the
Jews were not at all difpofed to make an Infur-
reftion in his Favour. Therefore he feemed to
be quite fatisfied as to the only Point, which he
wifhed to know, concerning the *Meffiah* of the
Jews.

After our Lord's Refurreftion, the droop-
ing Hopes, and continual Longings of the A-
poftles after a temporal Kingdom revived again.
For having found, that their Mafter was brought
to Life, contrary to all their Expeftations, they
from hence concluded, that the Scene of Power
was at laft going to begin, and that an aftonifhing
Difplay of Prodigies and Wonders would foon
take Place. " Therefore when they were come
" together,

" together, they afked him faying, Lord wilt " thou at this Time RESTORE the Kingdom to " *Ifrael?*" To which he returned an Anfwer, by no Means fatisfactory as to the Point of their Inquiry, and yet fufficiently explicit to intimate to them, that there were certain Secrets in the Difpenfations of Providence relative to a future Kingdom of the *Meffiah*, which it was their Duty at prefent not to pry into; becaufe they were not proper for them to know. " He faid unto " them, it is not for *you* to know the Times and " the Seafons, which the Father hath put in his " own Power. But ye fhall receive Power, " after that the Holy Ghoft is come upon you : " And ye fhall be Witneffes unto me, both in " *Jerufalem*, and in all *Judea*, and *Samaria*, " and to the uttermoft Part of the Earth."— *Acts* I. 6, 7, and 8 Verfes.

Now in all thefe Converfations, which our Lord had both with the *Jews*, and with his own Apoftles,—with thofe who confidered him as a vile Impoftor, and thofe who believed him to be the true MESSIAH, and that very King of the *Jews* fo long expected [fo that they need not look for another.]—I fay, in all thefe feveral Converfations, fet on Foot not only from different, but from *oppofite* Motives,—not a Word is hinted about *national Grievances*, or national Complaints of any Kind. For the Queftion

about

about the Payment of Tribute was not, Whether it was an unreafonable Tax, immoderate,
or oppreffive,—whether it was unequally laid,
or would be fquandered away, or improperly
applied [the ufual Topics in our Days] but whether they ought to pay *any* Tax at all, *much* or
little, to a Government, againft whofe Title
they objected, as founded on Violence and U-
furpation. In anfwer to which, the Words of
our Lord are as exprefs and determinate as
Words can be.—" If you allow, that Cæsar is
" now the Mafter of your Country (which you
" plainly do, by fubmitting to the Circulation of
" his Coin, an evident Proof of his fovereign
" Power!) you muft allow, that he has a Right
" to fome Tribute or other in that Coin, which
" bears his own Image and Superfcription. He
" is now in actual Poffeffion; his Government is
" peaceably eftablifhed; it is the Government
" under which you live, and under which you are
" protected. Render therefore to Cæsar the
" Things that are Cæsar's: For this is a fuf-
" ficient Warrant for, and Juftification of your
" Conduct; by what Means foever he may have
" acquired the fovereign Dominion over you."

Almost 30 Years after the Refurrection of
our Lord, the fame Controverfy concerning the
Legality, or rather the Validity of Cæsar's Title,
broke out a frefh. The *Jews* could not bear the
Thought

Thought of fubmitting with Patience to a Title, whofe only Recommendation was actual and peaceable Poffeffion. The *Judaizing Chriftians* were of courfe of the fame Way of Thinking. And there is no Doubt to be made, but that the other *Chriftian* Converts, and indeed that the whole *Roman* Empire, *Jews*, *Chriftians*, and *Pagans*, were no Strangers to the Manner, by which the firft CÆSARS mounted the Throne, and fubverted the antient Conftitution.

UNDER thefe Circumftances, it became of the utmoft Confequence to the *Chriftian* Caufe, to have it determined, what Part the *Chriftian* Converts, and more efpecially its Teachers and Profeffors, were to take. And I will add, that in every Age of Chriftianity to the prefent Hour, it is of the utmoft Importance to know, that the Religion of the Gofpel is " firft pure, then peace-" able, gentle, and eafy to be entreated, full of " Mercy, and good Fruits, without Partiality, " and without Hypocrify." Confequently its Profeffors and Teachers fhould ever reprefent it, as a Religion peculiarly calculated, not to difturb the Repofe and Happinefs of Mankind, but on the contrary, to cement them together, and to promote Unity, Peace, and Love, where ever it can.—And furely, as far as the mere Titles of the reigning Powers are concerned, this

this it can, and therefore this it actually doth, do. " Render therefore to Cæsar the Things " that are Cæsar's."

As to public Grievances, and well founded national Complaints, - what would have been the Gospel Doctrine concerning *the Extent* of passive Obedience, or *that Degree* of patient Submission, which ought to be paid to the higher Powers, in Case they were to be notoriously guilty in the Abuse of their Trust: This Question was never started: Therefore the Gospel of Christ is totally silent on that Head. And perhaps it would always be the better, and the safer Course, to leave these Points, as the Gospel has left them, totally undecided.—I say, it would be the *better* and the safer Course; because, as Obedience is a general Duty, and Disobedience or Resistance only an excepted Case, on some extraordinary Emergence, the natural Sense and Feelings of Mankind are seldom or ever wanting to apprize them in any Point where a Duty is to be relaxed. Nay, it is well if they are not too quick-sighted, and more officious than they ought to be in suggesting Exceptions, and Dispensations.

It is true, the Precepts in Scripture, which require Obedience to the higher Powers, urge such Motives, as by a natural Construction may imply, that where such Motives are wanting, there

there lies no Obligation to obey. And I freely grant, that fuch an Inference may be fairly made: But neverthelefs the Scriptures are filent about it: They make no fuch Inference, but leave the Relaxation of this Duty to thofe whom it may concern. Thus, for Example, the Reafons for obeying the civil Magiftrate, as alledged by St. PAUL, are, " Becaufe he is a Terror to " Evil-Doers, and for the Praife of them that " do well ; becaufe he is the Minifter of GOD " for Good, attending continually on this very " Thing : For which Purpofe he beareth not " the Sword in vain, being a Revenger to exe- " cute Wrath on them that do Evil." Now this being fuppofed as the Bafis of his Adminiftration, the Duty of Obedience follows of Courfe : And therefore the Apoftle adds, in the very next Verfe : " Wherefore we muft needs be fubject, " not only for Wrath, but alfo for Confcience " Sake."

On this Principle it is, that Kings and Magif-trates are reputed GOD's Vicegerents : On this Principle it is, that their Authority is derived from him : And confequently that their Subjects cannot even *fear* GOD, in the Manner they ought to do, without *honouring* his Minifters and Re-prefentatives here on Earth.

But fuppofing that thefe Vicegerents fhould act contrary to their Commiffion : Suppofing that

that they fhould no longer conduct themfelves, as the Minifters of GOD for *Good* : In fuch a Cafe, what is to be done ? I anfwer, it is very apparent from the Terms of their Commiffion, That they are no longer entitled to the Obedience of the Subject, as a Point of Duty and Confcience. But nothing farther can be inferred from the mere Words of Scripture ; all the reft being left to Men's natural Feelings, and Difcretion to do the beft they can in fuch an unhappy Situation : Only we fhould always bear in Mind this neceffary Caution, that tho' we are *free*, " we ought not to ufe our Liberty as a " Cloak for Malicioufnefs, but to behave as the " *Servants* of GOD."

AND as the Holy Scriptures are thus averfe to the giving any Countenance to popular Tumults and Infurrections,—it is very obfervable, that the *Englifh* Conftitution acts with the like Caution and Referve. For the boundary Line between Refiftance and Obedience is no more marked out by the Laws of *England*, than it is in the Gofpel of CHRIST :— Cafes and Exceptions there undoubtedly are, in which it would be right not to obey, and even to repel Force by Force. But neverthelefs the *Englifh* Conftitution doth not point out thofe Cafes, for fear Mankind fhould make a bad Ufe of fuch an Interpretation ;—for fear crafty and defigning Men fhould miflead the giddy Populace to
deem

deem that to be legal Liberty, which in Truth
and Reality is no better than a rampant Licentioufnefs, and lawlefs Anarchy;—and which
therefore muft, in the Courfe of Things, end in
the Defpotifm and Tyranny of fome cunning,
bold Ufurper. [See my Vol. of Sermons, Pages
321, 324, printed for RIVINGTON.]

THERE is but one Difficulty of Confequence,
as far as I can fee, which attends this Scripture
Doctrine [or perhaps, as fome would fay, *this
Interpretation* of a Scripture Doctrine] concern-
the Obedience due to our civil Governors; a
Difficulty in my poor Judgement much more
plaufible than real.

The Objection may thus be urged : According to the prefent Hypothefis, a *vile Ufurper*,
if once eftablifhed in quiet and peaceable Poffeffion, and behaving well in his public Capacity,
hath as good a Title to the Loyalty, and Obedience of the Subject, as the moft lawful Prince,
though invefted with the beft hereditary Right,
or even elected by the general Voice of the
People.—It is admitted that this Confequence
muft follow from the Premifes ; nor are we a-
fraid to meet it in its full Force. For *Julius
Cæfar*, *Auguftus*, *Tiberius*, *Caligula*, *Claudius*, and
Nero, were all Ufurpers, yet every one of them
was, in Effect, declared by the Scriptures to be
the

the *Ordinance* of God; as far, I mean, as the Duty of Allegiance and Subjection was concerned.

This Matter wants fome Illuftration ; and to fet it in a clear and juft Light, the following Confiderations ought to be attended to : That civil Government is *natural* to Man ;—and that political Subordinations of fome Kind, or under fome Form or other, muft neceffarily take Place :—Moreover, let the Contenders for Empire be whofoever they will, and their Titles (real or pretended) whatfoever they may (that is, whether founded on Confent. Election, Defcent or Conqueft) :—Still the actual Poffeffion of Government is no other than an Office held in Truft for the Good of the Governed. Confequently fuch an Office, or Trufteefhip, muft be fubject to all thofe Viciffitudes, Cafualties, or Accidents, to which every other public Charge is neceffarily expofed. Now, were a Guardian, a Tutor, a Steward, or any other fidu iary Agent to be rendered *incapable* of executing his Truft, whether by the afflicting Hand of God, or thro' the Wickednefs of Man, it is obvious to common Senfe, that [fuppofing the Office ☞ neceffary to be continued] recourfe muft be had to other Perfons, and to other Agents to fill up the Vacancy.—Apply now this Reafoning, *mutatis mutandis*, to the Cafe of

Sovereigns

Sovereigns and their Subjects.—Government there muſt be : This Point is aſſumed as a ſelf-evident Principle, from which no Departure can be made. And *Power*, *Wiſdom*, and *Goodneſs* are ſuch neceſſary Qualifications, for the Exerciſe of Government, at leaſt in ſome Degree, that no public Regimen, much leſs a good one, can ſubſiſt without a Mixture, or Combination of them. Suppoſe therefore that *Wiſdom*, through ſome unhappy DefeᏟ ſhould be wanting, and that inſtead thereof groſs *Idiotiſm* or *Inſanity* ſhould ſupervene] this is ſo total a Diſqualification, that all the World will unanimouſly agree in declaring ſuch unhappy Perſons to be entirely unfit to govern ; and therefore *they* muſt be governed, have Guardians appointed for themſelves. Suppoſe alſo that *Goodneſs*, the next eſſential Article, be wanting ; —if notoriouſly wanting, and to a very great Degree, a like Sentence of Deprivation ought to be pronounced againſt ſuch unworthy Governors, who forfeit all Pretenſions to be continued in an Office, the End and Deſign of which they manifeſtly pervert. Laſtly, ſuppoſe that *Power* be wanting : This, we will allow, may ſometimes be a Misfortune ; and not a Fault. But nevertheleſs the *Want of Power* in the Sovereign to proteᏟ, muſt extinguiſh the reciprocal Duty of Allegiance in the SubjeᏟ, as much as the Want of Wiſdom, or of Goodneſs.

Caſes

Cafes indeed may be put, proper to excite Compaffion, and draw forth Pity; but they cannot alter the Nature of Things. For after all, the Affair muft come to this,—That if the higher Powers in any Country, whofe Adminiftration anfwers to the apoftolic Defcription of being a Terror to evil Doers, and for the Praife of them that do well; –if, I fay, fuch Powers fhould be in Danger of being removed, depofed, or fubdued, either through the Machinations of fome internal Faction, or by the Arms of a Rival, or the Invafion of a foreign Enemy,—then, the firft and *immediate* Duty of every good, and confcientious Subject is, to fuccour and affift them to the utmoft of his Ability, and never to give the leaft Encouragement to the Adverfary. This, moft undoubtedly, is the firft and immediate Duty of every Subject. But fuppofe that, after the moft faithful Difcharge of his Duty in thefe Refpects, the foreign, or domeftic Enemy fhould neverthelefs fo far prevail, as to be eftablifhed in quiet and peaceable Poffeffion, What is the next Duty? The next, one would think, is fo clearly fet forth in the Writings of the New Teftament, that it would be impoffible to miftake it: " Let " every Soul be fubject to the higher Powers, the " *Powers that be:* For if CÆSAR is become the " Mafter of your Country, and if he protects " you in the Enjoyment of your Life and Pro- " perty, render to CÆSAR the Things that are " CÆSAR'S; and learn from thefe Circumftances

to

" to become his good and faithful Subjects for
" the future, without Equivocation, or Reserve.
" The Guilt of such a Revolution doth not fall
" upon *you:* For you did every Thing in your
" Power to have prevented it. Therefore you
" are no more responsible for the Injuries or In-
" justice thereby occasioned, whatever they may
" be, than you are for the Consequences of any
" other successful Villainy, which Providence
" hath permitted, and doth daily permit, in the
" Course of human Affairs. The Claims you
" make on this *new* Government, are only the
" Preservation of Life, Liberty, and Proper-
" ty. These are just Claims, which you have
" a Right to make, let who will be the ruling
" Powers: Because Government itself was in-
" stituted on purpose to preserve them." In
one Word, you have a Right to be *Quasi-*
Contractors, " if not *actual Contractors,* whatever
" Government shall prevail."

However, if this Casuistry should not be
deemed satisfactory, or if any one hath a Mind
to criticise upon it, let him try, if he can, to
substitute a better. " Cæsar is the actual and
" peaceable Possessor of the Throne. This is
" the Point to be supposed, and allowed : But
" it is also confessed, that his Title is founded in
" Bloodshed and Usurpation. What therefore is
" a private Person to do in such a Case?" He
hath but three Things to chuse : That is, he must
either

either refufe to yield to the Conqueror, and ob-
ftinately refolve to accept of no Protection and
no Quarter from him ;—or he muft fubmit in
Appearance, with an Intention neverthelefs to
rife up and rebel as foon as an Opportunity fhall
offer :—Or laftly, he muft fubmit in Sincerity,
and confcientioufly refolve to be faithful and obedient to the Power which prefides over, and protects him. Let us therefore now fee, which of
thefe deferves the Preference.—The firft, I believe, is what no Man, in his Senfes, would
efpoufe, or dare to recommend either as humane,
juft, or practicable.—The Second is the Doctrine
of the Jacobites on the one Extreme, and of our
modern Republicans on the other : For thefe
two Extremes meet at laft in the fame Point.
The Jacobite maintains an unalienable and indefeafible Right in one fingle Family, and indeed
in one fingle Perfon of that Family :—The Republican extends this wild Paradox, fo as to comprehend every Individual, and the whole human
Species : So that both thefe Factions, if they are
confiftent with their own Principles, muft be the
natural and irreconcileable Enemies to every
Government but their own. For according to
their Ideas of their refpective *unalienable Rights,*
all Ceffions, all Promifes, Oaths, Declarations,
Abjurations, &c. &c. are void, and null of
Courfe, when either the *right Heir* on the one
Side, fhall appear; or when the People fhall have
an Opportunity on the other of affembling to affert

fert their unalienable Birth-rights, and to chufe
their own Governors and Legiflators.—What
Scenes, firft of Hypocrify, Perfidy, and Treach-
ery! --and afterwards of Bloodfhed, Maffacres,
and Horror, are thefe two Syftems, the Jacobiti-
cal, and the Republican, capable of producing,
were they left to operate unreftrained, and uncon-
trolled!

Thirdly,—There is but one Choice more to
make, namely. That every Individual, if in the
Situation above defcribed, ought to be fubjeft in
Chriftian Sincerity, without Guile, or Fraud, to
the higher Powers, the Powers for the Time
being ; notwithftanding any Defeft of Title
imputed to them.—Of this third Choice therefore I fhall fay the lefs, as every Part of the foregoing Treatife has a Reference thereto.—Only
let me be permitted to remind my Readers at the
Clofe of the whole, that notwithftanding any little Cavils and Objeftions which may be made
againft this Doftrine,—It is the only Scheme that
ever was, or ever can be REDUCED TO PRAC-
TICE ;—And it is alfo the LAW OF THE LAND.

T H E   E N D.

THE
CONTENTS.
PART I.

CHAP. I.

CHAP. II.

CHAP. III.

C O N T E N T S.

P A R T II.

C H A P. I.

C H A P. II.

CONTENTS.

CHAP III.

CHAP. IV.

PART

CONTENTS.
PART III.
CHAP. I.

CHAP. II.

CHAP. III.

CHAP. IV.